Mastering phpMyAdmin 3.4 for Effective MySQL Management

A complete guide to getting started with
phpMyAdmin 3.4 and mastering its features

Marc Delisle

BIRMINGHAM - MUMBAI

Mastering phpMyAdmin 3.4 for Effective MySQL Management

Copyright © 2012 Packt Publishing

First published: February 2012

Production Reference: 1310112

Published by Packt Publishing Ltd.
Livery Place
35 Livery Street
Birmingham B3 2PB, UK.

ISBN 978-1-84951-778-2

www.packtpub.com

Cover Image by Michal Čihař (michal@cihar.com)

Credits

Author
Marc Delisle

Reviewers
Madhura Jayaratne

Rouslan Placella

Lead Technical Editors
Kartikey Pandey

Meeta Rajani

Technical Editor
Kedar Bhat

Project Coordinator
Jovita Pinto

Proofreader
Mario Cecere

Indexer
Tejal Daruwale

Production Coordinator
Arvindkumar Gupta

Cover Work
Arvindkumar Gupta

About the Author

Marc Delisle was awarded "MySQL Community Member of the year 2009" because of his involvement with phpMyAdmin. He started to contribute to the project in December 1998, when he made the multi-language version. He is involved with phpMyAdmin as a developer, translator, and project administrator and enjoys meeting phpMyAdmin users in person.

Marc is a system administrator at Cegep de Sherbrooke, Québec, Canada. He lives in Sherbrooke with his wife and they enjoy spending time with their four children.

In addition to the "*Mastering phpMyAdmin*" successive editions, Marc has written "*Creating your MySQL Database: Practical Design Tips and Techniques*" and "*phpMyAdmin Starter*", also with Packt Publishing.

I am truly grateful to the Packt team whose sound comments were greatly appreciated during the production. My thanks also go to the reviewers of all editions; their sharp eyes helped in making this book clearer and more complete.

Finally, I wish to thank all contributors to phpMyAdmin's source code, translations, and documentation; their dedication to this project continues to push me forward.

About the Reviewers

Madhura Jayaratne is a Computer Science and Engineering graduate of University of Moratuwa. Currently he works as a software engineer and is located in Colombo, Sri Lanka.

He is a member of phpMyAdmin team and has contributed with GIS support for the software, which will be a part of its future releases. He continues to contribute by coding and translating the software.

Rouslan Placella, based in Cork, Ireland, is currently completing an Honors degree in Software Development at the Cork Institute of Technology. Born in Saint Petersbourg in 1985, his enthusiasm for programming and electronics was nurtured from a very early age. He is passionate about high performance and secure software and has been contributing to open source software with phpMyAdmin and Geeklog. During the summer of 2011 he took part in the Google Summer of Code program, where he developed an improved interface for MySQL routines, triggers, and events for phpMyAdmin. He currently also teaches Math and programming to second and third-level students.

www.PacktPub.com

Support files, eBooks, discount offers, and more

You might want to visit www.PacktPub.com for support files and downloads related to your book.

Did you know that Packt offers eBook versions of every book published, with PDF and ePub files available? You can upgrade to the eBook version at www.PacktPub.com and as a print book customer, you are entitled to a discount on the eBook copy. Get in touch with us at service@packtpub.com for more details.

At www.PacktPub.com, you can also read a collection of free technical articles, sign up for a range of free newsletters and receive exclusive discounts and offers on Packt books and eBooks.

http://PacktLib.PacktPub.com

Do you need instant solutions to your IT questions? PacktLib is Packt's online digital book library. Here, you can access, read and search across Packt's entire library of books.

Why Subscribe?

- Fully searchable across every book published by Packt
- Copy and paste, print, and bookmark content
- On demand and accessible via web browser

Free Access for Packt account holders

If you have an account with Packt at www.PacktPub.com, you can use this to access PacktLib today and view nine entirely free books. Simply use your login credentials for immediate access.

This book is dedicated to Carole, André, Corinne, Annie, and Guillaume,
with all my love.

Table of Contents

Preface

phpMyAdmin is an open source web interface that handles the administration of MySQL. It can perform various tasks such as creating, modifying, or deleting databases, tables, columns, or rows. It can also execute SQL statements or manage users and their permissions. When it comes to exploiting phpMyAdmin to its full potential, even experienced developers and system administrators search for tutorials to accomplish their tasks.

Mastering phpMyAdmin 3.4 for Effective MySQL Management is an easy-to-read, step-by-step practical guide that walks you through every facet of this legendary tool—phpMyAdmin—and takes you a step ahead in taking full advantage of its potential. This book is filled with illustrative examples that will help you understand every phpMyAdmin feature in detail.

This book jump starts with installing and configuring phpMyAdmin, and then looks into phpMyAdmin's features. This is followed by configuring authentication in phpMyAdmin and setting parameters that influence the interface as a whole, including the new user preferences feature. You will first create two basic tables and then edit, delete data, tables, and databases. As backups are crucial to a project, you will create up-to-date backups and then look into importing the data that you have exported. You will also explore the various search mechanisms and query across multiple tables.

Now you will learn some advanced features such as defining inter-table relations, both with relation view and the Designer panel. Some queries are out of the scope of the interface; you will enter SQL command to accomplish these tasks.

You will also learn about synchronizing databases on different servers and managing MySQL replication to improve performance and data security. You will also store queries as bookmarks for their quick retrieval. Towards the end of the book you will learn to document your database, track changes made to the database, and manage user accounts using phpMyAdmin server management features.

This book is an upgrade from the previous version that covered phpMyAdmin version 3.3. Version 3.4.x introduced features such as a user preferences module, relation schema export to multiple formats, an ENUM/SET column editor, a simplified interface for export and import, AJAX interface on some pages, charts generation, and a visual query builder.

What this book covers

Chapter 1, Getting Started with phpMyAdmin, gives us the reasons why we should use phpMyAdmin as a means of managing MySQL databases. It then covers the downloading and installation procedures for phpMyAdmin. Installing the phpMyAdmin configuration storage is covered as well.

Chapter 2, Configuring Authentication and Security, provides an overview of various authentication types used in phpMyAdmin. It then covers the security issues related to phpMyAdmin.

Chapter 3, Over Viewing the Interface, gives us an overview of the phpMyAdmin interface. It includes the login panel, the navigation and main panels with the Light and the Full mode, and the Query window. The new user preferences module is examined in this chapter.

Chapter 4, Creating and Browsing Tables, is all about database creation. It teaches us how to create a table, how to insert data manually, and how to sort the data. It also covers how to produce charts from data.

Chapter 5, Changing Data and Structure, covers the aspects of data editing in phpMyAdmin. It teaches us handling NULL values, multi-row editing, and data deletion. Finally it explores the subject of changing the structure of tables, with focus on editing column attributes (including the new ENUM/SET editor) and index management.

Chapter 6, Exporting Structure and Data (Backup), deals with backups and exports. It lists various ways to trigger an export, available export formats, the options associated with export formats, and the various places where the export files may be sent.

Chapter 7, Importing Structure and Data, tells us how to bring back exported data created for backup and transfer purposes. It covers the various options available in phpMyAdmin to import data, and different mechanisms involved in importing SQL files, CSV files, and other formats. Finally, it covers the limitations that may be faced while importing files, and the ways to overcome them.

Chapter 8, Searching Data, presents the mechanisms that are useful for searching data effectively, per table or inside an entire database.

Chapter 9, Performing Table and Database Operations, covers ways to perform some operations that influence and can be applied on entire tables or databases as a whole. Finally, it deals with table maintenance operations for table repair and optimization.

Chapter 10, Benefiting from the Relational System, is where we start covering advanced features of phpMyAdmin. The chapter explains how to define inter-table relations and how these relations can help us while browsing tables, entering data, or searching for it.

Chapter 11, Entering SQL Statements, helps us enter our own SQL commands. The chapter also covers the Query window — the window used to edit an SQL query. Finally, it also helps us to obtain the history of typed commands.

Chapter 12, Generating Multi-table Queries, covers the multi-table query generator, which allows us to produces these queries without actually typing them. The visual query builder is covered as well.

Chapter 13, Synchronizing Data and Supporting Replication, teaches us how to synchronize databases on the same server or from one server to another. It then covers how to manage MySQL replication.

Chapter 14, Using Query Bookmarks, covers one of the features of the phpMyAdmin configuration storage. It shows how to record bookmarks and how to manipulate them. Finally, it covers passing parameters to bookmarks.

Chapter 15, Documenting the System, gives an overview of how to produce documentation which explains the structure of the databases, using the tools offered by phpMyAdmin.

Chapter 16, Transforming Data Using MIME, explains how to apply transformations to the data in order to customize its format at view time.

Chapter 17, Supporting Features Added in MySQL 5, covers phpMyAdmin's support for the MySQL features that are new in MySQL 5.0 and 5.1, such as views, stored procedures, and triggers.

Chapter 18, Tracking Changes, teaches us how to record structure and data changes done from the phpMyAdmin interface.

Chapter 19, Administrating the MySQL Server, is about the administration of a MySQL server, focusing on user accounts and privileges. The chapter discusses how a system administrator can use phpMyAdmin's server management features for day-to-day user account maintenance, server verification, and server protection.

Appendix, Troubleshooting and Support, explains how to troubleshoot phpMyAdmin by performing simple verifications. It also explains how to interact with the development team for support, bug reports, and contributions.

What you need for this book

You need to have access to a server or workstation that has the following installed:

- A web server with PHP 5.2 or later
- MySQL 5.0 or later

Who this book is for

If you are a developer, system administrator, or web designer who wants to manage MySQL databases and tables efficiently, then this book is for you. This book assumes that you are already well-acquainted with MySQL basics. This book is a must read for every serious phpMyAdmin user who would like to use this outstanding application to its full power.

Conventions

In this book, you will find a number of styles of text that distinguish between different kinds of information. Here are some examples of these styles, and an explanation of their meaning.

Code words in text are shown as follows: "If this information is not available, a good alternate choice is localhost."

A block of code is set as follows:

```
$i++;
$cfg['Servers'][$i]['host']   = '';
$cfg['Servers'][$i]['port']   = '';
$cfg['Servers'][$i]['socket'] = '';
```

When we wish to draw your attention to a particular part of a code block, the relevant lines or items are set in bold:

```
UPDATE `marc_book`.`book` SET `some_bits` = b '101'
WHERE `book`.`isbn` = '1-234567-89-0' LIMIT 1;
```

Any command-line input or output is written as follows:

```
tar -xzvf phpMyAdmin-3.4.5-all-languages.tar.gz
```

New terms and **important words** are shown in bold. Words that you see on the screen, in menus or dialog boxes for example, appear in the text like this: "There are various files available in the **Download** section."

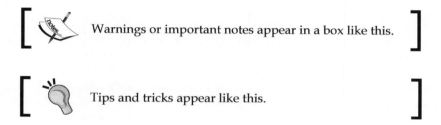

Warnings or important notes appear in a box like this.

Tips and tricks appear like this.

Reader feedback

Feedback from our readers is always welcome. Let us know what you think about this book—what you liked or may have disliked. Reader feedback is important for us to develop titles that you really get the most out of.

To send us general feedback, simply send an e-mail to feedback@packtpub.com, and mention the book title through the subject of your message.

If there is a topic that you have expertise in and you are interested in either writing or contributing to a book, see our author guide on www.packtpub.com/authors.

Customer support

Now that you are the proud owner of a Packt book, we have a number of things to help you to get the most from your purchase.

Errata

Although we have taken every care to ensure the accuracy of our content, mistakes do happen. If you find a mistake in one of our books—maybe a mistake in the text or the code—we would be grateful if you would report this to us. By doing so, you can save other readers from frustration and help us improve subsequent versions of this book. If you find any errata, please report them by visiting http://www.packtpub.com/support, selecting your book, clicking on the **errata submission form** link, and entering the details of your errata. Once your errata are verified, your submission will be accepted and the errata will be uploaded to our website, or added to any list of existing errata, under the Errata section of that title.

Piracy

Piracy of copyright material on the Internet is an ongoing problem across all media. At Packt, we take the protection of our copyright and licenses very seriously. If you come across any illegal copies of our works, in any form, on the Internet, please provide us with the location address or website name immediately so that we can pursue a remedy.

Please contact us at copyright@packtpub.com with a link to the suspected pirated material.

We appreciate your help in protecting our authors, and our ability to bring you valuable content.

Questions

You can contact us at questions@packtpub.com if you are having a problem with any aspect of the book, and we will do our best to address it.

1
Getting Started with phpMyAdmin

I wish you a warm welcome to this book! The goal of this first chapter is to:

- Know the position of this software product in the web spectrum
- Be aware of all its features
- Become proficient at installing and configuring it

PHP and MySQL: The leading open source duo

When we look at the web applications platforms currently offered by host providers, we will see that the most prevalent is the PHP/MySQL combination.

Well supported by their respective home sites — `http://www.php.net` and `http://www.mysql.com` — this duo has enabled developers to build a lot of ready-made open source web applications, and most importantly, enabled in-house developers to quickly put in place solid web solutions.

MySQL, which is mostly compliant with the SQL:2003 standard, is a database system well known for its speed, robustness, and a small connection overhead. This is important in a web context where pages must be served as quickly as possible.

PHP, usually installed as a module inside the web server, is a popular scripting language in which applications are written to communicate with MySQL (or other database systems) on the back end and browsers on the front end. Ironically, the acronym's significance has evolved along with the web evolution, from **Personal Home Page** to **Professional Home Page** to its current recursive definition — **PHP: Hypertext Preprocessor**. A blog posting about the successive name changes is available at `http://blog.roshambo.org/how-the-php-acronym-was-reborn`. PHP is available on millions of web domains and powers famous sites such as Facebook, Yahoo!, YouTube, and Wikipedia.

What is phpMyAdmin?

phpMyAdmin (official home page at `http://www.phpmyadmin.net`) is a web application written in PHP; it contains (like most web applications) XHTML, CSS, and JavaScript client code. This application provides a complete web interface for administering MySQL databases, and is widely recognized as the leading application in this field.

Being open source since its birth, it has enjoyed support from numerous developers and translators worldwide (being translated into 65 languages at the time of writing this book). The project is currently hosted at SourceForge.net and developed using their facilities by the phpMyAdmin team.

Host providers everywhere are showing their trust in phpMyAdmin by installing it on their servers. The popular cPanel (a website control application) contains phpMyAdmin. In addition, we can install our own copy of phpMyAdmin on our web server as long as our provider's server satisfies with the minimum requirements (refer to the *System requirements* section later in this chapter).

The goal of phpMyAdmin is to offer a complete web-based management of MySQL servers and data, and to keep up with MySQL and web standards evolution. While the product is always evolving, it supports all standard operations along with extra features.

The development team constantly fine-tunes the product based on the reported bugs and requested features, releasing new versions regularly.

phpMyAdmin offers features that cover basic MySQL database and table operations. It also has an internal system that maintains metadata to support advanced features. Finally, system administrators can manage users and privileges from phpMyAdmin. It is important to note that phpMyAdmin's choice of available operations depends on the rights the user has on a specific MySQL server.

Project documentation

Further information about phpMyAdmin is available on the home site's documentation page, located at `http://www.phpmyadmin.net/home_page/docs.php`. Moreover, the development team, helped by the community, maintains a wiki at `http://wiki.phpmyadmin.net`.

Installing phpMyAdmin

It's time to install the product and to configure it minimally for first-time use.

Our reason for installing phpMyAdmin could be one of the following:

- Our host provider did not install a central copy
- Our provider installed it but the version installed is not current
- We are working directly on our enterprise's web server

Note that we can dispense with the phpMyAdmin installation step, if we choose instead to install one of the AMP products that usually include phpMyAdmin as part of their offering. Further details are available at `http://en.wikipedia.org/wiki/List_of_AMP_packages`.

Required information

Some host providers offer an integrated web panel where we can manage accounts, including MySQL accounts, and also a file manager that can be used to upload web content. Depending on this, the mechanism we use to transfer phpMyAdmin source files to our web space may vary. We will need some of the following specific information before starting the installation:

- The web server's name or address. Here, we will assume it to be `www.mydomain.com`.
- Our web server's account information (username, password). This information will be used either for FTP or SFTP transfer, SSH login, or web control panel login.
- The MySQL server's name or IP address. If this information is not available, a good alternate choice is `localhost`, which means that the MySQL server is located on the same machine as the web server. We will assume this to be `localhost`.
- Our MySQL server's account information (username, password).

System requirements

The up-to-date requirements for a specific phpMyAdmin version are always stated in the accompanying `Documentation.html`. For phpMyAdmin 3.4, the minimum PHP version required is PHP 5.2 with **session** support, the **Standard PHP Library (SPL)** and **JSON** support. Moreover, the web server must have access to a MySQL server (version 5.0 or later)—either locally or on a remote machine. It is strongly recommended that the **PHP mcrypt** extension be present for improved performance in cookie-authentication mode (more on this in *Chapter 2*). In fact, on a 64-bit server, this extension is required.

On the browser side, cookie support must be activated, irrespective of any authentication mode we use.

Downloading the files

There are various files available in the **Download** section of `http://www.phpmyadmin.net`. There might be more than one version offered here and it is always a good idea to download the latest stable version. We only need to download one file, which works regardless of the platform (browser, web server, MySQL, or PHP version). For version 3.4, there are two groups of files—**english** and **all-languages**. If we need only the English interface, we can download a file whose name contains **english**, for example, **phpMyAdmin-3.4.5-english.zip**. On the other hand, if we have the need for at least one other language, choosing **all-languages** would be appropriate.

If we are using a server supporting only PHP 4—for which the PHP team has discontinued support since 31st December, 2007—the latest stable version of phpMyAdmin is not a good choice for download. We can use version 2.11.x, which is the latest branch that supports PHP 4, although the phpMyAdmin team has discontinued supporting this version too.

The files offered have various extensions: `.zip`, `.tar.bz2`, `.tar.gz`, `.tar.xz`, and `.7z`. Download a file having an extension for which you have the corresponding extractor. In the Windows world, `.zip` is the most universal file format, although it is bigger than `.gz` or `.bz2` (common in the Linux/Unix world). The `.7z` extension denotes a 7-Zip file, which is a format that achieves a higher compression ratio than the other formats offered; an extractor is available at `http://www.7-zip.org`. In the following examples, we will assume that the chosen file was **phpMyAdmin-3.4.5-all-languages.zip**.

After clicking on the appropriate file, the nearest mirror site is chosen by SourceForge.net. The file will start to download, and we can save it on our computer.

Installing on different platforms

The next step depends on the platform you are using. The following sections detail the procedures for some common platforms. You may proceed directly to the relevant section.

Installing on a remote server using a Windows client

Using the Windows Explorer, we double-click on the phpMyAdmin-3.4.5-all-languages.zip file we just downloaded on the Windows client. A file extractor should start, showing us all the scripts and directories inside the main phpMyAdmin-3.4.5-all-languages directory.

Use whichever mechanism your file extractor offers to save all the files, including sub-directories, to some location on your workstation. Here, we have chosen C:\. Therefore, a C:\phpMyAdmin-3.4.5-all-languages directory has been created by the extractor.

Now, it's time to transfer the entire directory structure C:\phpMyAdmin-3.4.5-all-languages to the web server in our web space. We use our favorite SFTP or FTP software or the web control panel for the transfer.

The exact directory under which we transfer phpMyAdmin may vary. It could be our public_html directory or another directory where we usually transfer web documents to. For further instructions about the exact directory to be used or the best way to transfer the directory structure, we can consult our host provider's help desk.

After the transfer is complete, these files can be removed from our Windows machine as they are no longer needed.

Installing on a local Linux server

Let us say we chose phpMyAdmin-3.4.5-all-languages.tar.gz and downloaded it directly to some directory on the Linux server. We move it to our web server's document root directory (for example, /var/www/html) or to one of its sub-directories (for example, /var/www/html/utilities). We then extract it with the following shell command or by using any graphical file extractor that our window manager offers:

```
tar -xzvf phpMyAdmin-3.4.5-all-languages.tar.gz
```

We must ensure that the permissions and ownership of the directory and files are appropriate for our web server. The web server user or group must be able to read them.

Installing on a local Windows server (Apache, IIS)

The procedure here is similar to that described in the *Installation on a remote server using a Windows client* section, except that the target directory will be under our `DocumentRoot` (for Apache) or our `wwwroot` (for IIS). Of course, we do not need to transfer anything after modifications are made to `config.inc.php` (described in the next section), as the directory is already on the web space.

Apache is usually run as a service. Hence, we have to ensure that the user under which the service is running has normal read privileges to access our newly created directory. The same principle applies to IIS, which uses the `IUSR_machinename` user. This user must have read access to the directory. You can adjust permissions in the `Security/permissions` tab of the directory's properties.

Configuring phpMyAdmin

Here, we learn how to prepare and use the configuration file containing the parameters to connect to MySQL, and which can be customized as per our requirements.

Before configuring, we can rename the directory `phpMyAdmin-3.4.5-all-languages` to something like `phpMyAdmin` or something easier to remember. This way, we and our users can visit an easily remembered URL to start phpMyAdmin. On most servers, the directory part of URLs is case-sensitive so we should communicate the exact URL to our users. We can also use a symbolic link if our server supports this feature.

In the following examples, we will assume that the directory has been renamed to `phpMyAdmin`.

The config.inc.php file

This file contains valid PHP code, defining the majority of the parameters (expressed by PHP variables) that we can change to tune phpMyAdmin to our own needs. There are also normal PHP comments in it, and we can comment our changes.

 Be careful not to add any blank line at the beginning or end of the file; this would hamper the execution of phpMyAdmin.

Note that phpMyAdmin looks for this file in the first level directory—the same one where `index.php` is located.

A `config.sample.inc.php` file is included, which can be copied and renamed to `config.inc.php` to act as a starting point. However, it is recommended that you use the web-based setup script (explained in this chapter) instead, for a more comfortable configuration interface.

There is another file—`layout.inc.php`—containing some configuration information. As phpMyAdmin offers theme management, this file contains the theme-specific colors and settings. There is one `layout.inc.php` per theme, located in `themes/<themename>`, for example, `themes/pmahomme`. We will cover modifying some of those parameters in *Chapter 4*.

Avoiding false error messages about permissions on config.inc.php

In its normal behavior, phpMyAdmin verifies that the permissions on this file do not allow everyone to modify it. This means that the file should not be writable by the world. Also, it displays a warning if the permissions are not correct. However, in some situations (for example a NTFS file system mounted on a non-Windows server), the permission detection fails. In these cases, you should set the following configuration parameter to `false`:

```
$cfg['CheckConfigurationPermissions'] = false;
```

The following sections explain various methods to add or change a parameter in `config.inc.php`.

Configuration principles

phpMyAdmin maintains no user accounts of its own; rather, it uses MySQL's privilege system.

It might now be the time to browse `http://dev.mysql.com/doc/refman/5.1/en/privilege-system.html`, to learn the basics about MySQL's privilege system.

With the lack of a configuration file, phpMyAdmin displays the cookie-based login panel by default (more details on this in *Chapter 2*, which explains that with the default configuration, it's not possible to log in with an empty password):

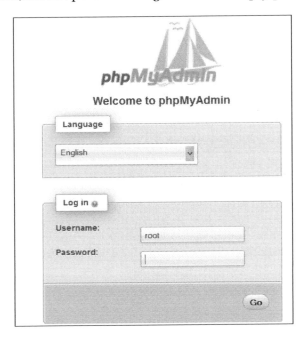

We can verify this fact by opening our browser and visiting `http://www.mydomain.com/phpMyAdmin`, and substituting the proper values for the domain part and the directory part.

If we are able to log in, it means that there is a MySQL server running on the same host as the web server (`localhost`), and we have just made a connection to it. However, not having created a configuration file means that we would not be able to manage other hosts through our installation of phpMyAdmin. Moreover, many advanced phpMyAdmin features (for example, query bookmarks, full-relational support, column transformation, and so on) would not be activated.

The cookie-based authentication method uses Blowfish encryption for storing credentials in browser cookies. When no configuration file exists, a Blowfish secret key is generated and stored in session data, which can open the door to security issues. This is why the following warning message is displayed:

The configuration file now needs a secret passphrase (blowfish_secret)

At this point, we have the following choices:

- Use phpMyAdmin without a configuration file
- Use the web-based setup script to generate a `config.inc.php` file
- Create a `config.inc.php` file manually

These two latter options are presented in the following sections. We should note that, even if we use the web-based setup script, we should familiarize ourselves with the `config.inc.php` file format as the setup script does not cover all the possible configuration options.

Web-based setup script

The web-based setup mechanism is strongly recommended in order to avoid syntax errors that could result from the manual creation of the configuration file. Also, as this file must respect PHP's syntax, it's common for new users to experience problems in this phase of the installation.

 A warning is in order here: The current version has only a limited number of translation languages for the setup interface.

To access the setup script, we must visit `http://www.mydomain.com/phpMyAdmin/setup`. On the initial execution, the following screenshot appears:

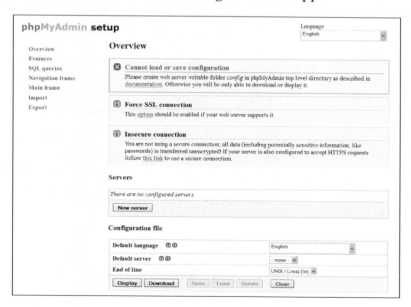

In most cases, the icons beside each parameter point to the respective phpMyAdmin official wiki and to the documentation, providing you with more information about this parameter and its possible values.

If **Show hidden messages** appears and we click on this link, messages that might have been shown earlier are revealed.

There are three warnings here. As taking care of the first message will require more manipulations, we will handle it in a moment. The second warning encourages you to use the ForceSSL option, which would automatically switch to HTTPS when using phpMyAdmin (not related to the setup phase).

Let us cover the third message—**Insecure connection**. This message appears if we are accessing the web server over HTTP—an insecure protocol. As we are possibly going to input confidential information, such as the user name and password in the setup phase, it's recommended that you communicate over HTTPS at least for this phase. HTTPS uses **SSL (Secure Socket Layer)** to encrypt the communication and make eavesdropping on the line impossible. If our web server supports HTTPS, we can simply follow the proposed link. It will restart the setup process, this time over HTTPS.

The first warning tells us that phpMyAdmin did not find a writable directory with the name config. This is normal as it was not present in the downloaded kit. Also, as the directory is not yet there, we observe that the **Save, Load,** and **Delete** buttons in the interface are grey. In this config directory, we can:

- Save the working version of the configuration file during the setup process
- Load a previously prepared config.inc.php file

It's not absolutely necessary that we create this configuration directory, as we can download the config.inc.php file produced by the setup procedure to our client machine. We can then upload it to phpMyAdmin in the first-level directory through the same mechanism (say, FTP) that we used to upload phpMyAdmin. For this exercise, we will create this directory.

The principle here is that the web server must be able to write to this directory. There is more than one way to achieve this. Here is one that would work on a Linux server—adding read, write, and execute permissions for everyone on this directory.

```
cd phpMyAdmin
mkdir config
chmod 777 config
```

Having done that, we refresh the page in our browser and get a screen resembling the following screenshot:

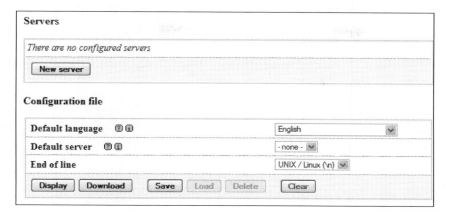

In the configuration dialog, a drop-down menu permits the user to choose the proper end-of-line format. We should pick up the format that corresponds to the platform (**UNIX / Linux** or **Windows**) on which we will open `config.inc.php` file with a text editor later.

A single copy of phpMyAdmin can be used to manage many MySQL servers but for now we will define parameters describing our first MySQL server. We click on **New server**, and the server configuration panel is shown.

A complete explanation of these parameters can be found in the following sections of this chapter. For now, we notice that the setup process has detected that PHP supports the `mysqli` extension. Therefore, this is the one that is chosen by default. This extension is the programming library used by PHP to communicate with MySQL.

We assume that our MySQL server is located on `localhost`. Hence, we keep this value and all the proposed values intact, except for the following:

- **Basic settings | Verbose name of this server** — we enter **my server**
- **Authentication | User for config auth** — we remove **root** and leave it empty, as the default authentication type is `cookie`, which ignores a username entered here

You can see that any parameter changed from its default value appears in a different color. Moreover, a small arrow becomes available, the purpose of which is to restore a field to its default value. Hence, you can feel free to experiment with changing parameters, knowing that you can easily revert to the proposed value. At this point, the **Basic settings** panel should resemble the following screenshot:

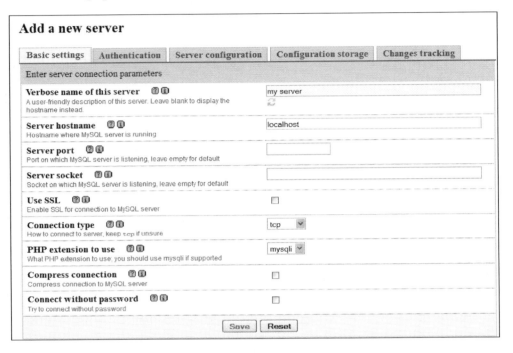

We then click **Save** and are brought back to the **Overview** panel. This save operation did not yet save anything to disk; changes were saved in memory. We are warned that a Blowfish secret key was generated. However, we don't have to remember it, as it's not keyed in during login process but is used internally. For the curious, you can switch to the **Features** panel and click on the **Security** tab to see which secret key was generated. Let us get back to the **Overview** panel. Now, our setup process knows about one MySQL server, and there are links that enable us to **Edit** or **Delete** these server settings as shown in the following screenshot:

Servers

#	Name	Authentication type	DSN	
1	my server	cookie	mysqli://localhost	Edit | Delete

We can have a look at the generated configuration lines by using the **Display** button; then we can analyze these parameters using the explanations given in the *Description of some configuration parameters* section later in this chapter.

At this point, this configuration is still just in memory, so we need to save it. This is done through the **Save** button on the **Overview** panel. It saves `config.inc.php` in the special `config` directory that we created previously. This is a directory strictly used for configuration purposes. If, for any reason, it was not possible to create this `config` directory, you just have to **download** the file by clicking on the **Download** button and upload it to the web server directory where phpMyAdmin is installed.

The last step is to copy `config.inc.php` from the `config` directory to the top-level directory—the one that contains `index.php`. By copying this file, it becomes owned by the user instead of the web server, ensuring that further modifications are possible. This copy can be done through FTP or through commands such as:

```
cd config
cp config.inc.php ..
```

As a security measure and until the configuration steps are not completed, it's recommended that you change the permission on the `config` directory, for example with the following command:

```
chmod ugo-rwx config
```

This is to block any unauthorized reading and writing in this directory.

Other configuration parameters can be set with these web-based setup pages. To do so, we would have to:

1. Enable read and write access to the `config` directory.
2. Copy the `config.inc.php` there.
3. Ensure that read and write access are provided to this file for the web server.
4. Start the web-based setup tool.

After the configuration steps are done, it's recommended to completely remove the `config` directory, as this directory is only used by the web-based setup script. phpMyAdmin displays the following warning on the home page (refer to *Chapter 3*) if it detects that this directory still exists:

Directory config, which is used by the setup script, still exists in your phpMyAdmin directory. You should remove it once phpMyAdmin has been configured.

You are invited to peruse the remaining menus to get a sense of the available configuration possibilities, either now or later when we cover a related subject.

In order to keep this book's text lighter, we will only refer to the parameters' textual values in the following chapters.

Manually creating config.inc.php

We can create this text file from scratch using our favorite text editor, or by using `config.sample.inc.php` as a starting point. The exact procedure depends upon which client operating system we are using. We can refer to the next section for further information.

The default values for all possible configuration parameters that can be located inside `config.inc.php` are defined in `libraries/config.default.php`. We can take a look at this file to see the syntax used as well as further comments about configuration. See the important note about this file in the *Upgrading phpMyAdmin* section of this chapter.

Tips for editing config.inc.php on a Windows client

This file contains special characters (Unix-style end of lines). Hence, we must open it with a text editor that understands this format. If we use the wrong text editor, this file will be displayed with very long lines. The best choice is a standard PHP editor such as NetBeans or Zend Studio for Eclipse. Another choice would be WordPad, Metapad, or UltraEdit.

Every time the `config.inc.php` file is modified, it will have to be transferred again to our web space. This transfer is done through an FTP or an SFTP client. You have the option to use a standalone FTP/SFTP client such as FileZilla, or save directly through FTP/SFTP if your PHP editor supports this feature.

Description of some configuration parameters

In this chapter and the next one, we will concentrate on the parameters that deal with connection and authentication. Other parameters will be discussed in the chapters where the corresponding features are explained.

PmaAbsoluteUri

The first parameter we will look at is `$cfg['PmaAbsoluteUri'] = '';`

Sometimes, phpMyAdmin needs to send an HTTP `Location` header and must know the absolute URI of its installation point. Using an absolute URI in this case is required by RFC 2616, section 14.30.

In most cases, we can leave this one empty as phpMyAdmin tries to auto-detect the correct value. If we browse a table later, then edit a row, and click on **Save**, we will receive an error message from our browser saying, for example, **This document does not exist**. This means that the absolute URI that phpMyAdmin built in order to reach the intended page was wrong, indicating that we must manually put the correct value in this parameter.

For example, we would change it to:

```
$cfg['PmaAbsoluteUri'] = 'http://www.mydomain.com/phpMyAdmin/';
```

Server-specific sections

The next section of the file contains server-specific configurations, each starting with the following code snippet:

```
$i++;
$cfg['Servers'][$i]['host'] = '';
```

If we examine only the normal server parameters (other parameters are covered in the *Installing phpMyAdmin configuration storage* section of this chapter), we see a section that resembles the following code block for each server:

```
$i++;
$cfg['Servers'][$i]['host']          = '';
$cfg['Servers'][$i]['port']          = '';
$cfg['Servers'][$i]['socket']        = '';
$cfg['Servers'][$i]['connect_type']  = 'tcp';
$cfg['Servers'][$i]['extension']     = 'mysqli';
$cfg['Servers'][$i]['compress']      = FALSE;
$cfg['Servers'][$i]['controluser']   = '';
$cfg['Servers'][$i]['controlpass']   = '';
$cfg['Servers'][$i]['auth_type']     = 'cookie';
$cfg['Servers'][$i]['user']          = '';
$cfg['Servers'][$i]['password']      = '';
$cfg['Servers'][$i]['only_db']       = '';
$cfg['Servers'][$i]['hide_db']       = '';
$cfg['Servers'][$i]['verbose']       = '';
```

In this section, we have to enter in `$cfg['Servers'][$i]['host']`, the hostname or IP address of the MySQL server, for example, `mysql.mydomain.com` or `localhost`. If this server is running on a non-standard port or socket, we fill in the correct values in `$cfg['Servers'][$i]['port']` or `$cfg['Servers'][$i]['socket']`. See the *connect_type, sockets, and port* section for more details about sockets.

The displayed server name inside phpMyAdmin's interface will be the one entered in `'host'` unless we enter a non-blank value in the following parameter, for example:

```
$cfg['Servers'][$i]['verbose'] = 'Test server';
```

This feature can thus be used to display a different server hostname as seen by the users on the login panel and on the main page, although the real server name can be seen as part of the user definition (for example, `root@localhost`) on the main page.

extension

The traditional-mechanism PHP uses to communicate with a MySQL server, as available in PHP before version 5, is the `mysql` extension. This extension is still available in PHP 5. However, a new extension called `mysqli` has been developed and should be preferred for PHP 5, due to its improved performance and its support of the full functionality of MySQL family 4.1.x. This extension is designed to work with MySQL version 4.1.3 and higher. As phpMyAdmin supports both extensions, we can choose either one for a particular server. We indicate the extension we want to use in `$cfg['Servers'][$i]['extension']`. The default value used is `mysqli`.

connect_type, socket, and port

Both the `mysql` and `mysqli` extensions automatically use a socket to connect to MySQL if the server is on `localhost`. Consider the following configuration:

```
$cfg['Servers'][$i]['host']         = 'localhost';
$cfg['Servers'][$i]['port']         = '';
$cfg['Servers'][$i]['socket']       = '';
$cfg['Servers'][$i]['connect_type'] = 'tcp';
$cfg['Servers'][$i]['extension']    = 'mysql';
```

The default value for `connect_type` is `tcp`. However, the extension will use a socket because it concludes that this is more efficient as the host is `localhost`. So in this case, we can use `tcp` or `socket` as the `connect_type`. To force a real TCP connection, we can specify `127.0.0.1` instead of `localhost` in the host parameter. Because the `socket` parameter is empty, the extension will try the default socket. If this default socket, as defined in `php.ini`, does not correspond to the real socket assigned to the MySQL server, we have to put the socket name (for example, `/tmp/mysql.sock`) in `$cfg['Servers'][$i]['socket']`.

If the hostname is not `localhost`, a TCP connection will occur; in this case, on the special port `3307`. However, leaving the port value empty would use the default `3306` port:

```
$cfg['Servers'][$i]['host']         = 'mysql.mydomain.com';
$cfg['Servers'][$i]['port']         = '3307';
$cfg['Servers'][$i]['socket']       = '';
$cfg['Servers'][$i]['connect_type'] = 'tcp';
$cfg['Servers'][$i]['extension']    = 'mysql';
```

compress

The protocol used to communicate between PHP and MySQL allows a compressed mode. Using this mode provides better efficiency. To take advantage of this mode, simply specify:

```
$cfg['Servers'][$i]['compress'] = TRUE;
```

PersistentConnections

Another important parameter (which is not server-specific but applies to all server definitions) is `$cfg['PersistentConnections']`. For every server we connect to using the `mysql` extension, this parameter, when set to TRUE, instructs PHP to keep the connection to the MySQL server open. This speeds up the interaction between PHP and MySQL. However, it is set to FALSE by default in `config.inc.php` as persistent connections are often a cause of resource depletion on servers (you would find MySQL refusing new connections). For this reason, the option is not even available for the `mysqli` extension. Hence, setting it to TRUE here would have no effect if you are connecting with this extension.

controluser

Defining the control user has the following two purposes:

- On a MySQL server running with `--skip-show-database`, the control user permits the use of multi-user authentication even though servers running with this option are not commonly seen. This aspect is described in *Chapter 2*.

- On all versions of MySQL server, this user is necessary to be able to use the advanced features of phpMyAdmin.

For authentication purposes, `controluser` is a special user (the usual name we choose for it is `pma`) who has the rights to read some fields in the special `mysql` database (which contains all the user definitions). phpMyAdmin sends queries with this special `controluser` only for the specific needs of authentication, and not for normal operation. The commands to create the control user are available in phpMyAdmin's `Documentation.html` and may vary from one version to the other. This documentation contains the most current commands.

When our `controluser` is created in the MySQL server, we fill in the parameters as in the following example, replacing xxx with a suitably complex password:

```
$cfg['Servers'][$i]['controluser'] = 'pma';
$cfg['Servers'][$i]['controlpass'] = 'xxx';
```

Standard password guidelines apply here. Please refer to `http://en.wikipedia.org/wiki/Password_strength` for suggestions.

Installing phpMyAdmin configuration storage

In addition to basic MySQL databases maintenance, phpMyAdmin offers advanced features that we will discover in the following chapters. These features require the installation of the phpMyAdmin configuration storage.

Goal of the configuration storage

The configuration storage consists of a set of tables that are used behind the scene by phpMyAdmin. They hold metadata which contains information to support special features such as query bookmarks and data transformation. Moreover, for tables using a storage engine that does not support foreign keys, relations between tables are kept in this configuration storage. The metadata is generated and maintained by phpMyAdmin on the basis of our actions from the interface.

Location of the configuration storage

There are two possible places to store these tables:

- A user's database—to facilitate every web developer owning a database to benefit from these features.
- A dedicated database called **pmadb (phpMyAdmin database)**. In a multi-user installation, this database may be accessible to a number of users while keeping the metadata private.

As this storage does not exist by default and because the phpMyAdmin team wants to promote it, the interface displays the following notice message on the home page:

> ⚠ The phpMyAdmin configuration storage is not completely configured, some extended features have been deactivated. To find out why click here.

This message can be disabled with the following parameter (which, by default, is set to FALSE):

```
$cfg['PmaNoRelation_DisableWarning'] = TRUE;
```

Performing the installation

The previous error message is displayed even if only a part of the configuration storage is lacking. Of course, on a fresh installation, all parts are lacking—our database has not yet heard of phpMyAdmin and needs to be outfitted with this configuration storage. Following the **here** link in the previous screenshot brings up a panel explaining that the pmadb, and the tables that are supposed to be a part of it, are either missing or undefined.

It's important to realize that the configuration storage will be functional only if the following two conditions are met:

- Proper definitions are present in config.inc.php
- The corresponding tables (and maybe the database) are created

To create the necessary structure that matches our current version of phpMyAdmin, a command file called create_tables.sql is available in the scripts sub-directory of the phpMyAdmin installation directory. However, we should not blindly execute it before understanding the possible choices—single-user installation or multi-user installation.

 In subsequent chapters, we will assume that the multi-user installation has been chosen.

Installing for a single user

Even if we are entitled to only one database by the system administrator, we can still use all the advanced features of phpMyAdmin. In this setup, we will use our existing database to store the metadata tables.

We need to modify a local copy of the `scripts/create_tables.sql` file to populate our database with all the needed tables. They will have the prefix `pma_` to make them easily recognizable. We need to remove the following lines:

```
CREATE DATABASE IF NOT EXISTS `phpmyadmin`
  DEFAULT CHARACTER SET utf8 COLLATE utf8_bin;
USE phpmyadmin;
```

This is done because we won't be using a `phpmyadmin` database but our own. Next, we should open our own database in phpMyAdmin. We are now ready to execute the script. There are two ways of doing this:

- As we already have the script in our editor, we can just copy the lines and paste them in the query box of the **SQL** page. More details on this in *Chapter 11*.

- Another way is to use the import technique shown in *Chapter 7*. We select the `create_tables.sql` script that we just modified.

After the creation, the navigation panel shows us the special `pma_` tables along with our normal tables.

It is now time to adjust all the configuration storage related parameters in `config.inc.php`. This can be done easily with the setup script as seen in this chapter, or by pasting the appropriate lines from the `config.sample.inc.php` file. The database is our own and the table names are the ones that have just been created:

```
$cfg['Servers'][$i]['pmadb']            = 'mydatabase';
$cfg['Servers'][$i]['bookmarktable']    = 'pma_bookmark';
$cfg['Servers'][$i]['relation']         = 'pma_relation';
$cfg['Servers'][$i]['table_info']       = 'pma_table_info';
$cfg['Servers'][$i]['table_coords']     = 'pma_table_coords';
$cfg['Servers'][$i]['pdf_pages']        = 'pma_pdf_pages';
$cfg['Servers'][$i]['column_info']      = 'pma_column_info';
$cfg['Servers'][$i]['history']          = 'pma_history';
$cfg['Servers'][$i]['tracking']         = 'pma_tracking';
$cfg['Servers'][$i]['designer_coords']  = 'pma_designer_coords';
$cfg['Servers'][$i]['userconfig']       = 'pma_userconfig';
```

 As table names are case sensitive, we must use the same names as the tables created by the installation script. We are free to change the table names (see the right-hand part of the configuration directives listed) provided we change them accordingly in the database.

The `pmadb` and each table have a specific function as listed next:

Function	Description	Explained in
pmadb	Defines the database where all tables are located	This chapter
bookmarktable	Contains the query bookmarks	*Chapter 14*
relation	Defines inter-table relations, as used in many of the phpMyAdmin's features	*Chapter 10*
table_info	Contains the display field	*Chapter 10*
table_coords and pdf_pages	Contains the metadata necessary for drawing a schema of the relations in a PDF format	*Chapter 15*
column_info	Used for column-commenting and MIME-based transformations	*Chapter 16*
history	Contains SQL query history information	*Chapter 11*
tracking	Contains the metadata and the actual SQL statements related to the tracked tables	*Chapter 18*
designer_coords	Holds the coordinates used by the **Designer** feature	*Chapter 10*
userconfig	Holds the user's preferences	*Chapter 3*

Between each phpMyAdmin version, the infrastructure may be enhanced — the changes are explained in `Documentation.html`. This is why phpMyAdmin has various checks to ascertain the structure of the tables. If we know we are using the latest structure, `$cfg['Servers'][$i]['verbose_check']` can be set to FALSE to avoid checks, thereby slightly increasing phpMyAdmin's speed.

Installing for multiple users

In this setup, we will have a distinct database — `pmadb` — to store the metadata tables. Our control user will have specific rights to this database. Each user will work with his/her login name and password which will be used to access his/her databases. However, whenever phpMyAdmin itself accesses `pmadb` to obtain some metadata, it will use the control user's privileges.

 Setting a multi-user installation is possible only for a MySQL system administrator who has the privileges of assigning rights to another user (here, the `pma` user).

We first ensure that the control user `pma` has been created and that its definition in `config.inc.php` is appropriate. We then copy `scripts/create_tables.sql` to our local workstation and edit it. We replace the following lines:

```
-- GRANT SELECT, INSERT, DELETE, UPDATE ON `phpmyadmin`.* TO
--   'pma'@localhost;
```

with these, removing the comment characters (double-dash):

```
GRANT SELECT, INSERT, DELETE, UPDATE ON `phpmyadmin`.* TO
   'pma'@localhost;
```

We then execute this script by importing it (refer to *Chapter 7*). The net effect is to create the `phpmyadmin` database, assign proper rights to user `pma`, and populate the database with all the necessary tables.

The last step is to adjust all the parameters in `config.inc.php` that relate to relational features. Please refer to the *Installing for a single user* section, except for the database name in the `pmadb` parameter, which will be as shown in the following code snippet:

```
$cfg['Servers'][$i]['pmadb'] = 'phpmyadmin';
```

The installation is now complete. We will test the features in the coming sections and chapters. We can do a quick check by logging out of phpMyAdmin, then logging in and displaying the home page; the warning message should be gone.

Upgrading phpMyAdmin

Normally, upgrading is just a matter of installing the newer version into a separate directory and copying the previous version's `config.inc.php` to the new directory.

 An upgrade path or the first-installation path, which should **not** be taken, is to copy `libraries/config.default.php` to `config.inc.php`. This is because the default configuration file is version-specific, and is not guaranteed to work for the future versions.

New parameters appear from version to version. They are documented in `Documentation.html` and defined in `libraries/config.default.php`. If a configuration parameter is not present in `config.inc.php`, its value from `libraries/config.default.php` will be used. Therefore, we do not have to include it in `config.inc.php` if the default value suits us.

Special care must be taken to propagate the changes we might have made to the `layout.inc.php` files depending on the themes used. We will have to copy our custom themes sub-directories if we added our own themes to the structure.

Summary

This chapter covered the popularity of PHP/MySQL for web applications. The chapter also gave an overview of why phpMyAdmin is recognized as a leading application to interface MySQL from the web. It then discussed common reasons for installing phpMyAdmin, steps for downloading it from the main site, basic configuration, uploading phpMyAdmin to our web server, and upgrading.

Now that the basic installation has been done, the next chapter will deal with the configuration subject in depth, by exploring the authentication and security aspects.

2
Configuring Authentication and Security

There are many ways of configuring authentication in phpMyAdmin—depending on our goals, the presence of other applications, and the level of security we need. This chapter explores the available possibilities.

Logging in to MySQL through phpMyAdmin

When we type in a username and password, although it seems that we are logging in to phpMyAdmin, we are not! We are merely using phpMyAdmin (which is running on the web server) as an interface that sends our username and password information to the MySQL server. Strictly speaking, we do not log in *to* phpMyAdmin, but *through* phpMyAdmin.

This is why in user-support forums about phpMyAdmin, people asking for help about authentication are often referred back to their MySQL server's administrator, because a lost MySQL user or password is not a phpMyAdmin problem.

This section explains the various authentication modes offered by phpMyAdmin.

Logging in to an account without a password

MySQL's default installation leaves a server open to intrusion because it creates a MySQL account named `root` without a password — unless a password has been set by the MySQL distributor. The recommended remedy for this weakness in security is to set a password for the `root` account. In the eventuality that we cannot set one or do not want to set one, we will have to make a configuration change to phpMyAdmin. Indeed, a server-specific configuration parameter, `$cfg['Servers']` `[$i]['AllowNoPassword']` exists. Its default value is `false`, which means that no account is permitted to log in without a password. Generally, this directive should remain `false` to avoid this kind of access through phpMyAdmin, as hackers are actively probing the web for insecure MySQL servers. Go through the *Securing phpMyAdmin* section for other ideas about protecting your server.

> If the `AllowNoPassword` parameter is left to `false` and a login attempt is made without a password, an **Access denied** message is displayed.

Authenticating a single user with config

We might have the need to automatically connect to a MySQL server via phpMyAdmin, using a fixed username and password, without even having been asked for it. This is the precise goal of the `config` authentication type.

For our first example, we will use this `config` authentication. However, in the *Authenticating multiple users* section, we will see more powerful and versatile ways of authenticating.

> Using the `config` authentication type leaves our phpMyAdmin open to intrusion, unless we protect it as explained in the *Securing phpMyAdmin* section of this chapter.

Here, we ask for `config` authentication, and enter our username and password for this MySQL server:

```
$cfg['Servers'][$i]['auth_type'] = 'config';
$cfg['Servers'][$i]['user']      = 'marc';
$cfg['Servers'][$i]['password']  = 'xxx';
```

We can then save the changes we made in `config.inc.php`.

Testing the MySQL connection

Now it's time to start phpMyAdmin and try connecting to it with the values we configured. This will test the following:

- The values we entered in the `config` file or on the web-based setup
- The setup of the PHP component inside the web server, if we did a manual configuration
- Communication between web and MySQL servers

We start our browser and point it to the directory where we installed phpMyAdmin, as in `http://www.mydomain.com/phpMyAdmin/`. If this does not work, we try `http://www.mydomain.com/phpMyAdmin/index.php`. (This would mean that our web server is not configured to interpret `index.php` as the default starting document.)

If you still get an error, refer to the *Appendix* for troubleshooting and support. We should now see phpMyAdmin's home page. *Chapter 3* gives an overview of the panels seen now.

Authenticating multiple users

We might want to allow a single copy of phpMyAdmin to be used by a group of persons, each having their own MySQL username and password, and seeing only the databases they have rights to. Or we might prefer to avoid having our username and password in clear text in `config.inc.php`.

Instead of relying on a username and password stored in `config.inc.php`, phpMyAdmin will communicate with the browser and get authentication data from it. This enables true login for all users defined in a specific MySQL server, without having to define them in the configuration file. There are three modes offered that allow a controlled login to MySQL via phpMyAdmin—`http`, `cookie`, and `signon`. We will have to choose the one that suits our specific situation and environment (more on this in a moment). The `http` and `cookie` modes may require that we first define a control user, as covered in *Chapter 1*.

Authenticating with HTTP

This mode—`http`—is the traditional mode offered in HTTP, in which the browser asks for the username and password, sends them to phpMyAdmin, and keeps sending them until all the browser windows are closed.

To enable this mode, we simply use the following line:

```
$cfg['Servers'][$i]['auth_type'] = 'http';
```

We can also define the HTTP **basic auth realm** (http://en.wikipedia.org/wiki/Basic_access_authentication), which is a message to be displayed to the user at login time, via `$cfg['Servers'][$i]['auth_http_realm']`. This can help indicate the purpose of this server.

This mode has the following limitations:

- PHP, depending on the version, might not support HTTP authentication for all kinds of web servers.

- If we want to protect phpMyAdmin's directory with a .htaccess file (refer to the *Securing phpMyAdmin* section in this chapter), this will interfere with HTTP authentication type; we cannot use both.

- Browsers usually store the authentication information to save retyping credentials but bear in mind that these credentials are saved in an unencrypted format.

- There is no support for proper logout in the HTTP protocol; hence we have to close all browser windows to be able to log in again with the same username.

Authenticating with cookie values

The `cookie` authentication mode is superior to `http` in terms of the functionalities it offers. This mode permits true login and logout, and can be used with PHP running on any kind of web server. It presents a login panel (as shown in the following screenshot) from within phpMyAdmin. This can be customized as we have the application source code. However, as you may have guessed, for `cookie` authentication, the browser must accept cookies coming from the web server—but this is the case for all authentication modes anyway.

This mode stores the username typed in the login screen into a permanent cookie in our browser while the password is stored as a temporary cookie. In a multi-server configuration, the username and password corresponding to each server are stored separately. To protect the username and password secrecy against attack methods that target cookie content, they are encrypted using the Blowfish cipher. So, to use this mode, we have to define (once) in `config.inc.php`, a secret string that will be used to securely encrypt all passwords stored as cookies from this phpMyAdmin installation.

This string is set via the `blowfish_secret` directive:

```
$cfg['blowfish_secret'] = 'jgjgRUD875G%/*';
```

In the previous example, an arbitrary string of characters was used; this string can be very complex as nobody will ever need to type it on a login panel. If we fail to configure this directive, a random secret string is generated by phpMyAdmin but it will last only for the current working session. Therefore, some features such as recalling the previous username on the login panel won't be available.

Then, for each server-specific section, use the following:

```
$cfg['Servers'][$i]['auth_type'] = 'cookie';
```

The next time we start phpMyAdmin, we will see the login panel as shown in the following screenshot:

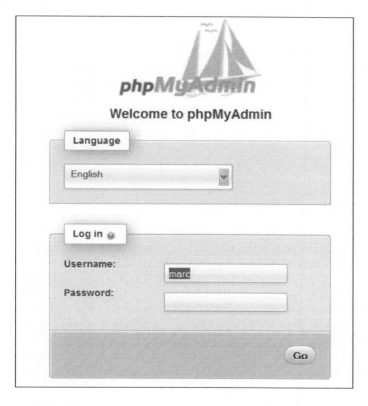

By default, phpMyAdmin displays (in the login panel) the last username for which a successful login was achieved for this particular server, as retrieved from the permanent cookie. If this behavior is not acceptable (someone else who logs in from the same workstation should not see the previous username), we can set the following parameter to FALSE:

```
$cfg['LoginCookieRecall'] = FALSE;
```

There is a security feature to add a specific time limit for the validity of a password. This feature helps to protect the working session. After a successful login, our password is stored (encrypted) in a cookie, along with a timer. Every action in phpMyAdmin resets the timer. If we stay inactive for a certain number of seconds, as defined in $cfg['LoginCookieValidity'], we are disconnected and have to log in again. Increasing this parameter does not work in all cases, because PHP's own session.gc_maxlifetime directive can get in the way. Please refer to http://php.net/manual/en/session.configuration.php for an explanation of this directive. Therefore, if phpMyAdmin detects that the value of session.gc_maxlifetime is less than the configured $cfg['LoginCookieValidity'], a warning is displayed on the main page. The default is 1440 seconds; this matches the php.ini's default value of the session.gc_maxlifetime parameter.

The Blowfish algorithm used to protect the username and password requires many computations. To achieve the best possible speed, the PHP's mcrypt extension and its accompanying library must be installed on our web server.

To help users realize that this extension is really important, a message is displayed on the main page when phpMyAdmin detects its absence. The $cfg['McryptDisableWarning'] directive controls this message. By default, a value of false implies that the message is shown.

Authenticating with signon mode

During the course of a working session, a user may encounter several requests to authenticate, from different web applications. The reason is these applications don't talk to each other and this situation inconveniences most users.

The signon mode enables us to use the credentials from another application to skip the authentication phase of phpMyAdmin. In order for this to work, this other application has to store the proper credentials into PHP's session data to be retrieved later by phpMyAdmin.

Storing credentials in PHP's session is not guaranteed to be safe, according to the PHP manual: http://php.net/manual/en/session.security.php.

To enable this mode, we start with the following directive:

```
$cfg['Servers'][$i]['auth_type'] = 'signon';
```

Let us suppose that the authenticating application has used a session named FirstApp to store the credentials. We tell this to phpMyAdmin by adding the following line of code:

```
$cfg['Servers'][$i]['SignonSession'] = 'FirstApp';
```

We must take care of users that would try to access phpMyAdmin before the other application; in this case, phpMyAdmin will redirect users to the authenticating application. This is done with:

```
$cfg['Servers'][$i]['SignonURL'] = 'http://www.mydomain.com/FirstApp';
```

How does the authenticating application store credentials in a format that phpMyAdmin can understand? An example is included as scripts/signon.php. In this script, there is a simple HTML form to input the credentials and logic that initializes the session—we would use FirstApp as a session name, and create the user, password, host, and port information into this session, shown as follows:

```
$_SESSION['PMA_single_signon_user']     = $_POST['user'];
$_SESSION['PMA_single_signon_password'] = $_POST['password'];
$_SESSION['PMA_single_signon_host']     = $_POST['host'];
$_SESSION['PMA_single_signon_port']     = $_POST['port'];
```

> Note that the authenticating first application does not need to ask the MySQL's credentials to the user. These could be hard coded inside the application, as they are secret or there is a known correspondence between the credentials of this application and that of MySQL's.

To pass additional configuration parameters to the signon module, $_SESSION['PMA_single_signon_cfgupdate'] can receive an array containing any additional server parameters that are permitted in $cfg['Servers'][$i].

The authenticating application then uses a way of its choosing—a link or a button—to let its users start phpMyAdmin. If an error happens during the login (for example, a denied access), the signon module saves into $_SESSION['PMA_single_signon_error_message'] the appropriate error message.

In another example, scripts/openid.php shows how to log in using the popular OpenID mechanism.

Configuring for multiple server support

The `config.inc.php` file contains at least one server-specific section; however, we can add more, enabling a single copy of phpMyAdmin to manage many MySQL servers. Let us see how to configure more servers.

Defining servers in the configuration file

In the server-specific sections of the `config.inc.php` file, we see lines referring to `$cfg['Servers'][$i]` for each server. Here, the variable `$i` is used so that one can easily cut and paste whole sections of the configuration file to configure more servers. While copying such sections, we should take care that the `$i++;` instruction, which precedes each section and is crucial to delimit the server sections, is also copied.

Then, at the end of the sections, the following line controls the startup:

```
$cfg['ServerDefault'] = 1;
```

The default value, 1, means that phpMyAdmin will use by default the first server defined. We can specify any number, for the corresponding server-specific section. We can also enter the value 0, signifying no default server; in this case a list of available servers will be presented at login time.

This configuration can also be done via web-based setup. Given here is an example of a multi-server definition, with the default server being set to **let the user choose**:

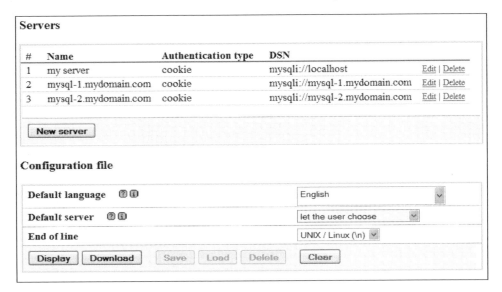

With no default server defined, phpMyAdmin will present a server choice:

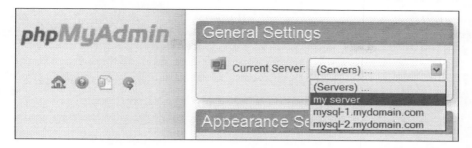

Authenticating through an arbitrary server

Another mechanism can be used if we want to be able to connect to an undefined MySQL server. First, we have to set the following parameter:

```
$cfg['AllowArbitraryServer'] = TRUE;
```

We also have to put back the default value of 1 into $cfg['ServerDefault']. Then, we need to use the cookie authentication type. We will be able to choose the server and enter a username and a password.

 Allowing an arbitrary server implies that any MySQL server accessible from our web server could be connected to via phpMyAdmin. Therefore, this feature should be used in conjunction with a reinforced security mechanism (refer to the *Securing phpMyAdmin* section).

As seen here, we still can choose one of the defined servers in **Server Choice**. In addition, we can also enter an arbitrary server name, a username, and a password:

Logging out

A mechanism is available to tell phpMyAdmin which URL it should reach after a user has logged out. This feature eases integration with other applications and works for all authentication types that permit to log out. Here is an example:

```
$cfg['Servers'][$i]['LogoutURL'] = 'http://www.mydomain.com';
```

This directive must contain an absolute URL, including the protocol.

Securing phpMyAdmin

Security can be examined at the following various levels:

- How we can protect the phpMyAdmin installation directory
- Which workstations can access phpMyAdmin
- The databases that a legitimate user can see

Protecting phpMyAdmin at directory level

Suppose an unauthorized person is trying to use our copy of phpMyAdmin. If we use the simple `config` authentication type, anyone knowing the URL of our phpMyAdmin will have the same effective rights to our data as we do. In this case, we should use the directory protection mechanism offered by our web server (for example, `.htaccess`, a file name with a leading dot) to add a level of protection. More details are available at `http://en.wikipedia.org/wiki/Basic_access_authentication`.

If we decide on using `http` or `cookie` authentication types, our data would be safe enough. However, we should take normal precautions with our password (including its periodic change).

The directory where phpMyAdmin is installed contains sensitive data. Not only the configuration file but also all scripts stored there must be protected from alteration. We should ensure that apart from us, only the web server effective user has read access to the files contained in this directory, and that only we can write to them.

phpMyAdmin's scripts never have to modify anything inside this directory, except when we use the **Save export file to server** feature (explained in *Chapter 6*).

Another recommendation is to rename the default phpMyAdmin directory to something less obvious; this discourages probing of our server. This is called security by obscurity and can be very effective—but avoid choosing other obvious names such as admin.

Another possible attack is from other developers having an account on the same web server as we do. In this kind of attack, someone can try to open our config. inc.php file. As this file is readable by the web server, someone could try to include our file from their PHP scripts. This is why it is recommended to use PHP's open_ basedir feature, possibly applying it to all directories from which such attacks could originate. More details can be found at http://php.net/manual/en/ini.core. php#ini.open-basedir.

Displaying error messages

phpMyAdmin uses the PHP's custom error-handler mechanism. One of the benefits of this error handler is to avoid path disclosure, which is considered a security weakness. The default settings related to this are:

```
$cfg['Error_Handler']              = array();
$cfg['Error_Handler']['display'] = false;
```

You should let the default value for display be false, unless you are developing a new phpMyAdmin feature and want to see all PHP errors and warnings.

Protecting with IP-based access control

An additional level of protection can be implemented, this time verifying the **Internet Protocol (IP)** address of the machine from which the request is received. To achieve this level of protection, we construct rules allowing or denying access, and specify the order in which these rules will be applied.

Defining rules

The format of a rule is:

```
<'allow' | 'deny'> <username> [from] <source>
```

The `from` keyword being optional; here are some examples:

Rule	Description
allow Bob from 1.2.3/24	User Bob is allowed from any address matching the network 1.2.3 (this is CIDR IP matching, more details at http://en.wikipedia.org/wiki/CIDR_notation).
deny Alice from 4.5/16	User Alice cannot access when located on network 4.5.
allow Melanie from all	User Melanie can log in from anywhere.
deny % from all	all can be used as an equivalent to 0.0.0.0/0, meaning any host. Here, the % sign means any user.

Usually we will have several rules. Let us say we wish to have the following two rules:

```
allow Marc from 45.34.23.12
allow Melanie from all
```

We have to put them in `config.inc.php` (in the related server-specific section) as follows:

```
$cfg['Servers'][$i]['AllowDeny']['rules'] =
    array('allow Marc from 45.34.23.12', 'allow Melanie from all');
```

When defining a single rule or multiple rules, a PHP array is used. We must follow its syntax, enclosing each complete rule within single quotes and separating each rule from the next with a comma. Thus, if we have only one rule, we must still use an array to specify it. The next parameter explains the order in which rules are interpreted.

Order of interpretation for rules

By default, this parameter is empty:

```
$cfg['Servers'][$i]['AllowDeny']['order'] = '';
```

This means that no IP-based verification is made.

Suppose we want to allow access by default, denying access only to some username/IP pairs, we should use:

```
$cfg['Servers'][$i]['AllowDeny']['order'] = 'deny,allow';
```

In this case, all deny rules will be applied first, followed by allow rules. If a case is not mentioned in the rules, access is granted. Being more restrictive, we would want to deny by default. We can use:

```
$cfg['Servers'][$i]['AllowDeny']['order'] = 'allow,deny';
```

This time, all allow rules are applied first, followed by deny rules. If a case is not mentioned in the rules, access is denied. The third (and most restrictive) way of specifying rules order is:

```
$cfg['Servers'][$i]['AllowDeny']['order'] = 'explicit';
```

Now, deny rules are applied before allow rules. A username/IP address pair must be listed in the allow rules and must not be listed in the deny rules, for access to be granted.

Blocking root access

As the root user is present in almost all MySQL installations, it's often the target of attacks. A parameter permits us to easily block all phpMyAdmin logins of the MySQL's root account, using the following:

```
$cfg['Servers'][$i]['AllowRoot'] = FALSE;
```

Some system administrators prefer to disable the root account at the MySQL server level, creating another less obvious account possessing the same privileges. This has the advantage of blocking root access from all sources, not just from phpMyAdmin.

Protecting in-transit data

HTTP is not inherently immune to network sniffing (grabbing sensitive data off the wire). So, if we want to protect not only our username and password but all the data that travels between our web server and browser, then we have to use HTTPS.

To do so, assuming that our web server supports HTTPS, we just have to start phpMyAdmin by putting https instead of http in the URL as follows:

```
https://www.mydomain.com/phpMyAdmin/
```

If we are using `PmaAbsoluteUri` auto-detection, shown as follows:

```
$cfg['PmaAbsoluteUri'] = '';
```

phpMyAdmin will see that we are using HTTPS in the URL and react accordingly.

If not, we must put the `https` part in this parameter as follows:

```
$cfg['PmaAbsoluteUri'] = 'https://www.mydomain.com/phpMyAdmin';
```

We can automatically switch users to an HTTPS connection with the following setting:

```
$cfg['ForceSSL'] = TRUE;
```

Summary

This chapter gave us an overview of how to use a single copy of phpMyAdmin to manage multiple servers, and also of using authentication types to fulfill the needs of a users' group while protecting authentication credentials. The chapter also covered the ways of securing our phpMyAdmin installation.

In the next chapter, we will have a look at all the panels and windows that comprise the user interface of phpMyAdmin.

Over Viewing the Interface

3

Before delving into task-oriented chapters, such as searching and the like, it's appropriate to have a look at the general organization of phpMyAdmin's interface. We will also see configuration parameters and settings that influence the interface as a whole.

Over viewing panels and windows

The phpMyAdmin interface is composed of various panels and windows, each one having a specific function. We will first provide a quick overview of each panel, and then take a detailed look later in this chapter.

Login panels

The login panel that appears depends on the authentication type chosen. For the `http` type, it will take the form of our browser's HTTP authentication pop-up screen. For the `cookie` type, the phpMyAdmin-specific login panel will be displayed (covered in *Chapter 2*). For the external authentication (`signon`), the login panel is handled by the external application itself. By default, a **Server** choice dialog and a **Language** selector are present on this panel.

However, if we are using the `config` authentication type, no login panel is displayed, and the first displayed interface contains the navigation and the main panels.

Navigation and main panels

These panels go together and are displayed during most of our working session with phpMyAdmin. The **navigation panel** is our guide through the databases and tables. The **main panel** is the working area where the data is managed and results appear. Its exact layout depends on the choices made from the navigation panel and the sequence of operations performed. For the majority of languages (which are written from left to right) the navigation panel is located on the left side and the main panel is on the right, but for right-to-left languages such as Hebrew, these panels are reversed.

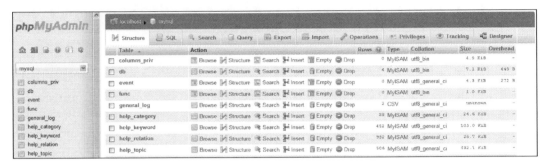

Home page

The main panel can take the form of the home page. The home page will then contain various links related to MySQL operations or phpMyAdmin information, a **Language** selector, and possibly the **Theme / Style** selector.

Views

In the main panel, we can see the `Database` view—where we can take various actions about a specific database, or the `Table` view—where we can access many functions to manage a table. There is also a `Server` view, useful for both system administrator and non-administrator users. All these views have a top menu, which takes the form of tabs that lead to different pages used to present information regrouped by common functions (table structure, privileges, and so on).

Query window

This is a distinct window that is usually opened from the navigation panel—and sometimes from the main panel when editing an SQL query. Its main purpose is to facilitate work on queries and display the results on the main panel.

Starting page

When we start phpMyAdmin, we will see one of the following panels (depending on the authentication type specified in `config.inc.php`, and on whether it has more than one server defined in it):

- One of the login panels
- The navigation and main panels with the home page displayed in the main panel

Customizing general settings

This section describes settings that have an impact on many panels. These settings modify the appearance of titles in windows, of information icons, and how the list of tables is sorted. The whole visual style of all pages is controlled by the theme system, which is covered in this section as well. This section also deals with how to restrict the list of databases seen by users.

Configuring window title

When the navigation and main panels are displayed, the window's title changes to reflect which MySQL server, database, and table are active. These directives control the following amount of information to be displayed: `$cfg['TitleDefault']`, `$cfg['TitleServer']`, `$cfg['TitleDatabase']`, and `$cfg['TitleTable']`.

If no server is selected, `$cfg['TitleDefault']` controls the title. When a server is selected (but no database), `$cfg['TitleServer']` controls what is displayed in the title bar. Then if a database is selected, `$cfg['TitleDatabase']` enters into play. Finally, `$cfg['TitleTable']` is effective if a table is selected.

These directives contain format strings that control which piece of information is shown. For example, here is the default value of one of these directives:

```
$cfg['TitleTable'] = '@HTTP_HOST@ / @VSERVER@ / @DATABASE@ / @TABLE@ |
    @PHPMYADMIN@';
```

The possible format strings and their meaning are described in `Documentation.html`, FAQ 6.27.

Natural sort order for database and table names

Usually, computers sort items in lexical order, which gives the following results for a list of tables:

```
table1
table10
table2
table3
```

phpMyAdmin implements **natural sort order** by default, as specified by `$cfg['NaturalOrder']` being TRUE. Thus the database and table lists in navigation and main panels are sorted as:

```
table1
table2
table3
table10
```

Creating site-specific header and footer

Some users may want to display a company logo, a link to their company's helpdesk, or other information on the phpMyAdmin interface. In the main phpMyAdmin directory, for this purpose, we can create two scripts— `config.header.inc.php` and `config.footer.inc.php`. We can put our own PHP or XHTML code in these scripts, and it will appear either at the beginning (for header) or at the end (for footer) of the `cookie` login and the main panel pages.

For example, creating a `config.footer.inc.php` containing these lines:

```
<hr />
<em>All the information on this page is confidential.</em>
```

Using such a sentence in the footer would produce the intended message on all pages as shown in the following screenshot:

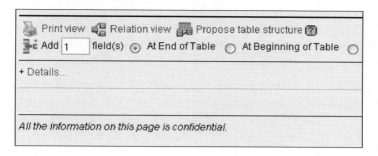

Themes

A theme system is available in phpMyAdmin. The color parameters and the various icons are located in a directory structure under the themes sub-directory. For each available theme, there is a sub-directory named after the theme. It contains:

- layout.inc.php for the theme parameters
- css directory with the various CSS scripts
- img directory containing any icons or other imagery (for example, logos)
- screen.png, a screenshot of this theme

The downloaded kit contains two themes but there are more available at http://phpmyadmin.net/home_page/themes.php. Installing a new theme is just a matter of downloading the corresponding .zip file and extracting it into the themes sub-directory.

 In case someone would like to build a custom theme that contains JavaScript code, please note that all phpMyAdmin 3.4 pages include the jQuery library.

Configuring themes

In config.inc.php, the $cfg['ThemePath'] parameter contains './themes' by default, indicating which sub-directory the required structure is located in. This could be changed to point to another directory where your company's specific phpMyAdmin themes are located.

The default chosen theme is specified in $cfg['ThemeDefault'], and is set to 'pmahomme'. If no theme selection is available for users, this theme will be used.

Selecting themes

On the home page, we can offer a theme selector to users. Setting
$cfg['ThemeManager'] to TRUE (the default) shows the selector as shown
in the following screenshot:

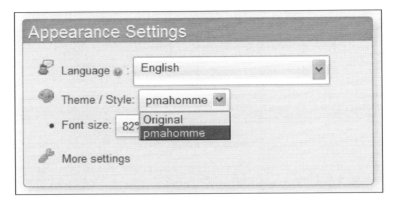

To help choose a suitable theme, the **Theme / Style** link displays a panel containing
screenshots of the available themes and a **Get more themes** link. We can then click
on **take it** under the theme we want. A reference to the chosen theme is stored in a
cookie and, by default, is applied to all servers we connect to.

To make phpMyAdmin remember one theme per MySQL server, we set
$cfg['ThemePerServer'] to TRUE.

Selecting a language

A **Language** selector appears on the login panel (if any) and on the home page. The
default behavior of phpMyAdmin is to use the language defined in our browser's
preferences, if there is a corresponding language file for this version.

The default language used, in case the program cannot detect one, is defined in
config.inc.php in the $cfg['DefaultLang'] parameter with 'en' (English). This
value can be changed. The possible values for language names are defined in the
libraries/select_lang.lib.php script in the PMA_langDetails() function.

Even if the default language is defined, each user (especially on a multi-user
installation) can choose his/her preferred language from the selector. The user's
choice will be remembered in a cookie whenever possible.

We can also force a single language by setting the $cfg['Lang']$ parameter with a value, such as 'fr' (French). Another parameter, $cfg['FilterLanguages']$, is available. Suppose we want to shorten the list of available languages to **English** and **Français—French**, as those are the ones used exclusively by the users of this phpMyAdmin's instance. This is accomplished by building a regular expression indicating which languages we want to display based on the ISO 639 codes of these languages. To continue with our example, we would use:

```
$cfg['FilterLanguages']  = '^(fr|en)';
```

In this expression, the caret (^) means "starting with" and the (|) means "or". The expression indicates that we are restricting the list to languages whose corresponding ISO codes start with fr or en.

By default, this parameter is empty, meaning that no filter is applied to the list of available languages.

Slider

On some pages, you will see a small plus sign followed by a controlling label—either **Options** or **Details**. A click on the label opens a slider to reveal a section of the interface, which is believed to be less often used in day-to-day work. As few people prefer to immediately see the whole interface at the expense of screen space, there is a configuration parameter that controls how the sliders are initially set:

```
$cfg['InitialSlidersState'] = 'closed';
```

The default value of closed means that sliders must be opened by a click on the label; you might have guessed that the reverse value is open. A third value, disabled, can be used by slider-allergic users.

Restricting the list of databases

Sometimes it is useful to avoid showing in the navigation panel, all the databases a user has access to. phpMyAdmin offers two ways of restriction—only_db and hide_db.

To specify the list of what can be seen, the only_db parameter is used. It may contain a database name or a list of database names. Only these databases will be seen in the navigation panel:

```
$cfg['Servers'][$i]['only_db'] = 'payroll';
$cfg['Servers'][$i]['only_db'] = array('payroll', 'hr');
```

The database names can contain MySQL wildcard characters such as _ and %. These wildcard characters are described at http://dev.mysql.com/doc/refman/5.1/en/account-names.html. If an array is used to specify many databases, they will be displayed on the interface in the same order they are listed in the array.

Another feature of `only_db` is that you can use it not to restrict the list, but instead to put emphasis on certain names that will be displayed on top of the list. Here, the `myspecial` database name will appear first, followed by all other names:

```
$cfg['Servers'][$i]['only_db'] = array('myspecial', '*');
```

We can also indicate which database names must be hidden with the `hide_db` parameter. It contains a regular expression (http://en.wikipedia.org/wiki/Regular_expression) representing what to exclude. If we do not want users to see any database whose name begins with `'secret'`, we would use:

```
$cfg['Servers'][$i]['hide_db'] = '^secret';
```

These parameters apply to all users for this server-specific configuration.

 These mechanisms do not replace the MySQL privilege system. Users' rights on other databases still apply, but they cannot use phpMyAdmin's navigation panel to reach their other databases or tables.

Deactivating Ajax

Certain pages are using **Asynchronous** JavaScript to improve user experience. We can deactivate this behavior by setting `$cfg['AjaxEnable']` to `false`; in this case, the pages for which a non-Ajax behavior has been programmed, will cease using Ajax, performing a full refresh instead. This may be perceived by the user as less fluid.

Character sets and collations

A **character set** describes how symbols for a specific language or dialect are encoded. A **collation** contains rules to compare and sort the characters of a character set. The character set used to store our data may be different from the one used to display it, leading to data discrepancies. Thus, a need to transform the data arises.

Since MySQL 4.1.x, the MySQL server does the character recoding work for us. Also, MySQL enables us to indicate the character set and collation for each database, each table, and even each field. A default character set for a database applies to each of its tables, unless it is overridden at the table level. The same principle applies to every column.

Effective character sets and collations

On the home page, we can see the **MySQL charset** information and a **MySQL connection collation** selector. Here is the **MySQL charset** information:

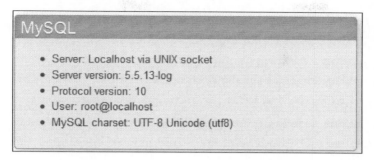

The character set information (as seen here after **MySQL charset**) is used to generate HTML information, which tells the browser what is the page's character set.

We can also choose which character set and collation will be used for our connection to the MySQL server using the **MySQL connection collation** dialog. This is passed to the MySQL server. MySQL then transforms the characters that will be sent to our browser into this character set. MySQL also interprets what it receives from the browser according to the character set information. Remember that all tables and columns have a character set information describing how their data is encoded.

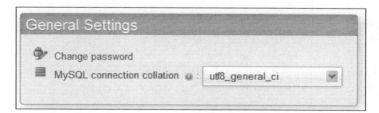

Normally, the default value should work. However, if we are entering some characters using a different character set, we can choose the proper character set in this dialog.

The following parameter defines both the default connection collation and character set:

```
$cfg['DefaultConnectionCollation'] = 'utf8_unicode_ci';
```

Navigation panel

The navigation panel contains the following elements:

- The logo
- The server list (if `$cfg['LeftDisplayServers']` is set to TRUE)
- The **Home** link or icon (takes you back to the phpMyAdmin home page)
- A **Log out** link or icon (if logging out is possible)
- A link or icon leading to the **Query window**
- Icons to display phpMyAdmin and MySQL documentation
- A **Reload** link or icon (to refresh just this panel)
- A table name filter (under certain conditions, see later in the *Table name filter* section)
- The names of databases and tables

If `$cfg['MainPageIconic']` is set to TRUE (the default), we see the icons. However, if it is set to FALSE, we see the links.

The navigation panel can be resized by clicking and moving the vertical separation line in the preferred direction to reveal more data, in case the database or table names are too long for the default navigation panel size.

We can customize the appearance of this panel. Many appearance-related parameters are located in `themes/<themename>/layout.inc.php`. The `$cfg['NaviWidth']` parameter contains the default width of the navigation panel in pixels. The background color is defined in `$cfg['NaviBackground']`. The `$cfg['NaviPointerColor']` parameter defines the pointer color. To activate the navigation pointer for any theme being used, a master setting, `$cfg['LeftPointerEnable']`, exists in `config.inc.php`. Its default value is TRUE.

Configuring the logo

The logo display behavior is controlled by a number of parameters. First, `$cfg['LeftDisplayLogo']` has to be set to TRUE, to enable any displaying of the logo. It is `true` by default. A click on this logo brings the interface to the page listed in the `$cfg['LeftLogoLink']` parameter, which is usually the main phpMyAdmin page (default value `main.php`), but can be changed to any URL. Finally, the `$cfg['LeftLogoLinkWindow']` parameter indicates in which window the new page appears after a click on the logo. By default, it's on the main page (value `main`). However, it could be on a brand new window by using the value `new`.

The logo image itself comes from the `logo_left.png` file, which is located in each specific theme directory structure.

Database and table list

The following example shows that no database has been chosen yet:

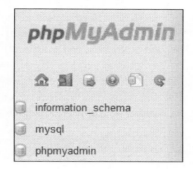

It is also possible to see a **No databases** message instead of the list of databases. This means that our current MySQL rights do not allow us to see any existing databases.

 A MySQL server always has at least one database (named **mysql**), but it may be the case that we do not have the rights to see it. Moreover, as MySQL 5.0.2, a special database called **information_schema** appears at all times in the database list — unless it is hidden via the `$cfg['Servers'][$i]['only_db']` or the `$cfg['Servers'][$i]['hide_db']` mechanisms. It contains a set of views describing the metadata visible for the logged-in users.

We may have the right to create one, as explained in *Chapter 4*.

Light mode

The navigation panel can be shown in two ways — the **Light** mode and the **Full** mode. The Light mode is used by default, defined by a TRUE value in `$cfg['LeftFrameLight']`. This mode shows a drop-down list of the available databases, and only tables of the currently chosen database are displayed. It is more efficient than Full Mode; the reason is explained in the *Full Mode* section appearing later in the chapter. In the following screenshot, we have chosen the **mysql** database:

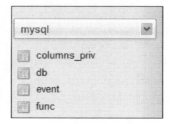

Clicking on a database name or selecting it opens the main panel in the `Database` view, and clicking on a table name opens the main panel in the `Table` view to browse this table. (Refer to the *Main panel* section for details.)

Tree display of database names

A user might be allowed to work on a single database, for example **marc**. Some system administrators offer a more flexible scheme by allowing user **marc** to create many databases, provided all have their names starting with **marc**, such as **marc_airline** and **marc_car**. In this situation, the navigation panel can be set to display a tree of these database names, as shown in the following screenshot:

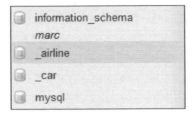

This feature is controlled by the following parameters:

```
$cfg['LeftFrameDBTree']      = TRUE;
$cfg['LeftFrameDBSeparator'] = '_';
```

The default value of TRUE in `$cfg['LeftFrameDBTree']` ensures that this feature is activated. A popular value for the separator is '_'. Should we need more than one set of characters to act as a separator, we just have to use an array:

```
$cfg['LeftFrameDBSeparator'] = array('_', '+');
```

Table name filter

If a database has too many tables, we might want to display just a subset of these, based on a filter text string. In Light mode only, if a database is currently selected, a table name filter is displayed just under the current database name, provided that the number of tables exceeds the value of `$cfg['LeftDisplayTableFilterMinimum']`, which is set to 30 by default. As we input a subset of the table names in this filter, the list of tables is reduced to match this subset. To try this feature, we set the directive's value to 15 and we input **time** in the filter field:

Full mode

The previous examples were shown in Light mode, but setting the
$cfg['LeftFrameLight'] parameter to FALSE produces a complete layout of our
databases and tables using collapsible menus (if supported by the browser) as shown
in the following screenshot:

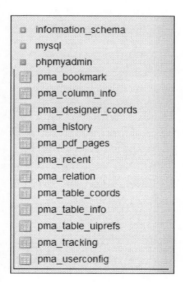

The Full mode is not selected by default; it can increase network traffic and server
load if our current rights give us access to a large number of databases and tables.
Links must be generated in the navigation panel to enable table access and quick
access to every table.

Table abridged statistics

Moving the cursor over a table name displays comments about the table (if any), and the number of rows currently within it as shown in the following screenshot:

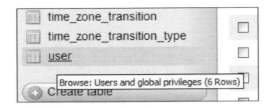

Table quick-access icon

It was established that the most common action on a table must be to browse it. Therefore, a click on the table name itself opens it in browse mode. The icon beside each table name is a quick way to do another action on each table, and by default, it brings us to `Structure` view.

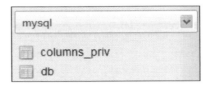

The `$cfg['LeftDefaultTabTable']` parameter controls this action. It has a default value of `'tbl_structure.php'`, which is the script that shows the table's structure. Other possible values for this parameter are listed in `Documentation.html`. If we prefer a setting in which a click on the table name opens it in the **Structure** page and a click on the quick-access icon leads to the **Browse** page, we have to set these directives:

```
$cfg['LeftDefaultTabTable'] = 'sql.php';
$cfg['DefaultTabTable']     = 'tbl_structure.php';
```

Nested display of tables within a database

MySQL's data structure is based on two levels—databases and tables. This does not allow subdivisions of tables per project. To work by project, users must rely on having multiple databases, but this is not always allowed by their provider. To help them with this regard, phpMyAdmin supports a **nested-levels** feature based on the naming of the table.

Let us say we have access to the **db1** database, and we want to represent two projects, **marketing** and **payroll**. Using a special separator (by default a double underscore) between the project name and the table name, we create the **marketing**, **payroll_employees** and **payroll_jobs** tables, achieving a visually interesting effect as shown in the following screenshot:

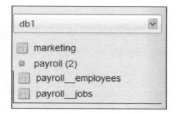

This feature is parameterized with $cfg['LeftFrameTableSeparator'] (set here to '__') to choose the characters that will mark each level change, and $cfg['LeftFrameTableLevel'] (set here to '1') for the number of sub-levels.

 The nested-level feature is intended only for improving the navigation panel's look. The proper way to reference the tables in MySQL statements stays the same, for example, db1.payroll__jobs.

A click on the navigation panel on the project name (here **payroll**) opens this project in the main panel, showing only those tables associated with that project.

Counting the number of tables

By default, $cfg['Servers'][$i]['CountTables'] is set to false, to speed up the display by not counting the number of tables per database. If set to true, this count is displayed in the navigation panel, next to each database name.

Choosing from the server list

If we have to manage multiple servers from the same phpMyAdmin window and often need to switch between servers, it is useful to always have the list of servers in the navigation panel.

For this, the `$cfg['LeftDisplayServers']` parameter must be set to TRUE. The list of servers can have two forms—a drop-down list or links. Which form appears depends on `$cfg['DisplayServersList']`. By default, this parameter is set to FALSE, so we see a drop-down list of servers. Setting `$cfg['DisplayServersList']` to TRUE produces a list of links to all defined servers.

Handling many databases or tables

This section describes some techniques to cope with a server holding a huge number of databases and tables.

Limits on the interface

It would be difficult to work with the interface if we had access to hundreds or even thousands of databases, or hundreds of tables in the same database. Two parameters, shown here with their default values, establish a limit on the number of databases and tables displayed, by adding a page selector and navigation links:

```
$cfg['MaxDbList']    = 100;
$cfg['MaxTableList'] = 250;
```

The effect of setting `$cfg['MaxTableList']` to a value of 5 can be seen on the navigation panel, shown here for a database having more than five tables:

The page selector and navigation links also appear in the main panel.

Improving fetch speed

Three configuration parameters have an effect on the speed of database name retrieval and table counting. The first one is:

```
$cfg['Servers'][$i]['ShowDatabasesCommand'] = 'SHOW DATABASES';
```

Every time phpMyAdmin needs to obtain the list of databases from the server, it uses the command listed in this parameter. The default command SHOW DATABASES is fine in ordinary situations. However, on servers with many databases, speed improvements can be observed by trying other commands such as one of the following:

```
SHOW DATABASES LIKE '#user#\_%'
SELECT DISTINCT TABLE_SCHEMA FROM information_schema.SCHEMA_
PRIVILEGES'
SELECT SCHEMA_NAME FROM information_schema.SCHEMATA
```

In the first example, #user# is replaced by the current username.

In extreme situations (thousands of databases), a user who installs his own copy of phpMyAdmin should put false in this parameter. This would block any database names' fetching, and would require to populate the $cfg['Servers'][$i]['only_db'] parameter with this user's database list.

Finally, some users experience speed issues (at least under MySQL 5.1) with information retrieval from INFORMATION_SCHEMA. Therefore, the $cfg['Servers'][$i]['DisableIS'] directive, with its default value of TRUE, disables the usage of INFORMATION_SCHEMA from a major portion of the phpMyAdmin code. For your server, it may be worth setting this to FALSE to see if response time improves.

Main panel

The **main panel** is the principal working area, and all the possible views for it are explained in the following sections. Its appearance can be customized. The background color is defined in $cfg['MainBackground'].

Home page

The home page may contain a varying number of links depending on the login mode and the user's rights. The **Home** link from the navigation panel is used to display this page. It shows the phpMyAdmin and MySQL versions, the MySQL server name, and the logged-in user. In order to reveal less information about our web server and MySQL server, we could set $cfg['ShowServerInfo']$ to FALSE. Another setting, $cfg['ShowPhpInfo']$, can be set to TRUE if we want to see the **Show PHP Information** link on the home page—by default its value is FALSE. In some cases, a **No privileges** message may appear here; the reason for this and how to fix this condition is covered in *Chapter 4*.

In this example, a normal user is allowed to change his/her password from the interface by using the **Change password** link which brings the following dialog:

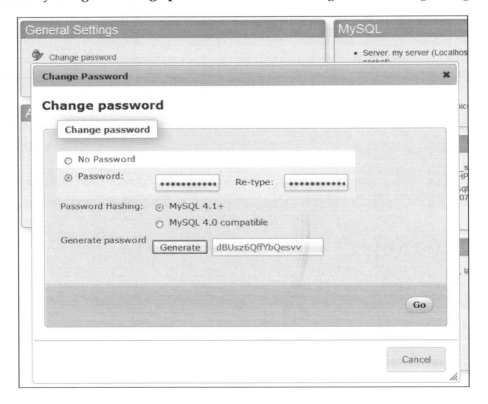

We can either choose our new password by typing it twice, or use the **Generate** button (only available in JavaScript-enabled browsers); in this case, the new password is shown in a clear field for us to take good note of it, and is automatically filled into the dialog for changing the password. It is highly recommended to generate passwords in this way, as they are most likely more secure than a human-chosen password. To disallow the **Change password** link from the home page, we set $cfg['ShowChgPassword']$ to FALSE. Privileged users have more options on the home page. They have more links to manage the server as a whole, for example, the **Privileges** link (more on this in *Chapter 19*).

Database view

phpMyAdmin goes into Database view (shown in the following screenshot) every time we click on a database name from the navigation panel.

This is where we can see an overview of the database—the existing tables, a dialog to create a table, the tabs to the Database view pages, and some special operations we might do on this database to generate documentation and statistics. There is a checkbox beside each table to make global operations on that table (covered in *Chapter 9*). The table is chosen by using the checkbox or by clicking anywhere on the row's background. We can also see each table's size, provided $cfg['ShowStats']$ is set to TRUE. This parameter also controls the display of table-specific statistics in the Table view.

The initial screen that appears here is the database **Structure** page. We note here that almost every column header—such as **Table**, **Records**, and **Size**—is a link which can be used to sort the corresponding column (*Chapter 4* covers sorting). While sorting by descending table name might not be that useful, sorting by descending size is definitely something we should do from time to time.

We might want a different initial page to appear while entering the Database view. This is controlled by the $cfg['DefaultTabDatabase']$ parameter, and the available choices are given in the configuration file as comments.

The number of rows is obtained using a quick method, the SHOW TABLE STATUS statement, and not by using a SELECT COUNT(*) FROM TABLENAME. This quick method is usually accurate, except for InnoDB tables, which returns an approximate number of records. To help get the correct number of records, even for InnoDB, the $cfg['MaxExactCount'] parameter is available. If the approximate number of records is lower than this parameter's value—by default, 20000—the slower SELECT COUNT(*) method will be used.

Do not put a value too high for the MaxExactCount parameter. You would get correct results but only after waiting for a few minutes, if there are many thousands of rows in your InnoDB table. To examine the number of rows as displayed for InnoDB, please refer to *Chapter 10*, where we actually have an InnoDB table to play with.

A user might be surprised when seeing the term **KiB** in the **Size** and **Overhead** columns. phpMyAdmin has adopted the **International Electrotechnical Commission** (IEC) binary prefixes (see http://en.wikipedia.org/wiki/Binary_prefix). The displayed values are defined in each language file.

Table view

This is a commonly used view, giving access to all table-specific pages. By default, the initial screen is the table's **Browse** screen, which shows the first page of this table's data. Note that the header for this screen always shows the current database and table names. We also see the comments set for the table, next to the table name:

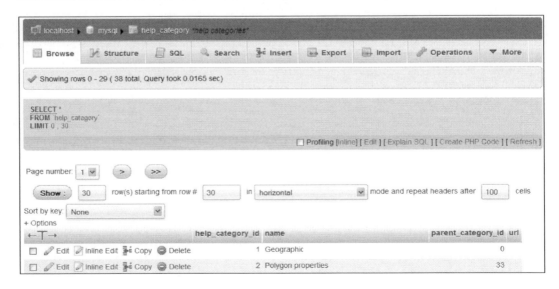

The $cfg['DefaultTabTable']$ parameter defines the initial page on the Table view. Some users prefer to avoid seeing the first page's data because in production they routinely run saved queries or enter the **Search** page (explained in *Chapter 8*).

Server view

This view is entered each time we go back to the home page. A privileged user will, of course, see more choices in the Server view. The Server view panel was created to group together related server management pages, and enable easy navigation between them.

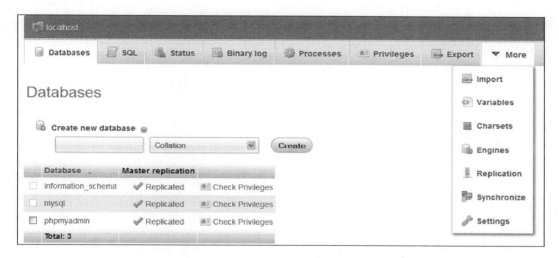

The default **Server** page is controlled by the $cfg['DefaultTabServer']$ parameter. This parameter defines the initial starting page as well. For multi-user installations, it is recommended to keep the default value (main.php), which displays the traditional home page. We could choose to display server statistics instead by changing this parameter to server_status.php, or to see the user's list with server_privileges. php. Other possible choices are explained in the configuration file, and the server administration pages are covered in *Chapter 19*.

Icons for home page and menu tabs

A configuration parameter, $cfg['MainPageIconic']$, controls the appearance of icons at various places of the main panel:

- On the home page
- At top of page when listing the **Server**, **Database**, and **Table** information
- On the menu tabs in Database, Table, and Server views

When the parameter is set to TRUE, which is by default, you will see the following screenshot:

Opening a new phpMyAdmin window

Sometimes we want to compare data from two tables at once or have other needs for more than one phpMyAdmin window. At the bottom of almost every page, a small icon is available to open another window in phpMyAdmin with the current panel's content. Moreover, this icon can be used to create a browser bookmark that points to the current phpMyAdmin page (but we should log in to access the data).

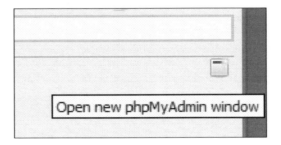

User preferences

One instance of phpMyAdmin can be installed to serve multiple users; however, before version 3.4.0, these users had to be content with the parameter values as chosen by the person in charge for this instance.

It's true that some pages on the interface has allowed tweaking specific parameters and that some of these were remembered in cookies, for example, the chosen language; but this version is the first to offer a global mechanism for adjusting and remembering preferences per user.

Even in the case where the instance has only one user, it's more convenient to be able to fine-tune preferences from the interface rather than manipulating the configuration file.

Accessing user preferences

From the home page, we click on **More settings**. From any page in Server view, we click on the **Settings** menu tab. Upon entering the **Settings** panel, we see the **Manage your settings** sub-page:

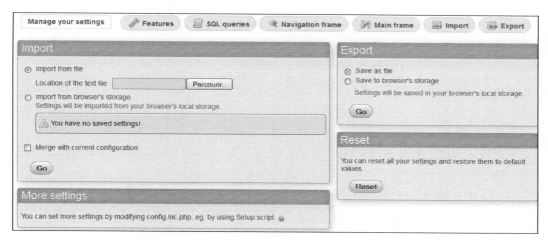

This sub-page is where we act globally on our preferences. Other sub-pages such as **Features** and **Main frame** are used to change specific preferences—refer to the *Changing settings* section.

The **Import** and **Export** dialogs will be covered in the *Possible locations for saving preferences* section. The **More settings** dialog reminds us that config.inc.php is the place to configure all possibilities, for example, specifying servers and authentication modes is out of scope for user preferences.

The **Reset** dialog enables us to go back to default values for all user preferences in one easy click.

Possible locations for saving preferences

There are three possible places where user preferences can be saved. Each one has pros and cons; this section covers these modes.

Saving in phpMyAdmin configuration storage

To enable this mode, `$cfg['Servers'][$i]['userconfig']` must be configured with the name of the table which holds these preferences, and the table must exist. This saving location is most useful because settings are immediately applied to the running instance upon login; moreover, it follows the user on whichever browser he happens to use.

If this storage is not configured, the settings page greets us with the following message:

Your preferences will be saved for current session only. Storing them permanently requires phpMyAdmin configuration storage.

Saving in a file

We always have the possibility of exporting our settings to a file and importing them back. The file follows the JSON format (see `http://json.org`). This method can be handy in the following situations:

- We plan to use these settings on another phpMyAdmin instance
- We want to keep a history of our settings; therefore, saving them from time to time in several files

Saving in the browser's local storage

Recent browsers, for example Firefox 6 and Internet Explorer 9, offer a local storage mechanism which is persistent between sessions. The first time we enter the **Manage your settings** sub-page, we see the **You have no saved settings!** message inside the **Import from browser's storage** dialog. However, after exporting settings to browser's local storage, the **Import** section tells us the date and time when settings were last saved using this mechanism.

In addition, when phpMyAdmin settings are found in the browser's storage and the phpMyAdmin configuration storage is not available, each phpMyAdmin page has the following message at the top:

Your browser has phpMyAdmin configuration for this domain. Would you like to import it for current session? Yes / No

A drawback of using this method is that our settings are only available when we are using this browser; moreover, if our browser's settings do not follow us when we change workstations, the settings are tied to this specific workstation (and apply to any other user running phpMyAdmin on it).

Changing settings

Upon entering a sub-page for specific preferences—in this case, the **Main frame** sub-page, we see a third level of menus related to this subject:

If a preference has been changed from its default value, the checkbox or data field has a different background color and a recycle icon is shown next to it, to quickly reset this preference to its default value. Quick explanations are given for each directive and links point to the documentation and the official wiki. As a general advice, we need to save any change we make on a page before changing to a different sub-page; however, in this example, we can switch from **Startup** to other third-level menus such as **Browse mode** and back without losing our changes.

Disallowing specific preferences

The person in charge of `config.inc.php` has the last word about which settings are changeable in the user preferences. To disallow some settings, we use the `$cfg['UserprefsDisallow']` directive. We place into it an array containing the keys in `$cfg` that represent the directives to disallow. As an example, we set this directive to:

```
$cfg['UserprefsDisallow'] = array('AjaxEnable', 'MaxDbList');
```

This produces a warning as shown in the following screenshot:

Showing developer settings

Some settings are sensitive and are intended only for the persons developing phpMyAdmin. For example, the possibility of displaying all errors, including PHP notices, can lead to disclose the full path of the phpMyAdmin instance. Therefore, in the **Features** sub-tab, the **Developer** menu is shown only if $cfg['UserprefsDeveloperTab'] is set to true.

Query window

It is often convenient to have a distinct window in which we can type and refine queries, and which is synchronized with the main panel. This window is called the **Query window**. We can open this window by using the small **SQL** icon, or the **Query window** link from the navigation panel's icons or links zone. This feature only works for a JavaScript-enabled browser.

The **Query window** itself has sub-pages, and it appears here over the main panel, as shown in the following screenshot:

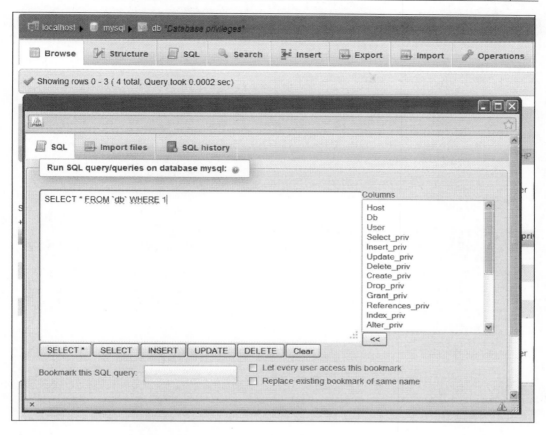

We can choose the dimensions (in pixels) of this window with $cfg['QueryWindowWidth'] and $cfg['QueryWindowHeight']. *Chapter 11* explains the Query window in more detail, including the available SQL query history features.

Summary

This chapter covered:

- The language-selection system
- The purpose of the navigation and main panels
- The contents of the navigation panel, including Light mode and Full mode
- The contents of the main panel, with its various views depending on the context
- The user preferences feature
- The Query window

The next chapter will guide you with simple steps to accomplish with a freshly-installed phpMyAdmin—initial table creation, data insertion, and retrieval.

4

Creating and Browsing Tables

Having seen the overall layout of phpMyAdmin, we are ready to create a database, create our first table, insert some data into it, and browse it. These first steps are intentionally simple, but they will give you the foundation on which more complex operations will be achieved later. At the end of the chapter, we will have at our disposal the two basic tables on which the remaining exercises are based.

Creating a database

Before creating a table, we must ensure that we have a database for which the MySQL server's administrator has given us the CREATE privilege. The following possibilities exist:

- The administrator has already created a database for us, and we see its name in the navigation panel; we don't have the right to create an additional database.

- We have the right to create databases from phpMyAdmin.

- We are on a shared host, and the host provider has installed a general web interface (for example, cPanel) to create MySQL databases and accounts; in this case, we should visit this web interface now and ensure we have created at least one database and one MySQL account.

The **Databases** panel in Server view is the place to go to find the database creation dialog. Note that a configuration parameter, $cfg['ShowCreateDb'], controls the display of the **Create new database** dialog. By default, it is set to true, which shows the dialog.

No privileges

If you do not have the privilege to create a database, the panel displays a **No privileges** message under the **Create new database** label. This means that you must work with the databases already created for you, or ask the MySQL server's administrator to give you the necessary CREATE privilege.

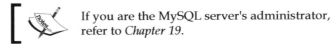 If you are the MySQL server's administrator, refer to *Chapter 19*.

First database creation is authorized

If phpMyAdmin detects that we have the right to create a database, the dialog appears as shown in the following screenshot:

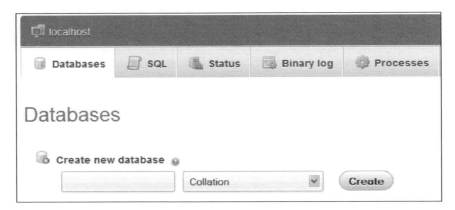

In the input field, a suggested database name appears if the $cfg['SuggestDBName'] parameter is set to TRUE, which is the default setting. The suggested database name is built according to the privileges we possess.

If we are restricted to the use of a prefix, the prefix might be suggested in the input field. (A popular choice for this prefix is the username, which might or might not be followed by an underscore character.) Note that, in this case, the prefix is followed by an ellipsis mark, added by phpMyAdmin. We should remove this ellipsis mark and complete the input field with an appropriate name.

The **Collation** choice can be left unchanged for now. With this dialog, we could pick a default character set and collation for this database. This setting can be changed later (refer to *Chapter 9* for more information on this).

We will assume here that we have the right to create a database named **marc_book**. We enter **marc_book** in the input field and click on **Create**. Once the database has been created, we will see the following screen:

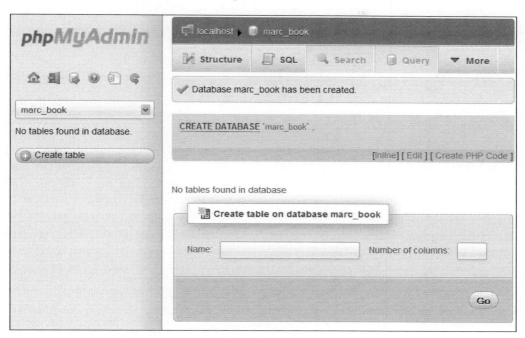

Notice the following:

- The title of the main panel has changed to reflect the fact that we are now located in this database
- A confirmation message regarding the creation is displayed
- The navigation panel has been updated; we see **marc_book**
- By default, the SQL query sent to the server by phpMyAdmin to create the database is displayed in color

phpMyAdmin displays the query it generated, because `$cfg['ShowSQL']` is set to TRUE. Looking at the generated queries can be a good way of learning SQL.

As the generated queries could be large and take much of the on-screen room, the `$cfg['MaxCharactersInDisplayedSQL']` acts as a limit. Its default value of `1000` should be a good balance between seeing too few and seeing too many of the queries, especially when doing large imports.

It is important to examine the phpMyAdmin feedback to ascertain the validity of the operations we make through the interface. This way, we can detect errors like typos in the names, or creation of a table in the wrong database. phpMyAdmin retrieves error messages from the MySQL server and displays them on the interface.

Creating our first table

Now that we have a new database, it's time to create a table in it. The example table we will create is named **book**.

Choosing the columns

Before creating a table, we should plan the information we want to store. This is usually done during database design. In our case, a simple analysis leads us to the following book-related data we want to keep:

- International Standard Book Number (ISBN)
- Title
- Number of pages
- Author identification

For now, it is not important to have the complete list of columns for our **book** table. We will modify it by prototyping the structure now and refining it later. At the end of the chapter, we will add a second table, `author`, containing information about each author.

Creating a table

We have chosen our table name and we know the number of columns. We enter this information in the **Create table** dialog and click on **Go** to start creating the table. At this point, it does not matter if the number of columns is exactly known, as a subsequent panel will permit us to add columns while creating the table.

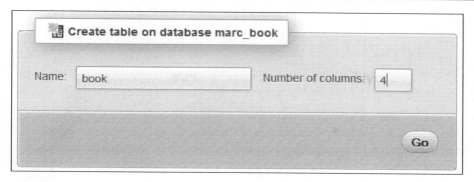

We then see a panel specifying column information. As we asked for four columns, we get four input rows. Each row refers to information specific to one column. The following screenshot represents the left side of this panel:

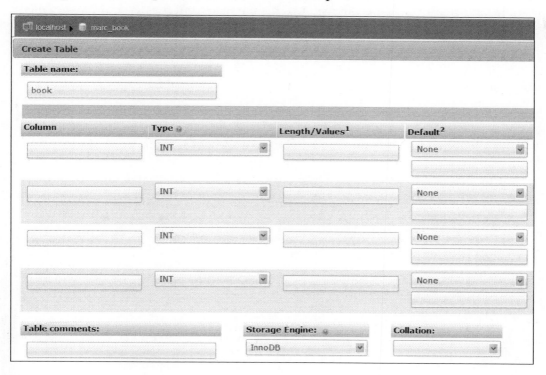

And the next one represents the right side:

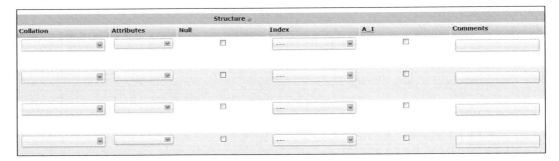

The MySQL documentation explains valid characters for the table and column names (if we search for "Legal names"). This may vary depending on the MySQL version. Usually, any character that is allowed in a file name (except the dot and the slash) is acceptable in a table name, and the length of the name must not exceed 64 characters. The 64-character limit exists for column names as well, but we can use any character.

We enter our column names under the **Column** column. Each column has a type, and the most commonly used types are located at the beginning of the drop-down list.

The **VARCHAR** (variable character) type is widely used when the column content is alphanumeric, because the contents will occupy only the space needed for it. This type requires a maximum length, which we specify. If we forget to do so, a small pop-up message reminds us later when we save. For the page count and the author identification, we have chosen **INT** type (integer), as depicted in the following screenshot:

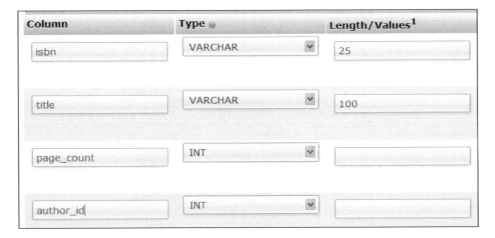

There are other attributes for columns, but we will leave them empty in this example. You might notice the **Add 1 column(s)** dialog at the bottom of the screen. We can use it to add some columns to this table-creation panel by entering the appropriate value and hitting **Go**. The number of input rows would change according to the new number of columns, leaving intact the information already entered about the first four columns. Before saving the page, let us define some keys.

Choosing keys

A table should normally have a primary key (a column with unique content that represents each row). Having a primary key is recommended for row identification, better performance, and possible cross-table relations. A good value here is the ISBN; so, in the **Index** dialog we select **PRIMARY** for the **isbn** column. Other possibilities for index type include **INDEX**, **UNIQUE**, and **FULLTEXT** (more on this in *Chapter 5*).

 Index management (also referred to as Key management) can be done at initial table creation, or later in the **Structure** page of `Table` view.

To improve the speed of the queries that we will make by **author_id**, we should add an index on this column. The right part of our screen now looks as shown in the following screenshot:

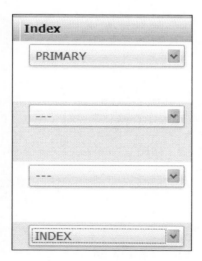

At this point, we could pick a different **Storage Engine** from the corresponding drop-down menu. However, for the time being, we will just accept the default storage engine.

Now we are ready to create the table by clicking on **Save**. If all goes well, the next screen confirms that the table has been created; we are now in the **Structure** page of the current database.

Of the various links shown for the **book** table, some are not active, because it would not make sense to browse or search a table if there are no rows in it.

Inserting data manually

Now that we have a table, let us put some data in it manually. Before we do that, here are some useful references on data manipulation within this book:

- *Chapter 5* explains how to change data and structure, including how to use the **Function** selector
- *Chapter 7* explains how to import data from existing files
- *Chapter 9* explains how to copy data from other tables
- *Chapter 10* explains the relational system (in our case, we will want to link to the author table)

For now, click on the **Insert** link, which will lead us to the data-entry (or edit) panel. This screen has room to enter information for two rows, that is, two books in our example. This is because the default value of $cfg['InsertRows']$ is 2. In the lower part of the screen, the dialog **Continue insertion with 2 rows** can be used if the default number of rows does not suit our needs. By default, the **Ignore** checkbox is ticked, which means that the second group of input fields will be ignored. As soon as we enter some information in one field of this group and exit the field, the **Ignore** box is automatically unchecked if JavaScript is enabled in the browser.

We can enter the following sample information for two books:

- ISBN: 1-234567-89-0, title: A hundred years of cinema (volume 1), 600 pages, author ID: 1
- ISBN: 1-234567-22-0, title: Future souvenirs, 200 pages, author ID: 2

The **Value** column width obeys the maximum length for the character columns. For this example, we keep the lower drop-down selector to its default value of **Insert as new row**. We then click on **Go** to insert the data. There is a **Go** button after each set of columns that represent a row, and another one on the lower part of the screen. All these have the same effect of saving the entered data but are provided for convenience.

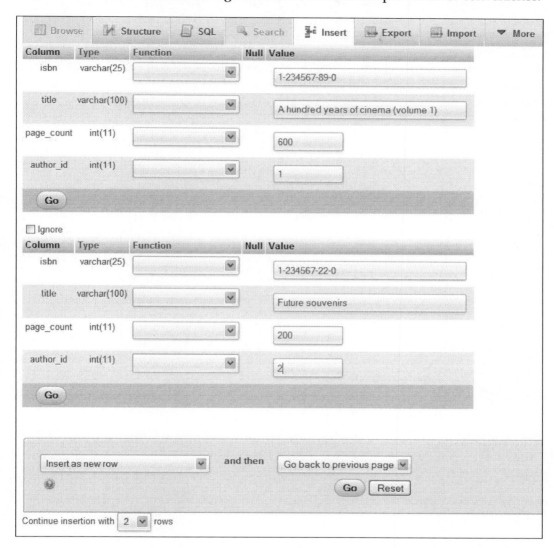

If our intention had been to enter data for more books after these two, we would have selected **Insert another new row** from the second drop-down before clicking on **Go**. This would then insert the data we have provided and reload the screen to insert more.

Data entry panel tuning for CHAR and VARCHAR

By default, phpMyAdmin displays an input field on a single line for the column types CHAR and VARCHAR. This is controlled by setting $cfg['CharEditing'] to 'input'. Sometimes, we may want to insert line breaks (new lines) within the field. This can be done by setting $cfg['CharEditing'] to 'textarea'. This is a global setting, and will apply to all the columns of all the tables, for all users of this copy of phpMyAdmin. In this mode, insertion of line breaks may be done manually with the *Enter* key, or by copying and pasting lines of text from another on-screen source. Applying this setting would generate a different **Insert** screen, shown as follows:

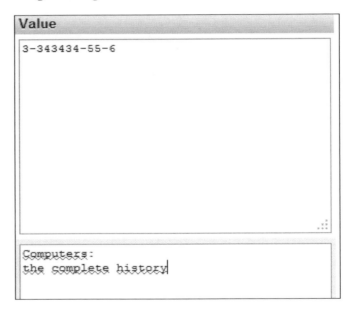

With this entry mode, the maximum length of each column no longer applies visually. It would be enforced by MySQL at insert time.

Browse mode

There are many ways to enter this mode. In fact, it is used each time the query results are displayed. We can enter this mode by clicking on the table name on the navigation panel, or by clicking **Browse** when we are in `Table` view for a specific table.

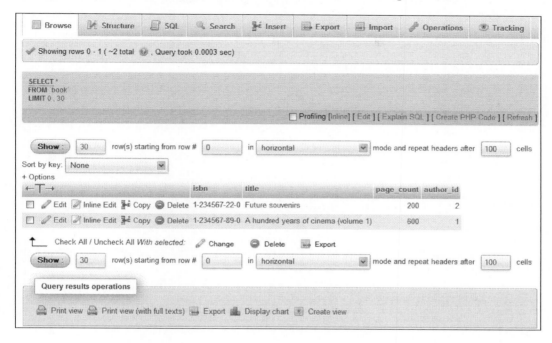

SQL query links

In the **Browse** results, the first part displayed is the query itself, along with a few links. The displayed links may vary depending on our actions and some configuration parameters.

The following points describe the function of each link:

- The **Profiling** checkbox is covered in the *Profiling queries* section of this chapter.
- The **Inline** link permits to put the query inside a text area without reloading the page; then the query may be edited and the new query may be executed.
- The **Edit** link appears if `$cfg['SQLQuery']['Edit']` is set to TRUE. Its purpose is to open the **Query window** so that you can edit this query (refer to *Chapter 11* for more details).
- **Explain SQL** is displayed if `$cfg['SQLQuery']['Explain']` is set to TRUE. We will see in *Chapter 5* what this link can be used for.
- The **Create PHP Code** link can be clicked to reformat the query to the syntax expected in a PHP script. It can then be copied and pasted directly at the place where we need the query in the PHP script we are working on. Note that after a click, this link changes to **Without PHP Code** (as shown in the following screenshot), which would bring back the normal query display. This link is available if `$cfg['SQLQuery']['ShowAsPHP']` is set to TRUE.

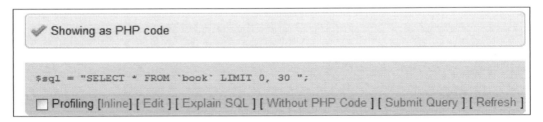

- **Refresh** is used to execute the same query again. The results might change, as a MySQL server is a multi-user server, and other users or processes might be modifying the same tables. This link is shown if `$cfg['SQLQuery']['Refresh']` is set to TRUE.

Navigation bar

The Navigation bar is displayed at the top of results and also at the bottom. Column headers can be repeated at certain intervals among results depending on the value entered in **repeat headers after** field.

The bar enables us to navigate from page to page, displaying an arbitrary number of rows, starting at some point in the results. As we entered browse mode by clicking **Browse**, the underlying query that generated the results includes the whole table. However, this is not always the case.

We are currently using a table containing a small number of rows. With larger tables, we could see a more complete set of navigation buttons. To simulate this, let us use the **Show** dialog to change the default number of rows from **30** to **1**; we then click on **Show**. We can see that the navigation bar adapts itself as shown in the following screenshot:

This time, there are buttons labeled **<<**, **<**, **>**, and **>>** for easy access to the first page, previous page, next page, and the last page of the results respectively. The buttons appear only when necessary; for example, the **first page** button is not displayed if we already are on the first page. These symbols are displayed in this manner as the default setting of $cfg['NavigationBarIconic']$ is TRUE. A FALSE here would produce buttons such as **Next** and **End**, whereas a value of 'both' would display **> Next** and **>> End**.

 Note that the $cfg['NavigationBarIconic']$ directive controls only the behavior of these navigation buttons; other buttons and links such as **Edit** are controlled by other configuration directives.

There is also a **Page number** drop-down menu, to go directly to one of the pages located near the current page. As there can be hundreds or thousands of pages, this menu is kept small and contains the commonly requested pages: a few page numbers before and after the current page, a few pages at the beginning and at the end plus a sample of page numbers based on a computed interval.

By design, phpMyAdmin always tries to give quick results, and one way to achieve this result is to add a LIMIT clause in SELECT. If a LIMIT clause is already there in the original query, phpMyAdmin will respect it. The default limit is 30 rows, set in $cfg['MaxRows']$. If there are many users on the server, limiting the number of rows returned helps keeping the server load to a minimum.

Another button is available on the navigation bar, but must be activated by setting $cfg['ShowAll'] to TRUE. It would be very tempting for users to use this button often. Hence, on a multi-user installation of phpMyAdmin, it is recommended that the button be left to its default value of disabled (FALSE). When enabled, the navigation bar is augmented with a **Show all** button. Clicking on this button retrieves all the rows of the current results set, which might hit the execution time limit in PHP or a memory limit in the server; most browsers would also crash when asked to display thousands of rows. The exact number of rows that can be safely displayed cannot be predicted as it depends on the actual data present in columns and on the browser's capabilities.

 If we enter a big number in the **Show __ rows** dialog, the same results will be achieved (and we may face the same problems).

Query results operations

A section labeled **Query results operations** is located under the results. It contains links to print the results (with or without the FULL TEXT columns), to export these results (refer to *Exporting partial query results* section in *Chapter 6*), or to create a view from this query (more on this in *Chapter 17*).

Displaying data as a chart

Another operation available is **Display chart**. To practice this, we will use a different query that selects only two columns. For this we can use the **Inline** link shown next to the query and change the query to:

```
SELECT page_count, author_id from book
```

Clicking on **Go** produces a result set with only those two columns; next we click on **Display chart**, which generates the following panel:

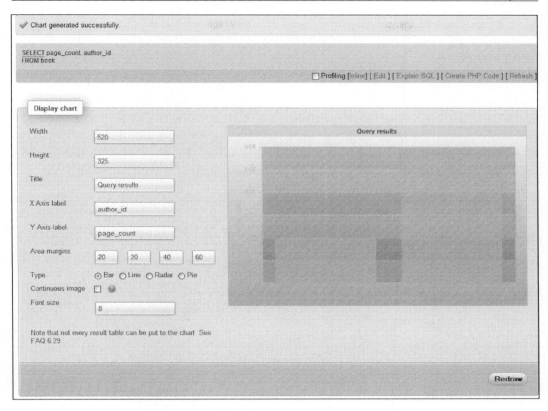

More details are available at `http://wiki.phpmyadmin.net/pma/Charts`.

Sorting results

In SQL, we can never be sure of the order in which the data is retrieved, unless we explicitly sort the data. Some implementations of the retrieving engine may show results in the same order as the one in which data was entered, or according to a primary key. However, a sure way to get results in the order we want is by sorting them explicitly.

When browsing results are displayed, any column header can be clicked to sort on this column, even if it is not part of an index. Let us click on the **author_id** column header.

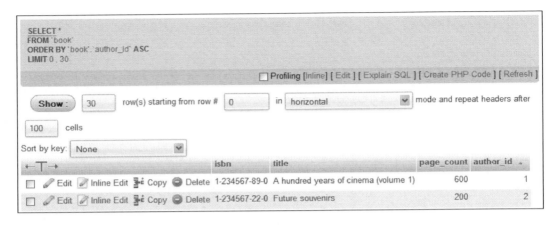

We can confirm that the sorting has occurred, by watching the SQL query at the top of screen; it contains an **ORDER BY** clause.

We now see a small triangle pointing upwards beside the **author_id** header. This means that the current sort order is 'ascending'. Hovering the mouse over the **author_id** header makes the triangle change direction, to indicate what will happen if we click on the header again—a sort by descending **author_id** values.

Another way to sort is by key. The **Sort** dialog shows all the keys already defined. Here we see a key named **PRIMARY**—the name given to our primary key on the **isbn** column when we checked **Primary** for this column at creation time:

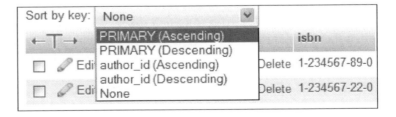

This might be the only way to sort on multiple columns at once
(for multi-columns indexes).

The initial sort order is defined in $cfg['Order'] with ASC for ascending, DESC for
descending, or SMART; the latter is the default sort order, which means that columns
of type DATE, TIME, DATETIME, and TIMESTAMP would be sorted in descending order,
whereas other column types will be sorted in ascending order.

Headwords

Because we can change the number of rows displayed on a page, it is quite possible
that we do not see the whole data. In this case, it would help to see **headwords**—
indications about the first and last row of displayed data. This way, you can click on
Next or **Previous** without scrolling to the bottom of the window.

However, which column should phpMyAdmin base his headwords generation on?
A simple assumption has been made: if you click on a column's header to indicate
your intention of sorting on this column, phpMyAdmin uses this column's data as a
headword. For our current **book** table, we do not have enough data to clearly notice
the benefits of this technique. However, we can nonetheless see that after a sort, the
top part of the screen now contains this message:

Showing rows 0 - 1 (2 total, Query took 0.0006 sec) [author_id: 1 - 2]

Here, the message between square brackets means that **author_id** number **1** is on the
first displayed row and number **2** is on the last one.

Color-marking rows or columns

When moving the mouse between rows (or between column headers),
the row (or column) background color may change to the color defined
in $cfg['BrowsePointerColor']. This parameter can be found in
themes/<themename>/layout.inc.php. To enable this, browse pointer for all
themes—$cfg['BrowsePointerEnable']—must be set to TRUE (the default) in
config.inc.php.

It may be interesting to visually mark some rows when we have many columns in the table and must constantly scroll left and right to read data. Another usage is to highlight the importance of some rows for personal comparison of data, or when showing data to people. Highlighting is done by clicking on the row. Clicking again removes the mark on the row. The chosen color is defined by `$cfg['BrowseMarkerColor']` (see `themes/<themename>/layout.inc.php`). This feature must be enabled by setting `$cfg['BrowseMarkerEnable']` to TRUE, this time in `config.inc.php`. This sets the feature for all the themes. We can mark more than one row. Marking the row also activates the checkbox for this row.

Marking a column is done by clicking on the column header, but not on the column name itself.

Limiting the length of each column

In the previous examples, we always saw the full contents of each column, as each column had the number of characters within the limit defined by `$cfg['LimitChars']`. This is a limit enforced on all non-numeric columns. If this limit was low (say `10`), the display would be as follows:

This would help us see more columns at the same time (at the expense of seeing less of each column).

Display options

In order to see the full texts, we will now make use of the **Options** slider, which reveals some display options. All these options will be explained in the chapters that cover the corresponding notions. The option that concerns us at the moment is the **Partial Texts/Full Texts** pair; we can choose **Full Texts** to see all of the text that was truncated. Even if we elect not to change the `$cfg['LimitChars']` parameter, there will be a time when asking for full texts will be useful (when we work with TEXT column type—more on this in *Chapter 5*).

A quicker way of seeing the full texts is to click on the big **T** which is located just on top of the **Edit** and **Delete** icons. Another click on this **T** toggles the display from full to partial.

Browsing distinct values

There is a quick way to display all distinct values and the number of occurrences for each value of a column. This feature is available on the **Structure** page of a table. For example, we want to know how many different authors we have in our book table and how many books each one wrote. On the line describing the column we want to browse (here **author_id**), we open the **More** menu and click on the **Browse distinct values** link.

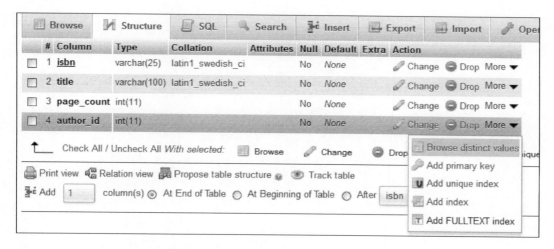

We have a limited test set, but can nonetheless see the results.

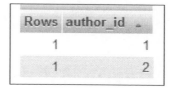

Profiling queries

Profiling support has been added in the MySQL versions 5.0.37 and 5.1.28. We have previously seen the **Profiling** checkbox appear in query results.

When this box is checked, phpMyAdmin will analyze every query (including the current one), and a report about the execution time of each MySQL internal operation is displayed as shown in the following screenshot:

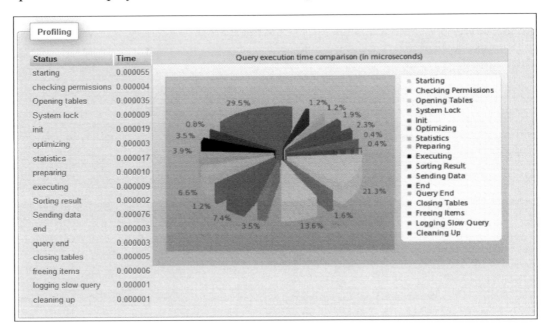

Although the profiling system can report additional information about operations (such as the CPU time, and even the internal server's function names), phpMyAdmin currently displays only the name of the operation and its duration.

Creating an additional table

In our (simple) design, we know that we need another table—the **author** table. The **author** table will contain:

- Author identification
- Full name
- Phone number

To create this table, we go back to the `Database` view for **marc_book** and request the creation of another table with three columns as indicated in the following screenshot:

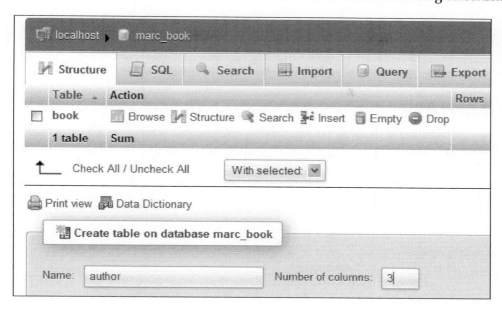

Using the same techniques used when creating the first table, we type this in:

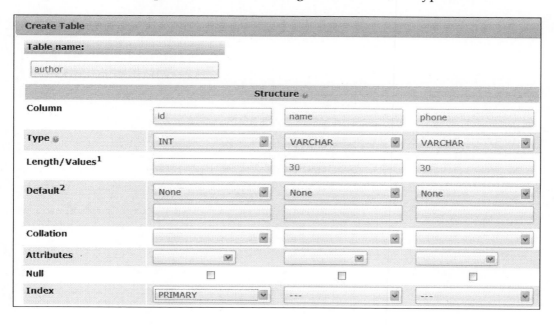

As we have three columns or less, the display is now in vertical mode (refer to the *Vertical mode* section in *Chapter 5* for more details).

The column name **id**, which is our primary key in this new table, relates to the author_id column from the book table. After saving the table structure, we enter some data for authors 1 and 2. Use your imagination for this!

Summary

This chapter explained how to create a database and tables, and how to enter data manually in the tables. It also covered how to confirm the presence of data by using the browse mode, which includes the SQL query links, navigation bar, sorting options, and row marking.

The next chapter explains how to edit data rows and covers the various aspects of deletion of rows, tables, and databases.

Changing Data and Structure

5

Data is not static, it changes often. This chapter focuses on editing and deleting data and its supporting structures—tables and databases.

The chapter is divided into two main parts. The first part covers all aspects of changing data. First we examine how to edit data, that is, how to enter the edit mode, how to edit more than one row at once, and how to benefit from inline editing. Next we see how to delete rows of data and how to delete tables and databases.

The second part explains how to modify the structure of tables. We examine how to add a column to a table; we then explore various column types such as TEXT, BLOB, ENUM, DATE, and BIT column types. Finally, we examine the management of indexes.

Changing data

In this section, we cover the various ways of editing and deleting data.

Entering edit mode

When we browse a table or view results from a search on any single-table query, small icons and links appear on the left or right of each table row as shown in the following screenshot:

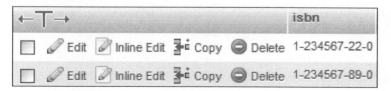

The row can be edited with one of the pencil-shaped icons (**Edit**) and deleted with the red icon (**Delete**). The exact form and location of these controls are governed by:

```
$cfg['PropertiesIconic']    = 'both';
$cfg['ModifyDeleteAtLeft']  = true;
$cfg['ModifyDeleteAtRight'] = false;
```

We can decide whether to display them on the left side, the right side, or on both sides. The $cfg['PropertiesIconic'] parameter can have the values TRUE, FALSE, or both. TRUE displays icons only, FALSE displays **Edit**, **Inline Edit**, **Copy**, and **Delete** (or their translated equivalent) as links, and both displays the icon and the text, as seen in the preceding screenshot.

The small checkbox beside each row is explained in the *Multi-row editing* and the *Deleting multiple rows* sections later in this chapter.

Clicking on the **Edit** icon or link brings the following panel, which is similar to the data entry panel (except for the lower part):

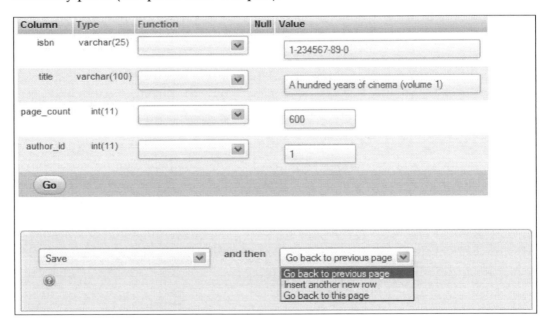

In this panel, we can change data by typing directly (or by cutting and pasting via the normal operating system mechanisms). We can also revert to the original contents using the **Reset** button.

By default, the lower drop-down menus are set to **Save** (so that we make changes to this row) and **Go back to previous page** (so that we can continue editing another row on the previous results page). We might want to stay on the current page after clicking on **Go**—in order to save and then continue editing—we can choose **Go back to this page**. If we want to insert yet another new row after saving the current row, we just have to choose **Insert another new row** before saving. The **Insert as new row** choice (below the **Save** choice) is explained in the *Duplicating rows of data* section later in this chapter.

Moving to next field with the tab key

People who prefer to use the keyboard can use the *Tab* key to go to the next field. Normally, the cursor goes from left to right and from top to bottom, so it would travel into the fields in the **Function** column (more on this in a moment). However, to ease data navigation in phpMyAdmin, the normal order of navigation has been altered. The *Tab* key first goes through each field in the **Value** column, and then through each one in the **Function** column.

Moving with arrows

Another way of moving between fields is with the *Ctrl + arrow* keys. This method might be easier than using the *Tab* key when many fields are on screen. For this to work, the $cfg['CtrlArrowsMoving']$ parameter must be set to true, which is the default value.

 In some situations, this technique cannot be used for moving between fields. For example, the Google Chrome browser does not support *Ctrl + arrow*. Also, on Mac OS X 10.5 with Spaces enabled, *Ctrl + arrow* is the default shortcut to switch between virtual desktops.

Handling NULL values

If the table's structure permits a NULL value inside a column, a small checkbox appears in the column's **Null** column. Selecting this puts a NULL value in the column. Whenever data is typed into this column's **Value**, the **Null** checkbox is cleared automatically. (This is possible in JavaScript-enabled browsers.)

In the following screenshot, we have modified the structure of the **phone** column in the `author` table, to permit a NULL value (refer to the *Editing column attribute* section in this chapter). The **Null** checkbox is not selected here:

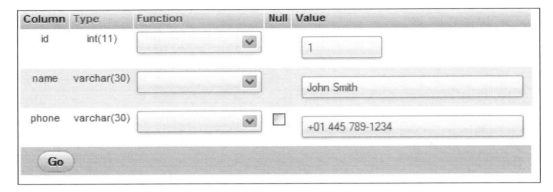

The corresponding data is erased after selecting the **Null** box.

Applying a function to a value

MySQL language offers some functions that we may apply to data before saving. Some of these functions appear in a drop-down menu beside each column, if `$cfg['ShowFunctionFields']` is set to TRUE.

The function list is defined in the `$cfg['Functions']` array. As usual, the default values for these arrays are located in `libraries/config.default.php`. We may change them by copying the needed section into `config.inc.php`. If we do so, as these values can change from version to version, we should take care of merging our changes with the values of the new version. The most commonly used functions for a certain data type are displayed first in the list. Some restrictions are defined in the `$cfg['RestrictColumnTypes']` and `$cfg['RestrictFunctions']` arrays.

As depicted in the following screenshot, we could apply the **UPPER** function to the **title** column when saving this row, which would convert the title to uppercase characters:

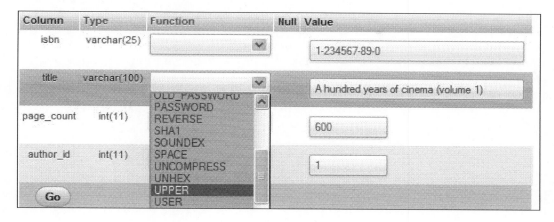

To gain some screen space, this feature may be disabled by setting `$cfg['ShowFunctionFields']` to FALSE. Moreover, the **Function** column header is clickable, so we can disable this feature on the fly.

When the feature is disabled—either by clicking or via the configuration parameter—a **Show : Function** link appears in order to display this **Function** column with a single click as shown in the following screenshot:

A similar feature is available for the **Type** column header, either by clicking on it or by configuring `$cfg['ShowFieldTypesInDataEditView']`.

Duplicating rows of data

During the course of data maintenance (for permanent duplication or for test purposes), we often have to generate a copy of a row. If this is done in the same table, we must respect the rules of key uniqueness.

Here is an example of row duplication. Our author has written volume 2 of his book about cinema. Hence, the columns that need a slight change are the ISBN, title, and page count. We bring the existing row on screen, change these three columns, and choose **Insert as new row**, as shown in the following screenshot:

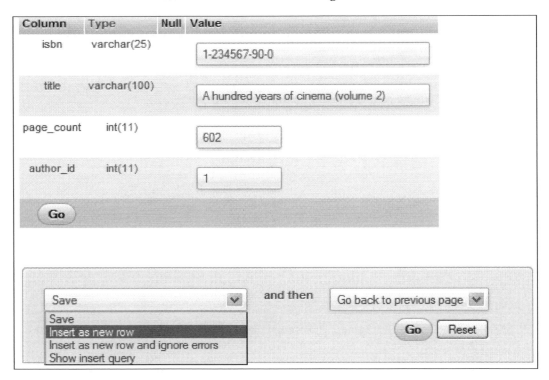

When we click on **Go**, another row is created with the modified information, leaving the original row unchanged, shown as follows:

isbn	title	page_count	author_id
1-234567-22-0	Future souvenirs	200	2
1-234567-89-0	A hundred years of cinema (volume 1)	600	1
1-234567-90-0	A hundred years of cinema (volume 2)	602	1

A shortcut link exists to achieve the same operation. When browsing the table, clicking on **Copy** for a specific row brings the edit panel for this row and selects **Insert as new row** instead of **Save**.

Multi-row editing

The multi-row edit feature enables us to use checkboxes on the rows we want to edit, and use the **Change** link (or the pencil-shaped icon) in the **With selected** menu. The **Check All / Uncheck All** links can also be used to quickly check or uncheck all the boxes. We can also click anywhere on the row's data to activate the corresponding checkbox. To select a range of checkboxes, we can click the first checkbox of the range, and then *Shift* + Click on the last checkbox of the range.

Upon clicking on **Change**, an edit panel containing all the chosen rows appears. The editing process may continue while the data from these rows is seen, compared, and changed. When we mark some rows with the checkboxes, we can also perform two other actions on them—**Delete** (refer to the *Deleting multiple rows* section in this chapter) and **Export** (refer to *Chapter 6*).

Editing the next row

Sequential editing is possible on tables that have a primary key on an integer column. Our `author` table meets the criteria. Let us see what happens when we start editing the row having the **id** value **1**:

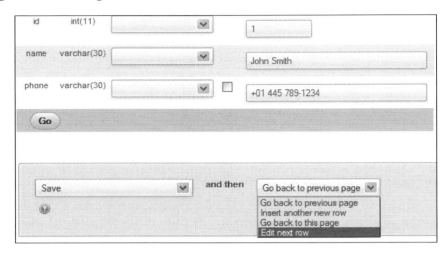

The editing panel appears, and we can edit author number **1**. However, in the drop-down menu, the **Edit next row** choice is available. If chosen, the next author—the first one whose primary key value is greater than the current primary key value—will be available for edit.

Inline row editing

Version 3.4 introduces inline row editing, that is, keeping in view the other rows of the results set while editing. This feature is available if `$cfg['AjaxEnable']` is set to `true`, via either `config.inc.php` or the user preferences. Clicking on **Inline Edit** for a row shows the following dialog:

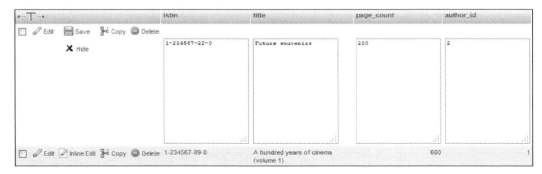

After editing the columns that need changes, we click on **Save**. Aborting the changes is also possible by using the **Hide** link.

Deleting data

phpMyAdmin's interface enables us to delete the following data:

- Single rows of data
- Multiple rows of a table
- All the rows in a table
- All the rows in multiple tables

Deleting a single row

We can use the red **Delete** icon beside each row to delete the row. If the value of $cfg['Confirm']$ is set to TRUE, every MySQL DELETE statement has to be confirmed before execution. This is the default, as it might not be prudent to allow a row to be deleted with just one click!

The form of the confirmation varies depending on the browser's ability to execute JavaScript. A JavaScript-based confirmation pop up would resemble the following screenshot:

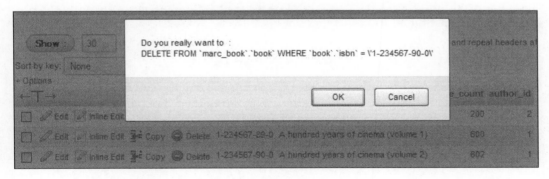

If JavaScript has been disabled in our browser, a distinct panel appears.

The actual DELETE statement will use whatever information is needed to ensure the deletion of only the intended row. In our case, a primary key had been defined and was used in the WHERE clause. In the absence of a primary key, a longer WHERE clause will be generated based on the value of each column. The generated WHERE clause might even prevent the correct execution of the DELETE operation, especially if there are TEXT or BLOB column types. This is because the HTTP transaction, used to send the query to the web server, may be limited in length by the browser or the server. This is another reason why defining a primary key is strongly recommended.

Deleting multiple rows

Let us say we examine a page of rows and decide that some rows have to be destroyed. Instead of deleting them one-by-one with the **Delete** link or icon and as sometimes the decision to delete must be made while examining a group of rows, there are checkboxes beside rows in Table view mode as shown in the following screenshot:

These are used with the **Delete** icon in the **With selected** menu. A confirmation screen appears listing all the rows that are about to be deleted.

Deleting all of the rows in a table

To completely erase all the rows in a table (leaving its structure intact), we first display the database **Structure** page by selecting the related database from the navigation panel. We then use the **Empty** icon or link located on the same line as the table we want to empty, shown as follows:

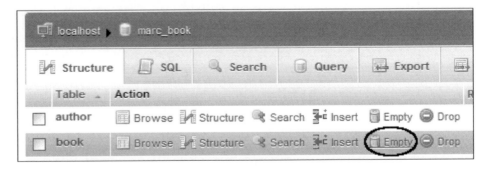

We get a message confirming the TRUNCATE statement (the MySQL statement used to quickly empty a table). For our exercise, we won't delete this precious data!

 Deleting data, either row-by-row or by emptying a table, is a permanent action. No recovery is then possible except by restoring a backup.

Deleting all rows in multiple tables

A checkbox is present on the left of each table name. We can choose some tables. Then, in the **With selected** menu, choose the **Empty** operation as shown in the following screenshot:

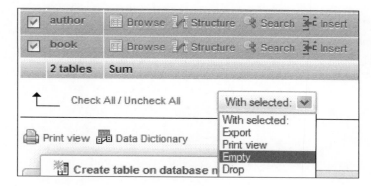

Of course, this decision must not be taken lightly!

Deleting tables

Deleting a table erases the data and the table's structure. In the Database view, we can delete a specific table by using the red **Drop** icon for that table. The same mechanism also exists for deleting more than one table (with the drop-down menu and the **Drop** action).

Deleting databases

We can delete an entire database (including all its tables) by going to the **Databases** page in `Server` view, selecting the checkbox beside the unwanted database and clicking on the **Drop** link:

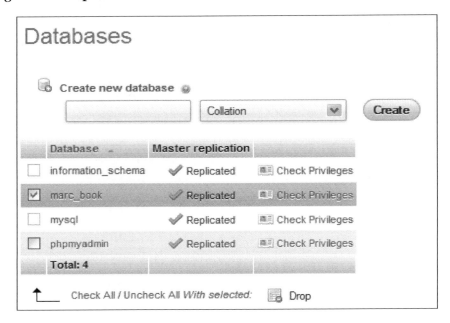

By default, `$cfg['AllowUserDropDatabase']` is set to `FALSE`. So, this panel does not permit unprivileged users to drop a database until this setting is manually changed to `TRUE`.

To help us think twice, a special message—**You are about to DESTROY a complete database!**—appears before a database is deleted.

 The database `mysql`, containing all user and privilege definitions, is highly important. Therefore, the checkbox is deactivated for this database, even for administrators.

Changing table structure

When developing an application, requirements about data structure often change because of new or modified needs. Developers must accommodate these changes through judicious table structure editing. This section explores the subject of changing the structure of tables. Specifically, it shows how to add a column to an existing table and edit the attributes of a column. We then build on these notions to introduce more specialized column types, and to explain their handling through phpMyAdmin. Finally, we will cover the topic of index management.

Adding a column

Suppose that we need a new column to store a book's language and, by default, the books on which we keep data are written in English. We call the column **language**, which will contain code composed of two characters (**en** by default).

In the **Structure** page of the `Table` view for the `book` table, we can find the **Add column** dialog. Here, we specify how many new columns we want, and where they will go.

The positions of the new columns in the table matter only from a developer's point of view. We usually group the columns logically, so that we can find them more easily in the list of columns. The exact position of the columns will not play a role in the intended results (output from the queries), as these results can be adjusted regardless of the table structure. Usually, the most important columns (including the keys) are located at the beginning of the table. However, it is a matter of personal preference.

We want to put the new column **At End of Table**. So, we check the corresponding radio button and click on **Go**.

Other possible choices would be **At Beginning of Table** and **After** (where we would have to choose from the drop-down menu, the column after which the new one must go).

We see the familiar panel for entering column's attributes. We fill it in. However, as we want to enter a default value this time, we do the following two actions:

- Change the **Default** drop-down menu from **None** to **As defined:**
- Enter the default value: **en**

We then click on **Save**.

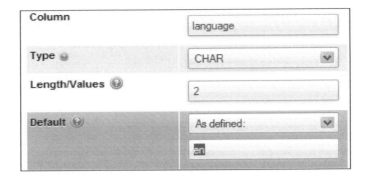

Vertical mode

The previous panel appeared in vertical mode because the default for $cfg['DefaultPropDisplay']$ is 3. This means that for three columns or less, the vertical mode is used, and for more than three, horizontal mode would be automatically selected. Here, we can use a number of our choosing.

If we set $cfg['DefaultPropDisplay']$ to 'vertical', the panel to add new columns (along with the panel to edit a column's structure) will be always presented in vertical order. This parameter can also take a value of 'horizontal' to force a horizontal mode.

Editing column attribute

On the **Structure** page, we can make further changes to our table:

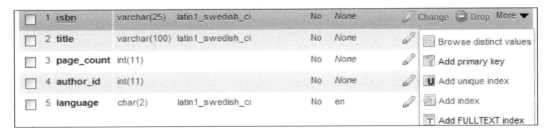

This panel does not allow every possible change to columns. It specifically allows:

- Changing one column structure, using the **Change** link on a specific column
- Removing a column, using **Drop** operation
- Adding a column to an existing **Primary** key

- Setting a non-unique **Index** or a **Unique** index on a column
- Setting a **FULLTEXT** index (offered only if the column type allows it)

These are quick links that may be useful in some situations, but they do not replace the full index management panel. Both of these are explained in this chapter.

We can use the checkboxes to choose columns. Then, with the appropriate **With selected** icons, we can edit the columns with **Change** or do a multiple column deletion with **Drop**. The **Check All / Uncheck All** option permits us to easily check or uncheck all boxes.

TEXT column type

We will now explore how to use the **TEXT** column type and the relevant configuration values to adjust for the best possible phpMyAdmin behavior. First, we add to the **book** table a **TEXT** column called **description**.

There are three configuration directives that control the layout of the text area that will be displayed in **Insert** or **Edit** mode for the **TEXT** column type. The number of display columns and rows for each column is defined by:

```
$cfg['TextareaCols'] = 40;
$cfg['TextareaRows'] = 15;
```

This gives (by default) space to work on a **TEXT** column type as shown in the following screenshot:

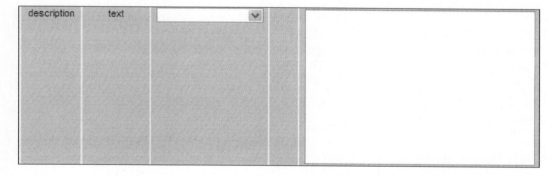

The settings impose only a visual limit on the text area, and a vertical scroll bar is created by the browser if necessary.

Although **MEDIUMTEXT**, **TEXT**, and **LONGTEXT** column types can accommodate more than 32 KiB of data, some browsers cannot always edit them with the text area—the mechanism offered by HTML. In fact, experimentation has convinced the phpMyAdmin development team to have the product display a warning message if the contents are larger than 32 KiB. The message warns users that the contents may not be editable.

The last configuration directive, `$cfg['LongtextDoubleTextarea']`, has an impact for **LONGTEXT** column types only. The default value of TRUE doubles the available editing space.

BLOB (Binary Large Object) column type

BLOB column types are generally used to hold binary data (such as images and sounds), even though the MySQL documentation implies that **TEXT** column types could be used for this purpose. The MySQL 5.1 manual says: "In some cases, it may be desirable to store binary data such as media files in BLOB or TEXT columns". However, another phrase: "BLOB columns are treated as binary strings (byte strings)", seems to indicate that binary data should really be stored in **BLOB** columns. Thus, phpMyAdmin's intention is to work with the **BLOB** column type to hold all binary data.

We will see in *Chapter 16* that there are special mechanisms available to go further with **BLOB** column type, including being able to view some images directly from within phpMyAdmin.

First, we add a **BLOB** column type named **cover_photo** to our book table. If we now browse the table, we can see the length information, **[BLOB - 0B]**, for each **BLOB** column type.

isbn	title	page_count	author_id	language	description	cover_photo
1-234567-22-0	Future souvenirs	200	2	en		[BLOB - 0B]

This is because the **Show BLOB** display option (do you remember the **Options** slider?) has no check mark by default. So, it blocks the display of **BLOB** contents in Browse mode. This behavior is intentional. Usually, we cannot do anything with binary data represented in plain text.

Uploading binary content

If we edit one row, we see the **Binary – do not edit** warning and a **Browse...** button. The exact caption on this button depends on the browser. Even though editing is not allowed, we can easily upload a text or binary file's contents into this **blob** column.

Let us choose an image file using the **Browse** button—for example, the `logo_left.png` file in a test copy of the `phpMyAdmin/themes/pmahomme/img` directory located on our client workstation. We now click on **Go**.

We need to keep in mind some limits for the upload size. Firstly, the **blob** column size is limited to 64 KiB, but in *Chapter 16* we will change the type of this column to accommodate bigger images. Hence, phpMyAdmin reminds us of this limit with the **Max: 64KiB** warning. Also, there could be limits inherent to PHP itself (refer to *Chapter 7* for more details). We have now uploaded an image inside this column for a specific row.

isbn	title	page_count	author_id	language	description	cover_photo
1-234567-22-0	Future souvenirs	200	2	en		[BLOB – 4.9KiB]

We notice that **BLOB – 4.9KiB** is a link; it permits to download any binary data to our workstation should the need arise.

If we put a check mark for the **Show BLOB Contents** display option, we now see the following in the **BLOB** column type:

 To really see the image from within phpMyAdmin, refer to *Chapter 16*.

The $cfg['ProtectBinary']$ parameter controls what can be done while editing binary columns (**BLOBs** and any other column with the binary attribute). The default value **blob** blocks the **BLOB** columns from being edited but allows us to edit other columns marked binary by MySQL. A value of all would block even binary columns from being edited. A value of FALSE would protect nothing, thus allowing us to edit all the columns. If we try the last choice, we see the following in the **Edit** panel for this row:

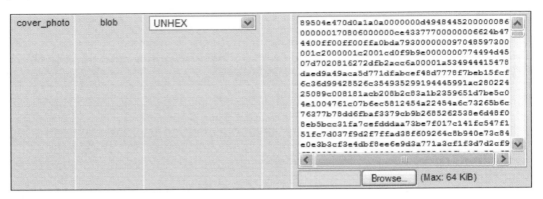

The content of this BLOB column type has been converted in hexadecimal and the **UNHEX** function is selected by default. We probably don't want to edit this image data in hexadecimal but this is the best way of safely representing binary data on screen. The reason for this hexadecimal representation is that the **Show binary contents as HEX display** option (in **Browse** mode) is currently marked. But we did not mark this option; it was checked because the $cfg['DisplayBinaryAsHex']$ directive is TRUE by default.

Should we decide instead to not mark this option, we would see the following pure binary data for this image:

There are chances that this is not our favorite image editor! In fact, data may be corrupted even if we save this row without touching the **BLOB** column type. But the possibility of setting $cfg['ProtectBinary']$ to FALSE exists, as some users put text in their **BLOB** columns, and they need to be able to modify this text. This is why phpMyAdmin can be configured to allow editing of **BLOB** columns.

MySQL **BLOB** data types are actually similar to their corresponding **TEXT** data types. However, we should keep in mind that a **BLOB** has no character set, whereas a **TEXT** column type has a character set that impacts sorting and comparison.

ENUM and SET column types

Both ENUM and SET column types are intended to represent a list of possible values. The difference is that the user can choose only one value from a defined list of values with **ENUM**, and more than one value with **SET**. With **SET**, all the multiple values go into one cell; but multiple values do not imply the creation of more than one row of data.

We add a column named **genre** to the book table and define it as an **ENUM**. For now, we choose to put short codes in the value list and make one of them, **F**, into the default value as shown in the following screenshot:

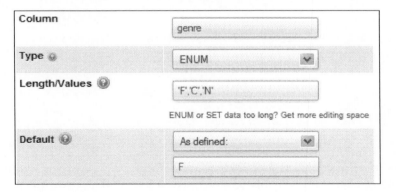

In the value list, we have to enclose each value within single quotes, unlike in the default value field. Starting with version 3.4.0, an editor targeted for ENUM/SET columns is available. With this editor, we don't need to bother enclosing values within single quotes. Clicking on **Get more editing space** brings this editor into action:

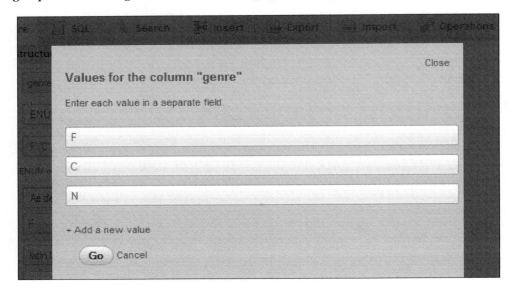

In our design, these values stand for **Fantasy**, **Child**, and **Novel**. However, for now, we want to see the interface's behavior with short code. In the **Insert** panel, we now see a radio box interface as shown in the following screenshot:

If we decide to have more self-describing values, we can go back to **Structure** mode and change the values definition for the **genre** column. We also have to change the default value to one of the possible values, to avoid getting an error message while trying to save this column structure's modification.

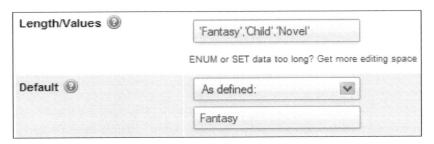

With the modified value list, the **Insert** panel now looks as follows:

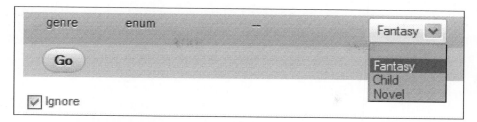

Observe that the radio buttons have been replaced by a drop-down list because the possible values are larger in length.

If we want more than one possible value selected, we have to change the column type to **SET**. The same value list may be used. However, using our browser's multiple value selector (control-click on a Windows or Linux desktop, command-click on a Mac), we can select more than one value as shown in the screenshot:

 In a normalized data structure, we would store only the **genre** code in the book table and would rely on another table to store the description for each code. We would not be using **SET** or **ENUM** in this case.

DATE, DATETIME, and TIMESTAMP column types

We could use a normal character column to store date or time information. But **DATE**, **DATETIME**, and **TIMESTAMP** are more efficient for this purpose. MySQL checks the contents to ensure valid date and time information, and offers special functions to work on these columns.

Calendar pop up

As an added benefit, phpMyAdmin offers a calendar pop up for easy data entry.

We will start by adding a **DATE** column type—**date_published**—to our book table. If we go into **Insert** mode, we should now see the new column where we could type a date. A **Calendar** icon is also available. This icon brings a pop-up window, synchronized to this **DATE** column type. If there is already a value in the column, the pop up is displayed accordingly. In our case, there is no value in the column, so the calendar shows the current date as shown in the following screenshot:

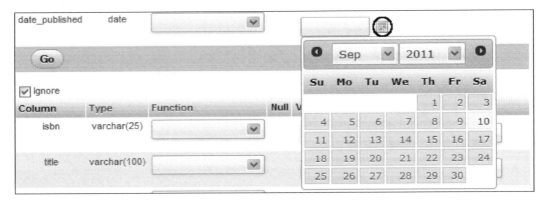

Small arrows permit easy scrolling through months and years. A simple click on the date we want transports it to our **date_published** column. For a **DATETIME** or **TIMESTAMP** column type, the pop up offers the ability to edit the time part.

If we type a date or time value, a validation is done if our browser is JavaScript-enabled; incorrect values are highlighted in red.

TIMESTAMP option

Starting with MySQL 4.1.2, there are more options that can affect a **TIMESTAMP** column type. Let us add to our book table, a column named **stamp** of type **TIMESTAMP**. In the **Default** drop-down, we could choose **CURRENT_TIMESTAMP**; but we won't for this exercise. However, in the **Attributes** column, we choose **on update CURRENT_TIMESTAMP**. More details are available at http://dev.mysql.com/doc/refman/5.5/en/timestamp.html.

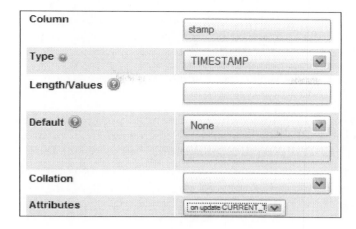

Bit column type

MySQL 5.0.3 introduced true bit columns. These take the same amount of space in the database as the number of bits in their definition. Let us say we have the following three pieces of information about each book, and each piece can only be true (1) or false (0):

- Book is hard cover
- Book contains a CD-ROM
- Book is available only in electronic format

We will use a single **BIT** column to store these three pieces of information. Therefore, we add a column having a length of **3** (which means 3 bits) to the book table:

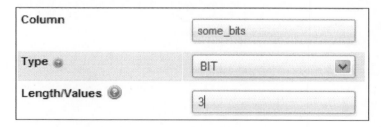

To construct and subsequently interpret the values we store in this column, we have to think in binary, respecting the position of each bit within the column. To indicate that a book is hard cover, does not contain a CD-ROM, and is available only in electronic format, we would use a value of 101.

phpMyAdmin handles `BIT` columns in a binary way. For example, if we edit one row and set a value of `101` to the **some_bits** column, the following query is sent at save time:

```
UPDATE `marc_book`.`book` SET `some_bits` = b '101'
WHERE `book`.`isbn` = '1-234567-89-0' LIMIT 1;
```

The highlighted part of this query shows that the column really receives a binary value. At browse time, the exact value (which in decimal is 5—a meaningless value for our purpose) is redisplayed in its binary form `101`, which helps to interpret each discrete bit value. More details about the notation for bit values are available at `http://dev.mysql.com/doc/refman/5.5/en/bit-type.html`.

Managing indexes

Properly maintained indexes are crucial for data retrieval speed. phpMyAdmin has a number of index management options, which will be covered in this section.

Single-column indexes

We have already seen how the **Structure** panel offers a quick way to create an index on a single column, thanks to some links such as **Add primary key**, **Add index**, and **Add unique index**. Under the columns list, there is a section of the interface available to manage indexes:

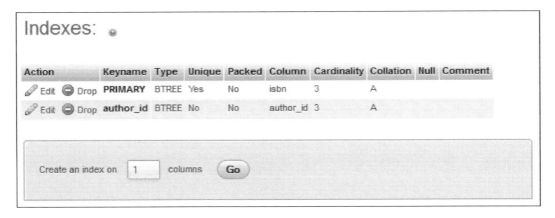

This section has links to edit or delete every index. Here, the **Column** part lists only one column per index, and we can see that the whole column participates in the index. This is because there is no size information after each column name, contrary to what will be seen in our next example.

We will now add an index on the title. However, we want to restrict the length of this index to reduce the space used by the on-disk index structure. The **Create an index on 1 columns** option is appropriate. So, we click on **Go**. In the next screen, we specify the index details as shown here:

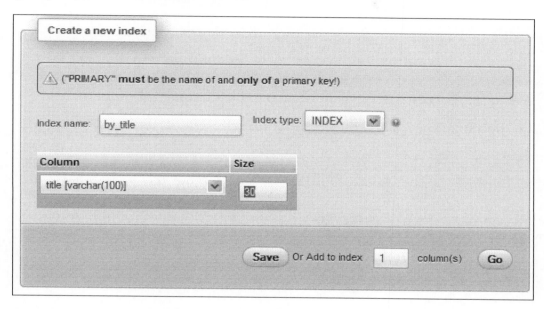

We fill in the following information in the options of this panel:

- **Index name**: A name we invent, that describes the purpose of this index
- **Index type**: We can choose **INDEX**
- **Column**: We select the column that is used as the index, which is **title**
- **Size**: We enter **30** instead of 100 (the complete length of the column) to save space in the table's physical portion that holds index data

After saving this panel, we can confirm from the following screenshot that the index is created and does not cover the entire length of the **title** column:

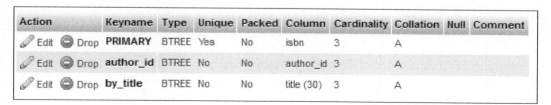

Action			Keyname	Type	Unique	Packed	Column	Cardinality	Collation	Null	Comment
Edit	Drop		PRIMARY	BTREE	Yes	No	isbn	3	A		
Edit	Drop		author_id	BTREE	No	No	author_id	3	A		
Edit	Drop		by_title	BTREE	No	No	title (30)	3	A		

Multi-column indexes and index editing

In the next example, we assume that in a future application we will need to find the books written by a specific author in a specific language. It makes sense to expand our **author_id** index, adding the **language** column to it.

We click on the **Edit** link (small-pencil icon) on the line containing the **author_id** index; this shows the current state of this index. The interface has room to add another column to this index. We could use the **Add to index 1 column(s)** feature should we need to add more than one column. In the selector, we pick **language**. This time we do not have to enter a size, as the whole column will be used in the index. For better documentation, we change the **Index name (author_language** is appropriate) as shown in the following screenshot:

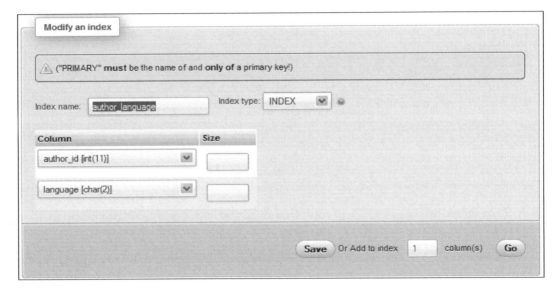

We save this index modification. In the list of indexes, we can confirm our index modification.

FULLTEXT indexes

This special type of index allows for full text searches. It is supported only on MyISAM tables for the **VARCHAR** and **TEXT** column types, but MySQL 5.6 should be offering this feature for InnoDB too. We can use the **Add FULLTEXT index** link in the columns list or go to the index management panel and choose **FULLTEXT** in the drop-down menu.

Optimizing indexes with EXPLAIN

In this section, we want to get some information about the index that MySQL uses for a specific query, and the performance impact of not having defined an index.

Let us assume we want to use the following query:

```
SELECT    *
FROM `book`
WHERE author_id = 2 AND language = 'es'
```

We want to know, which books written by the author whose id is 2, are in the es language—our code for Spanish.

To enter this query, we use the **SQL** tab from the database or the table menu, or the SQL Query window (refer to *Chapter 11*). We enter this query in the query box and click **Go**. Whether the query finds any results, is not important right now.

 You could obtain the same query by following explanations from *Chapter 8* to produce a search for **author_id 2** and language **es**.

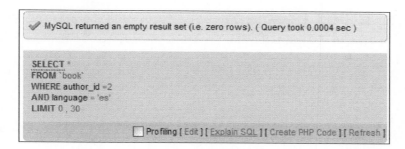

We will now use the **[Explain SQL]** link to get information about which index (if any) has been used for this query:

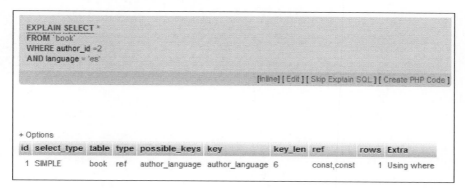

id	select_type	table	type	possible_keys	key	key_len	ref	rows	Extra
1	SIMPLE	book	ref	author_language	author_language	6	const,const	1	Using where

We can see that the **EXPLAIN** command has been passed to MySQL, telling us that the **key** used is **author_language.** Thus, we know that this index will be used for this type of query. If this index had not existed, the result would have been quite different.

id	select_type	table	type	possible_keys	key	key_len	ref	rows	Extra
1	SIMPLE	book	ALL	NULL	NULL	NULL	NULL	3	Using where

Here, **key (NULL)** and the **type (ALL)** mean that no index would be used, and all rows would need to be examined to find the desired data. Depending on the total number of rows, this could have a serious impact on the performance. We can ascertain the exact impact by examining the query timing that phpMyAdmin displays on each result page (**Query took x sec**), and comparing it with or without the index. However, the difference in time can be minimal if we only have limited test data, compared to a real table in production. For more details about the EXPLAIN output format, please refer to http://dev.mysql.com/doc/refman/5.5/en/explain-output.html.

Detecting index problems

To help users maintain an optimal index strategy, phpMyAdmin tries to detect some common index problems. For example, let us access the book table and add an index on the **isbn** column. When we display this table's structure, we get a warning as shown in the following screenshot:

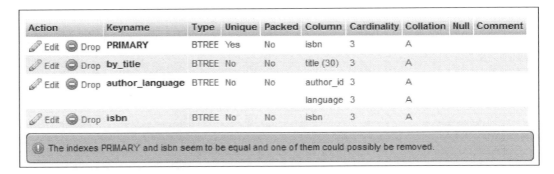

Action	Keyname	Type	Unique	Packed	Column	Cardinality	Collation	Null	Comment
Edit Drop	PRIMARY	BTREE	Yes	No	isbn	3	A		
Edit Drop	by_title	BTREE	No	No	title (30)	3	A		
Edit Drop	author_language	BTREE	No	No	author_id	3	A		
					language	3	A		
Edit Drop	isbn	BTREE	No	No	isbn	3	A		

The indexes PRIMARY and isbn seem to be equal and one of them could possibly be removed.

The intention here is to warn us about an inefficient index structure when considering the whole table. We don't need to have two indexes on the same column.

Summary

This chapter examined data-changing concepts, such as:

- Editing data
- Including the NULL column and using the *Tab* key
- Applying a function to a value
- Duplicating rows of data
- Deleting data, tables, and databases

We also got an overview of structure-changing techniques such as:

- How to add columns, including special column types such as TEXT, BLOB, ENUM, and SET
- How to use a calendar pop up for DATE, DATETIME, and TIMESTAMP column types
- How to upload binary data into a BLOB column
- How to manage indexes (multi-column and full-text), and get feedback from MySQL about which indexes are used in a specific query

In the next chapter, we will learn how to export a table's structure and data for backup purposes, or to use as a gateway to another application.

6
Exporting Structure and Data (Backup)

Keeping good backups is crucial to a project. Backups consist of up-to-date backups and intermediary snapshots taken during development and production phases. The export feature of phpMyAdmin can generate backups, and can also be used to send data to other applications.

> Please note that phpMyAdmin's export feature produces backups on demand and it is highly recommended to implement an automatic and scripted backup solution which takes backups on a regular schedule. The precise way to implement such a solution depends on the server's OS.

Dumps, backups, and exports

Let us first clarify some vocabulary. In MySQL documentation, you will encounter the term **dump**, and in other applications, **backup** or **export**. All these terms have the same meaning in the phpMyAdmin context.

MySQL includes **mysqldump**—a command-line utility that can be used to generate export files. But the shell access needed for command-line utilities is not offered by every host provider. Also, access to the export feature from within the web interface is more convenient. This is why phpMyAdmin offers the export feature with more export formats than mysqldump. This chapter will focus on phpMyAdmin's export features.

Before starting an export, we must have a clear picture of the intended goal of the export. The following questions may be of help:

- Do we need the complete database or just some tables?
- Do we need just the structure, just the data, or both?
- Which utility will be used to import back the data?
- Do we want only a subset of the data?
- What is the size of the intended export, and what is the link speed between us and the server?

Scope of the export

When we click an **Export** link from phpMyAdmin, we can be in one of these views or contexts—`Database` view, `Table` view, or `Server` view (more on this later in *Chapter 19*). According to the current context, the resulting export's scope will be a complete database, a single table, or even a multi-database as in the case of `Server` view. We will first explain database exports and all the relevant export types. Then we will go on with table and multi-database exports, underlining the difference for these modes of exporting.

Exporting a database

In the `Database` view, click on the **Export** link. Since version 3.4.0, the default export panel appears as shown in the following screenshot:

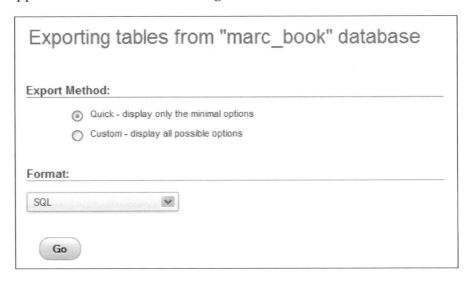

[126]

By default, $cfg['Export']['method']$ is set to `'quick'` and $cfg['Export']$ `['format']` is set to `'sql'`. Usability tests show that the most common goal of exporting is to produce a complete backup in SQL format and save it on our workstation; this is accomplished by just clicking on **Go**.

Other values for $cfg['Export']['method']$ are `'custom'`, which would show the detailed export options, and `'custom-no-form'` which would also show the detailed options but without the possibility of selecting a quick export—this being the behavior of versions prior to 3.4.0.

In custom mode, sub-panels are shown. The **Table(s)**, **Output**, and **Format** sub-panels occupy the top part of the page. The **Format-specific options** sub-panel varies in order to show the options for the export format chosen. Following screenshot shows the SQL format panel:

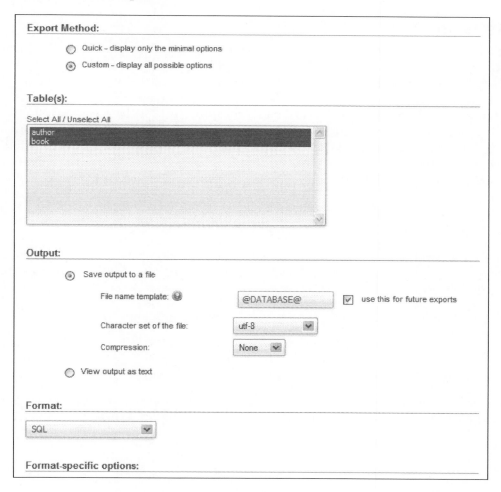

The Table(s) sub-panel

This sub-panel contains a table selector, from which we choose the tables that we want. By default, all tables are selected and we can use the **Select All / Unselect All** links to change our choice.

The Output sub-panel

The default behavior is to transmit the export file via HTTP (the **Save output to a file** radio button being selected). This triggers a **Save** dialog into the browser, which ultimately saves the file on our local machine. An alternative option would have been to select **View output as text**, which can be done as a testing procedure, provided that the exported data is of a reasonable size.

File name template

The name of the proposed file will obey the **File name template** field. In this template, we can use the special **@SERVER@**, **@DATABASE@**, and **@TABLE@** placeholders. These placeholders will be replaced by the current server, database, or table name (for a single-table export). Note that there is one "at sign" character before and after the words. We can also use any special character from the PHP strftime function; this is useful for generating an export file based on the current date or hour. Finally, we can put any other string of characters (not part of the strftime special characters), which will be used literally. The file extension is generated according to the type of export. In this case, it will be .sql. Following are some examples for the template:

- @DATABASE@ would generate marc_book.sql
- @DATABASE@-%Y%m%d would give marc_book-20110920.sql

The **use this for future exports** option, when activated, stores the entered template settings into cookies (for database, table, or server exports) and brings them back the next time we use the same kind of export.

The default templates are configurable, via the following parameters:

```
$cfg['Export']['file_template_table']    = '@TABLE@';
$cfg['Export']['file_template_database'] = '@DATABASE@';
$cfg['Export']['file_template_server']   = '@SERVER@';
```

The possible placeholders such as @DATABASE@ are the same as those that can be used for the window title and are described in Documentation.html, FAQ 6.27.

Choosing a character set

It is possible to choose the exact character set for our exported file. phpMyAdmin verifies that the conditions for recoding are met. For the actual recoding of data, the PHP component of the web server must support the `iconv` or the `recode` module. The `$cfg['RecodingEngine']` parameter specifies the actual recoding engine—the choices being `none`, `auto`, `iconv`, and `recode`. If it is set to `auto`, phpMyAdmin will first try the `iconv` module and then the `recode` module. If set to `none`, the character set dialog is not shown.

Kanji support

If phpMyAdmin detects the use of the Japanese language, it checks whether PHP supports the `mb_convert_encoding()` multibyte string function. If it does, additional radio buttons are displayed on the export and import pages and on the query box, so that we can choose between the `EUC-JP` and `SJIS` Japanese encodings.

Here is an example taken from the **Export** page:

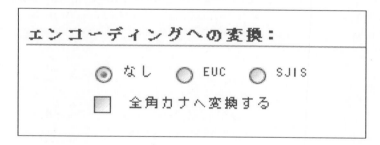

Compression

To save transmission time and get a smaller export file, phpMyAdmin can compress to ZIP, GZIP, or BZIP2 formats. These formats are offered only if the PHP server has been compiled with the `--with-zlib` (for ZIP and GZIP) or `--with-bz2` (for BZ2) configuration option respectively. The following parameters control which compression choices are presented in the panel:

```
$cfg['ZipDump']   = TRUE;
$cfg['GZipDump']  = TRUE;
$cfg['BZipDump']  = TRUE;
```

A system administrator installing phpMyAdmin for a number of users could choose to set all these parameters to FALSE, so as to avoid the potential overhead incurred by a lot of users compressing their exports at the same time. This situation usually causes more overhead than if all the users were transmitting their uncompressed files at the same time.

In older phpMyAdmin versions, the compression file was built in the web server memory. Some problems caused by this were:

- File generation depended on the memory limits assigned to running PHP scripts.
- During the time the file was generated and compressed, no transmission occurred. Hence, users were inclined to think that the operation was not working and that something had crashed.
- Compression of large databases was impossible to achieve.

The $cfg['CompressOnFly'] parameter (set to TRUE by default) was added to generate (for GZIP AND BZIP2 formats) a compressed file containing more headers. Now, the transmission starts almost immediately. The file is sent in smaller chunks so that the whole process consumes much less memory. The downside of this is a slightly larger resulting file.

Export formats

We shall now discuss the formats (and the options available once they have been chosen) that can be selected with the **Format** sub-panel.

 Even if we can export into many formats, only some of these formats can be imported back using phpMyAdmin.

SQL

The SQL format is useful, as it creates standard SQL commands that would work on any SQL server.

If the **Display comments** checkbox is selected, comments are included in the export file. The first part of the export comprises comments (starting with the -- characters) that detail the utility (and version) that created the file, the date, and other environment information. We then see the CREATE and INSERT queries for each table.

phpMyAdmin generates ANSI-compatible comments in the export file. These comments start with --. They help with importing the file back on other ANSI SQL-compatible systems.

SQL options are used to define exactly what information the export will contain. The following screenshot depicts the general SQL options:

The general SQL options are:

- **Additional custom header comment**: We can add our own comments for this export (for example, **Monthly backup**), which will show in the export headers (after the PHP version number). If the comment has more than one line, we must use the special character \n to separate each line.

- **Display foreign key relationships**: In *Chapter 10*, we will see that it's possible to define relations even for tables under the MyISAM storage engine; this option would export these relationship's definition as comments. These cannot be directly imported, but nonetheless are valuable as human-readable table information.

- **Display MIME types**: This adds information (in the form of SQL comments), to describe which MIME type has been associated to columns. *Chapter 16* explains this further.

- **Enclose export in a transaction**: Starting with MySQL 4.0.11, we can use the START TRANSACTION statement. This command, combined with SET AUTOCOMMIT=0 at the beginning and COMMIT at the end, asks MySQL to execute the import (when we will re-import this file) in one transaction, ensuring that all the changes are done as a whole.

- **Disable foreign key checks**: In the export file, we can add DROP TABLE statements. However, normally a table cannot be dropped if it is referenced in a foreign key constraint. This option overrides the verification by adding SET FOREIGN_KEY_CHECKS=0 to the export file. This override only lasts for the duration of the import.
- **Database system or older MySQL server to maximize output compatibility with**: This lets us choose the flavor of SQL that we export. We must know about the system onto which we intend to import this file. Among the choices are **MySQL 3.23, MySQL 4.0, ORACLE,** and **ANSI.**

We may want to export the structure, the data, or both; this is performed with the **Dump table** option. Selecting **Structure** generates the section with CREATE queries, and selecting **Data** produces INSERT queries.

If we select **Structure**, the **Object creation options** sub-panel appears, as depicted in the following screenshot:

Object creation options

Add statements:

☐ Add DROP TABLE / VIEW / PROCEDURE / FUNCTION / EVENT statement

☑ Add CREATE PROCEDURE / FUNCTION / EVENT statement

☑ CREATE TABLE options:

☑ IF NOT EXISTS

☑ AUTO_INCREMENT

☑ Enclose table and field names with backquotes *(Protects field and table names formed with special characters or keywords)*

The structure options are:

- **Add DROP TABLE / VIEW / PROCEDURE / FUNCTION / EVENT**: Adds a DROP ... IF EXISTS statement before each CREATE statement, for example, DROP TABLE IF EXISTS `author`;. This way, we can ensure that the export file is executed on a database in which the same element already exists, updating its structure but destroying the previous element's contents.
- **Add CREATE PROCEDURE / FUNCTION / EVENT**: This includes all procedures, functions, and event definitions found in this database, in the export.

- **CREATE TABLE OPTIONS / IF NOT EXISTS**: Adds the IF NOT EXISTS modifier to CREATE TABLE statements, avoiding an error during import if the table already exists.

- **CREATE TABLE OPTIONS / AUTO_INCREMENT**: Puts auto-increment information from the tables into the export, ensuring that the inserted rows in the tables will receive the next exact auto-increment ID value.

- **Enclose table and field names with backquotes**: In the MySQL world, backquotes are the normal way of protecting table and column names that may contain special characters. In most cases, it is useful to have them. However, backquotes are not recommended if the target server (where the export file will be imported) is running a SQL engine that does not support backquotes.

The following screenshot displays options relevant to a **Data** export:

Data dump options

Instead of INSERT statements, use:

☐ INSERT DELAYED statements ⊛

☐ INSERT IGNORE statements ⊛

Function to use when dumping data: INSERT ▾

Syntax to use when inserting data:

○ include column names in every INSERT statement
Example: INSERT INTO tbl_name (col_A,col_B,col_C) VALUES (1,2,3)

○ insert multiple rows in every INSERT statement
Example: INSERT INTO tbl_name VALUES (1,2,3), (4,5,6), (7,8,9)

◉ both of the above
Example: INSERT INTO tbl_name (col_A,col_B) VALUES (1,2,3), (4,5,6), (7,8,9)

○ neither of the above
Example: INSERT INTO tbl_name VALUES (1,2,3)

Maximal length of created query   50000

☑ Dump binary columns in hexadecimal notation *(for example, "abc" becomes 0x616263)*

☑ Dump TIMESTAMP columns in UTC *(enables TIMESTAMP columns to be dumped and reloaded between servers in different time zones)*

The options available in the **Data** section are:

- **INSERT DELAYED statements**: Adds the DELAYED modifier to INSERT statements. This accelerates the INSERT operation as it is queued to the server, which will execute it when the table is not in use. This is a MySQL non-standard extension, available only for MyISAM, MEMORY, and ARCHIVE tables.

- **INSERT IGNORE statements**: Normally, at import time, we cannot insert duplicate values for unique keys, as this would abort the insert operation. This option adds the IGNORE modifier to INSERT and UPDATE statements, thus skipping the rows that generate duplicate key errors.

- **Function to use when dumping data**: The choices are **INSERT, UPDATE,** and **REPLACE.** The most well-known of these types is the default **INSERT**— using INSERT statements to import back our data. At import time, however, we could be in a situation where a table already exists and contains valuable data, and we just want to update the columns that are in the current table we are exporting. **UPDATE** generates statements, such as the following line of code, updating a row when the same primary or unique key is found:

```
UPDATE `author` SET `id` = 1, `name` = 'John Smith', `phone` =
'111-1111' WHERE `id` = '1';
```

    The third possibility, **REPLACE**, produces statements such as REPLACE INTO `author` VALUES (1, 'John Smith', '111-1111'); These act similar to an INSERT statement for new rows and update existing rows, based on primary or unique keys.

- **Syntax to use when inserting data**: There are several choices here. By including column names in every statement, the resulting file is bigger, but will prove more portable on various SQL systems with the added benefit of being better documented. Inserting multiple rows with a statement is faster than using multiple INSERT statements, but is less convenient as it makes reading the resultant file harder. It also produces a smaller file, but each line of this file is not executable in itself as each line does not have an INSERT statement. If you cannot import the complete file in one operation, you cannot split the file with a text editor and import it chunk by chunk.

- **Maximal length of created query**: The single INSERT statement generated for **Extended inserts** might become too big and could cause problems. Hence, we set a limit to the number of characters for the length of this statement.

- **Dump binary columns in hexadecimal notation**: This option makes phpMyAdmin encode the contents of BLOB columns in 0x format. Such a format is useful as, depending on the software that will be used to manipulate the export file (for example a text editor or mail program), handling a file containing 8-bit data can be problematic. However, using this option will produce an export of BLOB column type that is twice the size.

- **Dump TIMESTAMP columns in UTC**: This is useful if the export file is to be imported back on a server located in a different time zone.

CSV

This format is understood by a lot of programs, and you may find it useful for exchanging data. Note that it is a data-only format—no SQL structure here.

The available options are:

- **Columns separated with**: We put a comma here, which means that a comma will be placed after each column. The default value comes from $cfg['Export']['csv_separator'].

- **Columns enclosed with**: We place an enclosing character here (double quotes) to ensure that a column containing the terminating character (comma) is not taken for two columns. The default value comes from $cfg['Export']['csv_enclosed'].

- **Columns escaped with**: If the export generator finds the **Columns enclosed with** character inside a column, this character will be placed before it in order to protect it. For example, "John \"The Great\"Smith". The default value comes from $cfg['Export']['csv_escaped'].

- **Lines terminated with**: This decides the character that ends each line. We should use a proper line delimiter here depending on the operating system on which we will manipulate the resulting export file. The default value of this option comes from the $cfg['Export']['csv_terminated'] parameter, which contains 'AUTO' by default. The 'AUTO' value produces a value of \r\n if the browser's OS is Windows, and \n otherwise. However, this might not be the best choice if the export file is intended for a machine with a different OS.

- **Replace NULL with**: This determines which string occupies the place in the export file of any NULL value found in a column.

- **Remove carriage return/line feed characters within columns**: As a column can contain carriage return or line feed characters, this determines if such characters should be removed from the exported data.

- **Put column names in the first row**: This gets some information about the meaning of each column. Some programs will use this information to name the column. For the exercise, we select this option.

Finally, we select the author table.

Clicking on **Go** produces a file containing the following lines:

```
"id","name","phone"
"1","John Smith","+01 445 789-1234"
"2","Maria Sunshine","+01 455 444-5683"
```

CSV for Microsoft Excel

This export mode produces a CSV file specially formatted for Microsoft Excel (using semicolons instead of commas). We can select the exact Microsoft Excel edition as shown in the following screenshot:

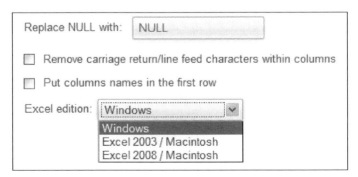

PDF

It's possible to create a PDF report of a table by exporting in PDF. This feature always produces a file. Since phpMyAdmin 3.4.7, we can also export a complete database or multiple tables in one sweep. We can add a title for this report, and it also gets automatically paginated. Non-textual (BLOB) data as in the book table is discarded from this export format.

Here, we test it on the author table, asking to use "The authors" as a title. PDF is interesting because of its inherent vectorial nature—the results can be zoomed. Let us have a look at the generated report, as seen from the Adobe Reader:

Microsoft Word 2000

This export format directly produces a .doc file suitable for all software that understands the Word 2000 format. We find options similar to those in the Microsoft Excel export, and a few more. We can independently export the table's **Structure** and **Data**.

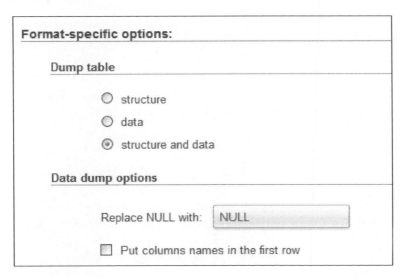

Note that, for this format and the Excel format, we can choose many tables for one export. However, unpleasant results happen if one of these tables has non-textual data. Here are the results for the author table:

Database marc_book

Table structure for table author

Field	Type	Null	Default
id	int(11)	Yes	
name	varchar(30)	Yes	
phone	varchar(30)	Yes	NULL

Dumping data for table author

1	John Smith	+01 445-789-1234
2	Maria Sunshine	333-3333

LaTeX

LaTeX is a typesetting language. phpMyAdmin can generate a .tex file that represents the table's structure and/or data in a sideways tabular format.

 Note that this file is not directly viewable, and must be processed further or converted for the intended final media.

The available options are:

Option	Description
Include table caption	Displays captions in the tabular output
Structure and **Data**	The familiar choice to request structure, data, or both
Table caption	The caption to go on the first page
Table caption (continued)	The caption to go on, page after page
Display foreign key relationships, comments, MIME types	Other structure information we want as output. These choices are available if the phpMyAdmin configuration storage is in place

XML

This format is very popular these days for data exchange. We can choose which data definition elements (such as functions, procedures, tables, triggers, or views) we want exported. What follows is the output for the `author` table.

```xml
<?xml version="1.0" encoding="utf-8"?>
<!--
- phpMyAdmin XML Dump
- version 3.4.5
- http://www.phpmyadmin.net
-
- Host: localhost
- Generation Time: Sep 16, 2011 at 03:18 PM
- Server version: 5.5.13
- PHP Version: 5.3.8
-->

<pma_xml_export version="1.0" xmlns:pma="http://www.phpmyadmin.net/
some_doc_url/">
  <!--
  - Structure schemas
  -->
  <pma:structure_schemas>
  <pma:database name="marc_book" collation="latin1_swedish_ci"
    charset="latin1">
  <pma:table name="author">
  CREATE TABLE `author` (
    `id` int(11) NOT NULL,
    `name` varchar(30) NOT NULL,
    `phone` varchar(30) DEFAULT NULL,
    PRIMARY KEY (`id`)
  ) ENGINE=InnoDB DEFAULT CHARSET=latin1;
  </pma:table>
  </pma:database>
  </pma:structure_schemas>

  <!--
  - Database: 'marc_book'
  -->
  <database name="marc_book">
  <!-- Table author -->
  <table name="author">
  <column name="id">1</column>
  <column name="name">John Smith</column>
```

```
        <column name="phone">+01 445 789-1234</column>
        </table>
        <table name="author">
        <column name="id">2</column>
        <column name="name">Maria Sunshine</column>
        <column name="phone">333-3333</column>
        </table>
        </database>
    </pma_xml_export>
```

Open document spreadsheet

This spreadsheet format is a subset of the open document (`http://en.wikipedia.org/wiki/OpenDocument`), which was made popular with the `OpenOffice.org` office suite. We need to choose only one table to be exported in order to have a coherent spreadsheet. The following screenshot shows our `author` table, exported into a file named `author.ods`, and subsequently looked at from OpenOffice:

A1		*f(x)* Σ =	1
	A	**B**	**C**
1	1	John Smith	+01 445-789-1234
2	2	Maria Sunshine	333-3333
3			

Open document text

This is another subset of the open document standard, this time oriented towards text processing. Our `author` table is now exported and viewed from OpenOffice.

Database marc_book

Table structure for table author

Field	Type	Null	Default	Comments
id	int(11)	Yes		
name	varchar(30)	Yes		
phone	varchar(30)	Yes	NULL	

Dumping data for table author

id	name	phone
1	John Smith	+01 445-789-1234
2	Maria Sunshine	333-3333

YAML

YAML stands for **YAML Ain't Markup Language**. YAML is a human-readable data serialization format; its official site is `http://www.yaml.org`. This format has no option that we can choose from within phpMyAdmin. Here is the YAML export for the `author` table:

```
1:
  id: 1
  name: John Smith
  phone: +01 445-789-1234
2:
  id: 2
  name: Maria Sunshine
  phone: 333-3333
```

CodeGen

This choice might some day support many formats related to code development. Currently, it can export in NHibernate **Object-relation mapping (ORM)** format. For more details, please refer to `http://en.wikipedia.org/wiki/Nhibernate`.

Texy! text

Texy! is a formatting tool (`http://texy.info/en/`) with its own simplified syntax. The following block of code is an example of export in this format:

```
===Database marc_book

== Table structure for table author
|------
|Field|Type|Null|Default
|------
|//**id**//|int(11)|Yes|NULL
|name|varchar(30)|Yes|NULL
|phone|varchar(30)|Yes|NULL

== Dumping data for table author
|1|John Smith|+01 445 789-1234
|2|Maria Sunshine|333-3333
```

PHP array

In PHP, associative arrays can hold text data; therefore, a PHP-array export format is available. The following is a PHP array export of the `author` table:

```php
<?php
// marc_book.author
$author = array(
  array('id'=>1,'name'=>'John Smith','phone'=>'+1 445 789-1234'),
  array('id'=>2,'name'=>'Maria Sunshine','phone'=>'333-3333')
);
```

MediaWiki table

MediaWiki (`http://www.mediawiki.org/wiki/MediaWiki`) is a popular wiki package, which supports the ubiquitous Wikipedia. This wiki software implements a formatting language in which it's possible to describe data in tabular format. Choosing this export format in phpMyAdmin produces a file which can be pasted on a wiki page we are editing.

JSON

The JavaScript Object Notation (`http://json.org`) is a data-interchange format popular in the web world. Exporting the `author` table in this format is shown in the following block of code:

```
/**
 Export to JSON plugin for PHPMyAdmin
 @version 0.1
 */

/* Database 'marc_book' */
/* marc_book.author */

[{"id": 1,"name": "John Smith","phone": "+01 445 789-1234"}, {"id":
2,"name": "Maria Sunshine","phone": "333-3333"}]
```

Exporting a table

The **Export** link in the `Table` view brings up the export sub-panel for a specific table. It is similar to the database export panel, but there is no table selector. However, there is an additional section for split exports (**Rows**) before the **Output** sub-panel, as depicted here:

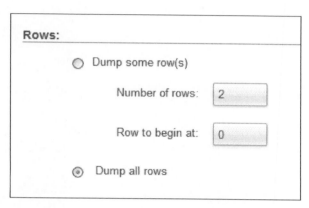

Split-file exports

The part of the dialog containing **Number of rows** and **Row to begin at** enables us to split the table into chunks. Depending on the exact row size, we can experiment with various values for the number of rows to find and how many rows can be put in a single export file before the memory or execution time limits are hit in the web server. We could then use names such as `book00.sql` and `book01.sql` for our export files. Should we decide to export all rows, we just select the **Dump all rows** radio button.

Exporting selectively

At various places in phpMyAdmin's interface, we can export the results that we see, or select the rows that we want to export. We will examine the various ways of exporting a selected portion of a table.

Exporting partial query results

When results are displayed from phpMyAdmin (here, the results of a query asking for the books from **author_id 2**), an **Export** link appears at the bottom of the page.

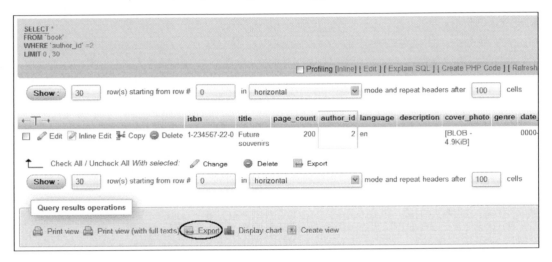

Clicking on this link brings up a special export panel containing the query on the top, along with the other table export options. An export produced via this panel would contain only the data from this result set.

> The results of single-table queries can be exported in all the available formats, while the results of multi-table queries can be exported in all the formats except SQL.

Exporting and checkboxes

Anytime we see the results (when browsing or searching, for example), we can check the boxes beside the rows that we want, and use the **With selected: Export** icon or link to generate a partial export file with just those rows.

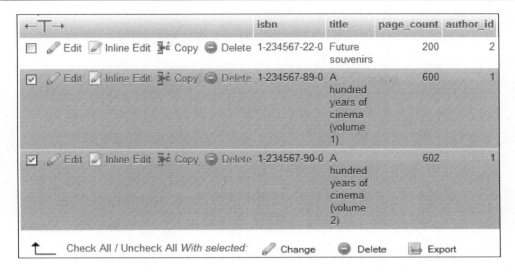

Exporting multiple databases

Any user can export the databases to which he/she has access, in one operation.

On the home page, the **Export** link brings us to the screen shown in the following screenshot. This has the same structure as the other export pages, except for the databases list.

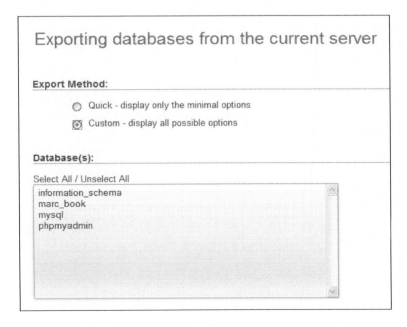

Exporting large databases may or may not work. It depends on their size, the options chosen, and the web server's PHP component settings (especially memory size and maximum execution time).

Saving the export file on the server

Instead of transmitting the export file over the network with HTTP, it is possible to save it directly on the file system of the web server. This could be quicker and less sensitive to execution time limits as the entire transfer from the server to the client browser is bypassed. Eventually, a file transfer protocol such as FTP or SFTP can be used to retrieve the file, as leaving it on the same machine would not provide good backup protection.

A special directory has to be created on the web server before saving an export file on it. Usually, this is a sub-directory of the main phpMyAdmin directory. We will use save_dir as an example. This directory must have the correct permissions. First, the web server must have write permissions for this directory. Also, if the web server's PHP component is running on safe mode, the owner of the phpMyAdmin scripts must be the same as that of save_dir.

On a Linux system, assuming that the web server is running as group apache, the following commands would do the trick:

```
# mkdir save_dir
# chgrp apache save_dir
# chmod g=rwx save_dir
```

 The proper ownership and permissions depends highly on the chosen web server and the **SAPI (Server Application Programming Interface)** (refer to http://en.wikipedia.org/wiki/Server_Application_Programming_Interface) used, which influences how directories and files are created and accessed. PHP could be using the scripts' owner as the accessing user, or the web server's user/group itself.

We also have to define the './save_dir' directory name in $cfg['SaveDir']. We are using a path relative to the phpMyAdmin directory here, but an absolute path would work just as well.

The **Output** section will appear with a new **Save on server...** section:

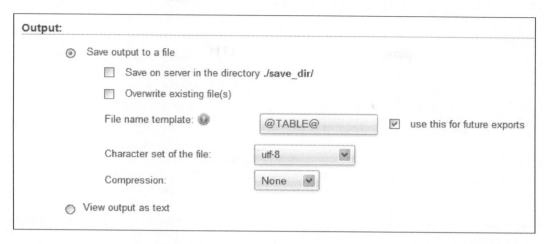

After clicking on **Go**, we will get a confirmation message or an error message (if the web server does not have the required permissions to save the file).

> For saving a file again using the same file name, check the **Overwrite existing file(s)** box.

User-specific save directories

We can use the special string, %u, in the $cfg['SaveDir'] parameter. This string will be replaced by the logged-in username. For example, as shown in the following line of code:

```
$cfg['SaveDir'] = './save_dir/%u';
```

This would give us an on-screen choice, **Save on server in the directory ./save_dir/ marc/**. These directories (one per potential user) must exist and must bear the proper permissions, as already seen in the previous section.

Memory limits

Generating an export file uses a certain amount of memory, depending on the size of the tables and on the chosen options. The $cfg['MemoryLimit'] parameter can contain a limit (in bytes) for the amount of memory used by PHP scripts in phpMyAdmin—the exporting/importing scripts and other scripts. By default, the parameter is set to 0, meaning that there is no limit. We could set here a limit of 20 MiB by using a value of 20M (the M suffix here is very important, to avoid setting a limit of 20 bytes!).

> Note that, if PHP has its safe mode activated, changing $cfg['MemoryLimit'] has no effect. Instead, the enforced limit comes from the memory_limit directive in php.ini.

In addition to memory limits, the execution time limit has an effect on exporting and can be controlled via the $cfg['ExecTimeLimit'] parameter.

Summary

In this chapter, we examined the various ways to trigger an export—from the Database view, the Table view, or a results page. We also listed the various available export formats, their options, the possibility of compressing the export file, and the various places where it might be sent.

In the next chapter, we will have the opportunity of importing back our structure and data, provided the chosen format is supported by phpMyAdmin.

Importing Structure and Data

In this chapter, we will learn how to import data that we may have exported for backup or transfer purposes. Exported data may also come from authors of other applications, and could contain the whole foundation structure of these applications, along with some sample data.

The current phpMyAdmin version (3.4) can import the following:

- Files containing MySQL statements (usually having a `.sql` suffix, but not necessarily so)
- CSV files (comma-separated values, although the separator is not necessarily a comma); these files can be imported by phpMyAdmin itself or via the MySQL `LOAD DATA INFILE` statement which enables the MySQL server to handle the data directly rather than having phpMyAdmin parse it first
- Open Document Spreadsheet files
- XML files (generated by phpMyAdmin)

The binary column upload covered in *Chapter 5* can be said to belong to the import family.

 Importing and uploading are synonyms in this context.

In general, an exported file can be imported to the same database it came from or to any other database; the XML format is an exception to this and a workaround is given in the XML section later in the chapter. Also, a file generated from an older phpMyAdmin version should have no problem being imported by the current version, but the difference between the MySQL version at time of export and the one at time of import might play a bigger role regarding compatibility. It's difficult to evaluate how future MySQL releases will change the language's syntax, bringing import challenges.

The import feature can be accessed from several panels:

- The **Import** menu available from the home page, the `Database` view, or the `Table` view
- The **Import files** menu offered inside the Query window (as explained in *Chapter 11*)

The default values for the `Import` interface are defined in `$cfg['Import']`.

Before examining the actual import dialog, let us discuss some limits issues.

Limits for the transfer

When we import, the source file is usually on our client machine and, therefore, must travel to the server via HTTP. This transfer takes time and uses resources that may be limited in the web server's PHP configuration.

Instead of using HTTP, we can upload our file to the server using a protocol such as FTP, as described in the *Reading files from a web server upload directory* section. This method circumvents the web server's PHP upload limits.

Time limits

First, let us consider the time limit. In `config.inc.php`, the `$cfg['ExecTimeLimit']` configuration directive assigns, by default, a maximum execution time of 300 seconds (five minutes) for any phpMyAdmin script, including the scripts that process data after the file has been uploaded. A value of 0 removes the limit, and in theory, gives us infinite time to complete the import operation. If the PHP server is running in safe mode, modifying `$cfg['ExecTimeLimit']` will have no effect. This is because the limits set in `php.ini` or in user-related web server configuration files (such as `.htaccess` or virtual host configuration files), take precedence over this parameter.

Of course, the time it effectively takes depends on two key factors:

- Web server load
- MySQL server load

The time taken by the file, as it travels between the client and the server, does not count as execution time as the PHP script only starts to execute after the file has been received on the server. Therefore, the $cfg['ExecTimeLimit']$ parameter has an impact only on the time used to process data (such as decompression or sending it to the MySQL server).

Other limits

The system administrator can use the `php.ini` file or the web server's virtual host configuration file to control uploads on the server.

The `upload_max_filesize` parameter specifies the upper limit or maximum file size that can be uploaded via HTTP. This one is obvious, but another less obvious parameter is `post_max_size`. As HTTP uploading is done via the POST method, this parameter may limit our transfers. For more details about the POST method, please refer to `http://en.wikipedia.org/wiki/Http#Request_methods`.

The `memory_limit` parameter is provided to prevent web server child processes from grabbing too much of the server's memory—phpMyAdmin runs inside a child process. Thus, the handling of normal file uploads, especially compressed dumps, can be compromised by giving this parameter a small value. Here, no preferred value can be recommended; the value depends on the size of uploaded data we want to handle and on the size of the physical memory. The memory limit can also be tuned via the `$cfg['MemoryLimit']` parameter in `config.inc.php`, as seen in *Chapter 6*.

Finally, file uploads must be allowed by setting `file_uploads` to `On`; otherwise, phpMyAdmin won't even show a dialog to choose a file. It would be useless to display this dialog as the connection would be refused later by the PHP component of the web server.

Handling big export files

If the file is too big, there are ways in which we can resolve the situation. If the original data is still accessible via phpMyAdmin, we could use phpMyAdmin to generate smaller export files, choosing the **Dump some row(s)** dialog. If this were not possible, we could use a spreadsheet program or a text editor to split the file into smaller sections. Another possibility is to use the **upload directory mechanism**, which accesses the directory defined in `$cfg['UploadDir']`. This feature is explained later in this chapter.

In recent phpMyAdmin versions, the **Partial import** feature can also solve this file size problem. By selecting the **Allow the interruption...** checkbox, the import process will interrupt itself if it detects that it is close to the time limit. We can also specify a number of queries to skip from the start, in case we successfully import a number of rows and wish to continue from that point.

Uploading into a temporary directory

On a server, a PHP security feature called open_basedir (which limits the files that can be opened by PHP to the specified directory tree) can impede the upload mechanism. In this case, or for any other reason, when uploads are problematic, the $cfg['TempDir'] parameter can be set with the value of a temporary directory. This is probably a sub-directory of phpMyAdmin's main directory, into which the web server is allowed to put the uploaded file.

Importing SQL files

Any file containing MySQL statements can be imported via this mechanism. This format is the more commonly used for backup/restore purposes. The dialog is available in the Server view, Database view, or the Table view, via the **Import** page, or in the Query window.

There is no relation between the currently selected table (here **author**) and the actual contents of the SQL file that will be imported. All the contents of the SQL file will be imported, and it is those contents that determine which tables or databases are affected. However, if the imported file does not contain any SQL statements to select a database, all statements in the imported file will be executed on the currently selected database.

Let us try an import exercise. First, we make sure that we have a current SQL export file of the book table (as explained in *Chapter 6*). This export file must contain the structure and the data. Then we drop the book table—yes, really! We could also simply rename it. (Refer to *Chapter 9* for the procedure.)

Now it is time to import the file back to the current database (the file could be imported for testing in a different database or even on another MySQL server). We should be on the **Import** page, where we can see the **File to import** dialog. We just have to hit the **Browse** button and choose our file.

phpMyAdmin is able to detect which compression method (if any) has been applied to the file. Depending on the phpMyAdmin version, and the extensions that are available in the PHP component of the web server, there is variation in the formats that the program can decompress.

However, to import successfully, phpMyAdmin must be informed of the character set of the file to be imported. The default value is **utf-8**. However, if we know that the import file was created with another character set, we should specify it here.

A **SQL compatibility mode** selector is available at import time. This mode should be adjusted to match the actual data that we are about to import, according to the type of server where the data was previously exported.

Another option, **Do not use AUTO_INCREMENT for zero values**, is marked by default. If we have a value of zero in a primary key and we want it to stay zero instead of being auto-incremented, we should use this option.

To start the import, we click on **Go**. The import procedure continues and we receive a message: **Import has been successfully finished, 2 queries executed**. We can browse our newly-created tables to confirm the success of the import operation.

An import file may contain the DELIMITER keyword. This enables phpMyAdmin to mimic the mysql command-line interpreter. The DELIMITER separator is used to delineate the part of the file containing a stored procedure, as these procedures can themselves contain semicolons.

Importing CSV files

In this section, we will examine how to import CSV files. There are two possible methods—**CSV** and **CSV using LOAD DATA**. The first method is implemented internally by phpMyAdmin and is the recommended one for its simplicity. With the second method, phpMyAdmin receives the file to be loaded, and passes it to MySQL. In theory, this method should be faster. However, it has more requirements due to MySQL itself (refer to the *Requirements* sub-section of the *CSV using LOAD DATA* section).

Differences between SQL and CSV formats

Usually, the SQL format contains both structure and data. The CSV file format contains data only, so if we import in `Table` view, we must already have an existing table in place. This table does not need to have the same structure as the original table (from which the data comes); the **Column names** dialog enables us to choose which columns are affected in the target table.

Since version 3.4, we can also import a CSV file in `Database` view. In this case, phpMyAdmin examines the CSV data and generates a table structure to hold this data (with generic column names such as `COL 1`, `COL 2` and a table name such as `TABLE 24`).

Exporting a test file

Before trying an import, let us generate an `author.csv` export file from the `author` table. We use the default values in the **CSV export** options. We can then use the **Empty** option to empty the `author` table—we should avoid dropping this table as we still need the table structure. The procedure to empty a table is covered in *Chapter 5*, in the *Deleting all of the rows in a table* section.

CSV

From the `author` table menu, we select **Import** and then **CSV**.

Format:

```
CSV                              ▽
```

Note: If the file contains multiple tables, they will be combined into one

Format-Specific Options:

☐   Replace table data with file

☐   Do not abort on INSERT error

Columns separated with: [,]

Columns enclosed with: ["]

Columns escaped with: [\ ]

Lines terminated with: [auto]

Column names: ⓘ   [   ]

We can influence the behavior of the import in a number of ways. By default, importing does not modify existing data (based on primary or unique keys). However, the **Replace table data with file** option instructs phpMyAdmin to use REPLACE statements instead of INSERT statements, so that existing rows are replaced with the imported data.

Using **Do not abort on INSERT error**, INSERT IGNORE statements are generated. These cause MySQL to ignore any duplicate key problems during insertion. A duplicate key from the import file does not replace existing data, and the procedure continues for the next line of CSV data.

We can then specify the character that terminates each column, the character that encloses data, and the character that escapes the enclosing character. Usually this is ****.

For **Lines terminated with** option, the **auto** choice should be tried first as it detects the end-of-line character automatically. We can also specify manually which characters terminate the lines. The usual choice is **\n** for UNIX-based systems, **\r\n** for DOS or Windows systems, and **\r** for Mac-based systems (up to Mac OS 9). If in doubt, we can use a hexadecimal file editor on our client computer (not part of phpMyAdmin) to examine the exact codes.

By default, phpMyAdmin expects a CSV file with the same number of columns and the same column order as the target table. This can be changed by entering a comma-separated list of column names in **Column names**, respecting the source file format. For example, let us say our source file contains only the author ID and the author name information:

```
"1","John Smith"
"2","Maria Sunshine"
```

We would have to put **id, name** in **Column names** to match the source file.

When we click on **Go**, the import is executed and we get a confirmation. We might also see the actual INSERT queries generated if the total size of the file is not too big.

```
Import has been successfully finished, 2 queries executed.
INSERT INTO `author` VALUES ('1', 'John Smith', '+01 445 789-1234'
)# 1 row(s) affected.

INSERT INTO `author` VALUES ('2', 'Maria Sunshine', '333-3333'
)# 1 row(s) affected.
```

CSV using LOAD DATA

With this method (only available in the Table view), phpMyAdmin relies on the server's LOAD DATA INFILE or LOAD DATA LOCAL INFILE mechanisms to do the actual import, instead of processing the data internally. These statements are the fastest way for importing text in MySQL. They cause MySQL to start a read operation either from a file located on the MySQL server (LOAD DATA INFILE) or from another place (LOAD DATA LOCAL INFILE), which in this context, is always the web server's file system. If the MySQL server is located on a computer other than the web server, we won't be able to use the LOAD DATA INFILE mechanism.

Requirements

Relying on the MySQL server has some consequences. Using LOAD DATA INFILE requires that the logged-in user possess a global FILE privilege. Also, the file itself must be readable by the MySQL server's process.

 Chapter 19 explains phpMyAdmin's interface, which can be used by system administrators to manage privileges.

Usage of the LOCAL modifier in LOAD DATA LOCAL INFILE must be allowed by the MySQL server and MySQL's client library used by PHP.

Both the LOAD methods are available from the phpMyAdmin LOAD interface, which tries to choose the best possible default option.

Using the LOAD DATA interface

We select **Import** from the author table menu. Choosing **CSV using LOAD DATA** option brings up the following dialog:

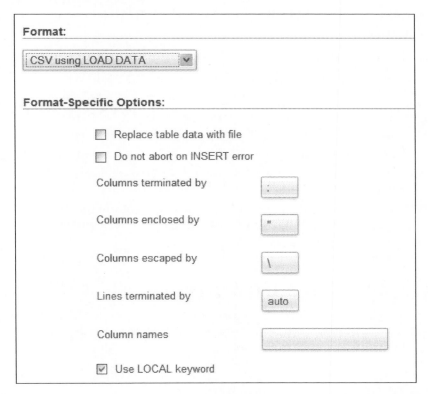

 The available options have already been covered in the *CSV* section.

In the **File to import** section, we choose our author.csv file.

Finally, we can choose the LOAD method, as discussed earlier, by selecting the **Use LOCAL keyword** option. We then click on **Go**.

If all goes well, we can see the confirmation screen as shown in the following screenshot:

Import has been successfully finished, 1 queries executed. (author.csv)

LOAD DATA LOCAL INFILE '/opt/php-upload-tmp/phpgW6kly' INTO TABLE `author` FIELDS TERMINATED BY ',' ENCLOSED BY '"' ESCAPED BY '\' LINES TERMINATED BY '\r\n' # 2 rows affected.

[Inline] [Edit] [Create PHP Code]

This screen shows the exact **LOAD DATA LOCAL INFILE** statement used. Here is what has happened:

1. We chose **author.csv**.
2. The contents of this file were transferred over HTTP and received by the web server.
3. The PHP component inside the web server saved this file in a work directory (here `/opt/php-upload-tmp/`) and gave it a temporary name.
4. phpMyAdmin, informed of the location of this working file, built a LOAD DATA LOCAL INFILE command, and sent it to MySQL. Note that just one query was executed, which loaded many rows.
5. The MySQL server read and loaded the contents of the file into our target table. It then returned the number of affected rows (**2**), which phpMyAdmin displayed on the results page.

Importing other formats

In addition to SQL and CSV formats, phpMyAdmin can import Open Document Spreadsheet and XML files. However, these files need to have been exported by phpMyAdmin itself, or closely follow what phpMyAdmin does when exporting.

Open Document Spreadsheet

By default, when we export via phpMyAdmin in this format, the **Put column names in the first row** option is not marked. This means that the exported file contains only data. At import time, a corresponding option **The first line of the file contains the table column names** is offered and should not be marked if the file does not contain the column names in its first line.

However, if the exported file does contain the column names, we can check this option. Therefore, when importing from the Database view, phpMyAdmin will do the following:

1. Create a table, using the file name (author.ods) as the table name (author).
2. Use the first line's column names as column names for this table.
3. Determine each column's type and appropriate size, based on the data itself.
4. Insert data into the table.

If we are in the Table view, only the data will be imported.

Other import options exist to indicate what should be done with empty rows and with data containing percentages or currency values.

XML

The amount of structural information that can be created by importing an XML file depends on the options that were chosen at export time. Indeed, if the **Tables** option of the **Object creation options** dialog was selected, then the exact CREATE TABLE statement is placed in the exported file. Therefore, the same table structure is available in the restored table.

Likewise, if the **Export contents** option was marked, the whole data is there in the XML file ready to be imported back. There are no options available at import time as XML is a self-describing format; therefore, phpMyAdmin can correctly interpret what is in the file and react appropriately.

As the original database name is part of the XML export, the current phpMyAdmin version only supports importing an XML file into the database from which the export originated. To import to a different database, we need to first use a text editor and change the database name inside the following line:

```
<pma:database name="marc_book" collation="latin1_swedish_ci"
charset="latin1">
```

Reading files from a web server upload directory

To get around cases where uploads are completely disabled by a web server's PHP configuration, or where upload limits are too small, phpMyAdmin can read upload files from a special directory located on the web server's file system.

We first specify the directory name of our choice in the $cfg['UploadDir'] parameter, for example, './upload'. We can also use the %u string, as described in *Chapter 6*, to represent the user's name.

Now, let us go back to the **Import** page. We get an error message:

The directory you set for upload work cannot be reached.

This error message is expected, as the directory does not exist. It is supposed to have been created inside the current phpMyAdmin installation directory. The message might also indicate that the directory exists, but can't be read by the web server.

> In PHP safe mode, the owner of the directory and the owner of the phpMyAdmin-installed scripts must be the same.

Using an SFTP or FTP client, we create the necessary directory, and can now upload a file there (for example **book.sql**) bypassing any PHP timeouts or upload maximum limits.

> Note that the file itself must have permissions that allow the web server to read it.

In most cases, the easiest way is to allow everyone to read the file.

Refreshing the **Import** page brings up the following screenshot:

Clicking on **Go** should execute the statements located in the file.

Automatic decompression is also available for the files located in the upload directory. The file names should have extensions such as .bz2, .gz, .sql.bz2, or .sql.gz.

 Using the double extensions (.sql.bz2) is a better way to indicate that a .sql file was produced and then compressed, as we see all the steps used to generate this file.

Displaying an upload progress bar

Especially when importing a large file, it's interesting to have a visual feedback on the progression of upload. Please note that the progress bar we are discussing here informs us only about the uploading part, which is a subset of the whole import operation.

Having a JavaScript-enabled browser is a requirement for this feature. Moreover, the web server's PHP component must have the JSON extension and at least one of these extensions:

- The well-know APC extension (http://pecl.php.net/package/APC), which is highly recommended anyway for its opcode caching benefits

- The uploadprogress extension (http://pecl.php.net/package/uploadprogress)

phpMyAdmin uses AJAX techniques to fetch progress information, then displays it as part of the **File to import** dialog. The number of bytes uploaded, total number of bytes, and percentage uploaded are displayed under the bar.

Configuring APC

A few php.ini directives play an important role for upload progress. First, the apc.rfc1867 directive must be set to On or true, otherwise this extension won't be reporting upload progress to the calling script. When set to On, this extension updates an APC user cache entry with the upload status information.

Also, the frequency of the updates can be set via the apc.rfc1867_freq directive, which can take the form of a percentage of the total file size (for example, apc.rfc1867_freq = "10%"), or a size in bytes (suffixes k for kilobytes, m for megabytes, and g for gigabytes are accepted). A value of 0 here indicates us to update as often as possible, which looks interesting but in reality may slow down the upload.

This very notion of update frequency explains why the bar progresses in chunks rather than continuously when using this mechanism.

Summary

This chapter covered:

- Various options in phpMyAdmin that allow us to import data
- The different mechanisms involved in importing files
- The limits that we might hit when trying a transfer, and ways to bypass these limits

The next chapter will explain how to do single-table searches (covering search criteria specification) and how to search in the whole database.

8
Searching Data

In this chapter, we present mechanisms that can be used to find the data we are looking for, instead of just browsing tables page-by-page and sorting them. In **Search** mode, application developers can look for data in ways not expected by the interface they are building—adjusting and sometimes repairing data. This chapter covers single-table searches and entire database searches. *Chapter 12* is a complement to this chapter and presents examples of searches involving multiple tables at once.

Single-table searches

This section describes the **Search** page where a single-table search is available. Searching in just one table is effective only in the situation where a single table regroups all the data on which we want to search. If the data is scattered in many tables, a database search should be launched instead, and this is covered later in the chapter.

Entering the search page

The **Search** page can be accessed by clicking on the **Search** link in the `Table` view. This has been done here for the `book` table:

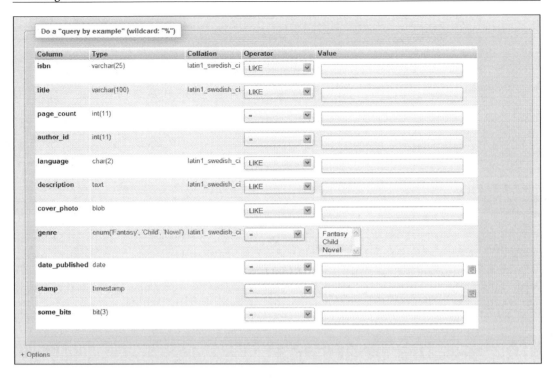

The most commonly used section of the **Search** interface (**query by example**) is the one immediately displayed, whereas other dialogs are hidden in a slider that can be activated by the **Options** link (more on these dialogs later in this chapter).

Searching criteria by column—query by example

The main use of the **Search** panel is to enter criteria for some columns so as to retrieve only the data we are interested in. This is called **query by example** because we give an example of what we are looking for. Our first retrieval will concern finding the book with ISBN **1-234567-89-0**. We simply enter this value in the **isbn** box and set the **Operator** field to =.

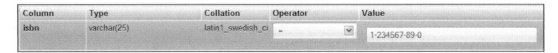

Clicking on **Go** gives these results (shown partially in the following screenshot):

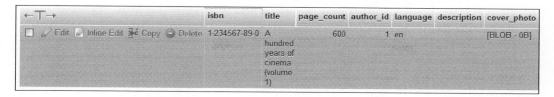

This is a standard results page. If the results ran in pages, we could navigate through them, and edit and delete data for the subset we have chosen during the process. Another feature of phpMyAdmin is that the columns used as the criteria are highlighted by changing the border color of the columns to better reflect their importance on the results page.

It isn't necessary to specify that the **isbn** column be displayed even though this is the column in which we search. We could have selected only the **title** column for display (refer to the *Selecting the columns to be displayed* section) and chosen the **isbn** column as a criterion.

Searching for empty / non-empty values

Two handy operators are present in the operator's list when the column has a character type such as CHAR, VARCHAR, or TEXT:

- = ' '
- ! = ' '

Those are the ones to use when you want to search for an empty (= ' ') or not empty (! = ' ') value in some column. Normally, typing nothing in a column's **Value** field means that this column does not participate in the search process. However, with one of these operators, this column is included in the generated search query.

> Please do not confuse this method with searching for a NULL value, which is quite different. Indeed, a NULL value (refer to http://en.wikipedia.org/wiki/Null_(SQL) for a more complete explanation) is a special value that conveys that some information is missing in this column.

Producing reports with Print view

We see the **Print view** and **Print view (with full texts)** links on the results page. These links produce a more formal report of the results (without the navigation interface) directly to the printer. In our case, using **Print view** would produce the following:

SQL result

Host: localhost
Database: marc_book
Generation Time: Dec 06, 2011 at 12:36 PM
Generated by: phpMyAdmin 3.4.5 / MySQL 5.5.13
SQL query: SELECT * FROM `book` WHERE `isbn` = '1-234567-89-0' LIMIT 0, 30 ;
Rows: 1

isbn book number	title	page_count approximate	author_id cf author table	language	description	cover_photo	genre	date_published	stamp	some_bits
1-234567-89-0	A hundred years of cinema (volume 1)	600	1	en		[BLOB - 0B]	Fantasy	0000-00-00 00:00:00	2011-12-06 12:34:40	101

This report contains information about the server, database, time of generation, version of phpMyAdmin, version of MySQL, and generated SQL query. The other link, **Print view (with full texts)**, would print the contents of the TEXT columns in their entirety.

Searching with wildcard characters

Let us assume we are looking for something less precise—all books with "cinema" in their title. First, we go back to the search page. For this type of search, we will use SQL's **LIKE** operator. This operator accepts wildcard characters—the % character (which matches any number of characters) and the underscore (_) character (which matches a single character). Thus we can use **%cinema%** to let phpMyAdmin find any substring that matches the word "cinema". If we left out both wildcard characters, we would get exact matches with only that single word.

This substring matching is easier to access, being part of the **Operator** drop-down list. We only have to enter the word **cinema** and use the operator **LIKE %...%** to perform that match. We should avoid using this form of the **LIKE** operator on big tables (comprising of thousands of rows), as MySQL does not use an index for data retrieval in this case, leading to wait times that depend on the server hardware and its current load. This is why this operator is not the default one in the drop-down list, even though this method of search is commonly used on smaller tables.

The following screenshot shows how we ask for a search on **cinema** with the **LIKE** %...% operator:

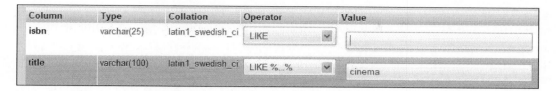

 The LIKE operator can be used for other types of wildcard searches, for example History%, which would search for this word at the beginning of a title. As the expression does not start with a wildcard character, MySQL will try to use an index if it finds one that speeds up data retrieval. For more details about MySQL's use of indexes, please refer to http://dev. mysql.com/doc/refman/5.1/en/mysql-indexes.html.

Using either of these methods of performing the query produces the following results:

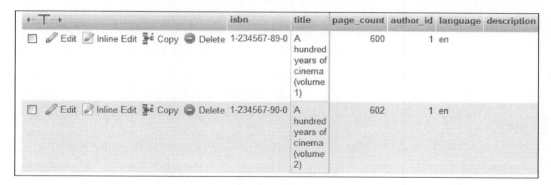

The % and _ wildcard characters may be repeated in a search expression; for example, histo__ (two underscores) would match history whereas histo% would match history and historian. The MySQL manual gives more examples at http://dev. mysql.com/doc/refman/5.1/en/string-comparison-functions.html.

Case sensitivity and search

In the previous example, we could have replaced "cinema" with "CINEMA" and achieved similar results. The reason is that the collation of the **title** column is **latin1_swedish_ci**. This collation comes from the collation set, by default, at database creation unless the server's default collation has been changed (refer to http://dev.mysql.com/doc/refman/5.1/en/charset-mysql.html). Here, **ci** means that comparisons are done in a case-insensitive way. Please refer to http://dev.mysql.com/doc/refman/5.1/en/case-sensitivity.html for more details.

Combining criteria

We can use multiple criteria for the same query (for example, to find all the English books of more than 300 pages). There are more comparative choices in **Operator** because the **page_count** column is numeric, as shown in the following screenshot:

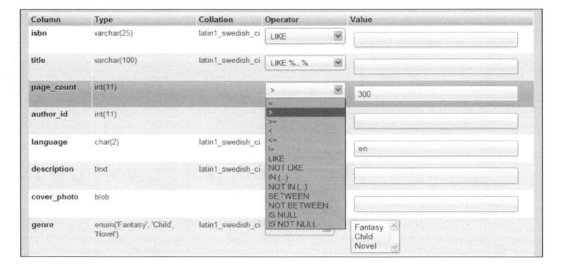

Search options

The **Options** slider reveals additional panels to further refine the search process.

Selecting the columns to be displayed

In the **Options** slider, a **Select columns** panel facilitates selection of the columns to be displayed in the results. All columns are selected by default, but we can *Ctrl* + Click on other columns to make the necessary selections. Mac users would use *Command* + Click to select/unselect the columns.

Following are the columns of interest in this example:

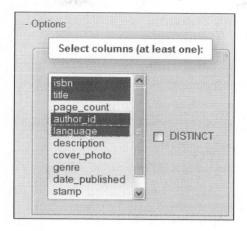

We can also specify the number of rows per page in the textbox next to the column selection. The **Add search conditions** box will be explained in the *Applying a WHERE clause* section, which will follow shortly.

Ordering the results

The **Display order** dialog permits the specification of an initial sorting order for the results to come. In this dialog, a drop-down menu contains all the table's columns; it's up to us to select the one on which we want to sort. By default, the sorting will be in **Ascending** order, but a choice of **Descending** order is also available.

It should be noted that on the results page, we can change the sort order using the techniques explained in *Chapter 4*.

Applying a WHERE clause

Sometimes, we may want to enter a search condition that is not offered in the **Function** list of the **query by example** section. The list cannot contain every possible variation in the language. Let us say we want to find all the English or French books using the IN clause. To do this, we can use the **Add search conditions** section.

The complete search expression is generated by combining the search conditions and other criteria (entered in the **query by example** lines) with a logical AND operator.

We could have a more complex list of search conditions that would be entered in the same textbox, possibly with brackets and operators such as AND or OR.

A **Documentation** link points to the MySQL manual where we can see a huge choice of available functions. (Each function is applicable to a specific column type.)

Avoiding repeated results

The normal behavior of the SELECT statement is to fetch all entries corresponding to the criteria, even if some entries are repeated. Sometimes, we may want to avoid getting the same results more than once. For example, if we want to know in which cities we have clients, displaying each city name once would be enough. Here, we want to know in which languages our books are written. In the **Select columns** dialog, we choose just the **language** column, and we check **DISTINCT**, as shown in the following screenshot:

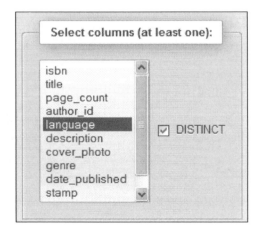

Clicking on **Go** produces a results page where we see **en** just once; without the **DISTINCT** option, the row containing **en** would have appeared three times.

If we select more than one column (for example author_id and language) and mark the DISTINCT option, we will now see two lines in the results as there are two books in English (but from different authors). Results are still not repeated.

Performing a complete database search

In the previous examples, searching was limited to one table. This assumes knowledge of the exact table (and columns) where the necessary information might be stored.

When the data is hidden somewhere in the database, or when the same data can be presented in various columns (for example, a **title** column or a **description** column), it is easier to use the database search method.

We enter the **Search** page in the Database view for the marc_book database:

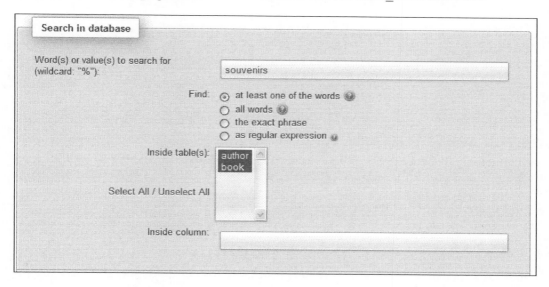

In the **Word(s) or value(s)** section, we enter what we want to find. The % wildcard character can prove useful here—but remember the performance advice about wildcard characters given earlier in this chapter. We enter **souvenirs**.

In the **Find** section, we specify how to treat the values entered. We might need to find **at least one of the words** entered, **all words** (in no particular order), or **the exact phrase** (words in the same order, somewhere in a column). Another choice is to use **as regular expression**, which is a more complex way of doing pattern matching. More details are available at http://dev.mysql.com/doc/refman/5.1/en/regexp.html and http://www.regular-expressions.info/. We will keep the default value—**at least one of the words**.

We can choose the tables to restrict the search or select all the tables. As we only have two (small) tables, we select both.

As the search will be done on each row of every table selected, we might hit some time limits if the number of rows or tables is too big. Thus, this feature can be deactivated by setting `$cfg['UseDbSearch']` to FALSE. (It is set to TRUE by default).

Clicking on **Go** finds the following result for us:

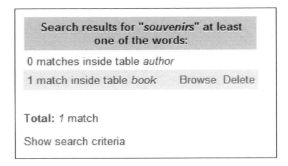

This is an overview of the number of matches and the relevant tables. We might get some matches in the tables in which we may not be interested. However, for the matches that look promising, we can click on **browse** to browse the results page, or we can choose **delete** to delete the unwanted rows. The **show search criteria** link would bring back our criteria panel.

Restricting search to a column

Sometimes, a particular column name is part of one (or many) tables, and we want to search only inside this column. For example, suppose that we are looking for "marc"; but this name could be also part of a book's title. So, we want to restrict the search to only the "name" column in all the chosen tables. This can be achieved by entering "name" in the **inside column** choice.

Stopping an errant query

Suppose we launch a complex search and notice that the browser is waiting for the results. This might happen with a database search but also with a single-table search. We can instruct the browser to stop but this will only tell the web server to cease handling our request. However, at this point the MySQL server process is busy, possibly doing a complex join or a full table scan. Here is a method to stop this errant query:

1. We open a different browser (for example, the errant query was launched via Firefox and we open Internet Explorer).

2. We log in via phpMyAdmin to MySQL with the same account.

3. On the home page, we click on **Processes**.

4. At this point, we should see a process identified by **Query** under the **Command** column and containing the errant query (other than SHOW PROCESSLIST which is not the one to kill).

5. We click on **Kill** for this process.

6. To verify, we can immediately click again on **Processes** and the chosen process should now be identified as **Killed** instead of **Query**.

Summary

In this chapter, we took an overview of single table searches with "query by example" criteria and additional criteria specification—selecting displayed values and ordering results. We also looked at wildcard searches and full database search.

The next chapter will explain how to perform the operations on tables, for example, changing a table's attributes, such as its storage engine. The subjects of repairing and optimizing tables are covered in this chapter as well.

9
Performing Table and Database Operations

In the previous chapters, we dealt mostly with table columns. In this chapter, we will learn how to perform some operations that influence tables or databases as a whole. We will cover table attributes and how to modify them, and will also discuss multi-table operations.

Various links that enable table operations have been put together on the **Operations** page of the Table view. Here is an overview of this page:

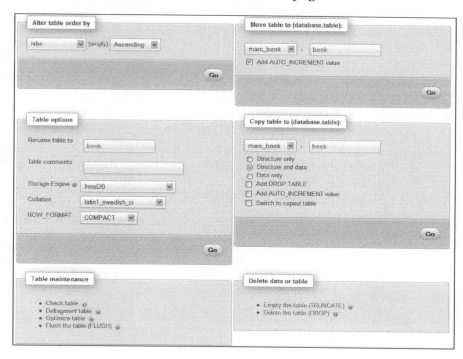

Maintaining a table

During its lifetime, a table repeatedly gets modified and is, therefore, continually growing and shrinking. Outages may occur on the server, leaving some tables in a damaged state.

Using the **Operations** page, we can perform various operations, which are listed next. However, not every operation is available for every storage engine.

- **Check table**: Scans all rows to verify that deleted links are correct. A checksum is also calculated to verify the integrity of the keys. If everything is all right, we will obtain a message stating **OK** or **Table is already up to date**; if any other message shows up, it's time to repair this table (refer to the **Repair table** bullet point).

- **Analyze table**: Analyzes and stores the key distribution; this will be used on subsequent JOIN operations to determine the order in which the tables should be joined. This operation should be periodically done (in case data has changed in the table) to improve JOIN efficiency.

- **Repair table**: Repairs any corrupted data for tables in the MyISAM and ARCHIVE engines. Note that a table might be so corrupted that we cannot even go into Table view for it! In such a case, refer to the *Multi-table operations* section for the procedure to repair it.

- **Defragment table**: Random insertions or deletions in an InnoDB table fragment its index. The table should be periodically defragmented for faster data retrieval. This operation causes MySQL to rebuild the table and only applies to InnoDB.

- **Optimize table**: This is useful when the table contains overheads. After massive deletions of rows or length changes for VARCHAR columns, lost bytes remain in the table. phpMyAdmin warns us in various places (for example, in the Structure view) if it feels the table should be optimized. This operation reclaims the unused space in the table. In the case of MySQL 5.x, the relevant tables that can be optimized use the MyISAM, InnoDB, and ARCHIVE engines.

- **Flush table**: This must be done when there have been many connection errors and the MySQL server blocks further connections. Flushing will clear some internal caches and allow normal operations to resume.

The operations are based on the available underlying MySQL queries—phpMyAdmin only calls those queries. More details are available at http://dev.mysql.com/doc/refman/5.5/en/table-maintenance-sql.html.

Changing table attributes

Table attributes are the various properties of a table. This section discusses the settings for some of them.

Table storage engine

The first attribute we can change is called **Storage Engine**.

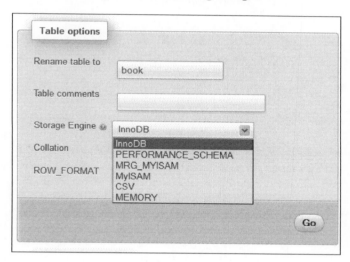

This controls the whole behavior of the table—its location (on disk or in memory), the index structure, and whether it supports transactions and foreign keys. The drop-down list varies depending on the storage engines supported by our MySQL server.

 Changing a table's storage engine may be a long operation if the number of rows is large.

Table comments

Table comments option allows us to enter comments for the table.

These comments will be shown at appropriate places, for example, in the navigation panel, next to the table name in the `Table` view, and in the export file. The following screenshot shows what the navigation panel looks like when the `$cfg['ShowTooltip']` parameter is set to its default value of TRUE:

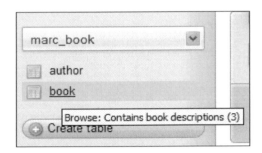

The default value (FALSE) of `$cfg['ShowTooltipAliasDB']` and `$cfg['ShowTooltipAliasTB']` produces the behavior we saw earlier—the true database and table names are displayed in the navigation panel and in the `Database` view for the **Structure** page. Comments appear as a tooltip (when the cursor is hovered over a database or table name). If one of these parameters is set to TRUE, the behavior is reversed—showing the comment by default and the true name as a tooltip. This is convenient when the real table names are not meaningful.

There is another possibility for `$cfg['ShowTooltipAliasTB']`—the `'nested'` value. Here is what happens if we use this feature:

- The true table name is displayed in the navigation panel
- The table comment (for example, `project__`) is interpreted as the project name and is displayed as it is (refer to the *Nested display of tables within a database* section in *Chapter 3*)

Table order

When we browse a table, or execute a statement such as SELECT * from book without specifying a sort order, MySQL uses the order in which the rows are physically stored. This table order can be changed with the **Alter table order by** dialog. We can choose any column and the table will be reordered once on this column. We choose **author_id** in the example, and after we click on **Go**, the table gets sorted on this column.

Reordering is convenient if we know that we will be retrieving rows in this order most of the time. Moreover, if we use an ORDER BY clause later on, and the table is already physically sorted on this column, we might get better performance.

This default ordering will last as long as there are no changes in the table (no insertions, deletions, or updates). This is why phpMyAdmin shows the **(singly)** warning.

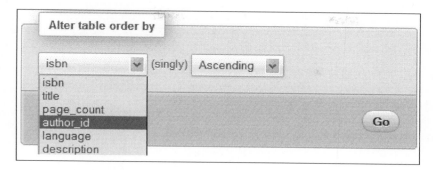

After the sort has been done on **author_id**, books for author **1** will be displayed first, followed by the books for author **2**, and so on (we are talking about a default browsing of the table without explicit sorting). We can also specify the sort order as **Ascending** or **Descending**.

If we insert another row, describing a new book from author **1**, and then click on **Browse**, the book will not be displayed along with the other books for this author because the sort was done before the insertion.

Table collation

Character-based columns have a collation attribute that describes which character set is used to interpret the contents, and rules for sorting. The **name** column currently has a **latin1_swedish_ci** collation, as can be seen via the **Structure** page. On the **Operations** page, if we change the collation for table author from **latin1_swedish_ci** to, say, **utf8_general_ci**, this generates the following statement:

```
ALTER TABLE `author` DEFAULT CHARACTER SET utf8 COLLATE
utf8_general_ci
```

Therefore, we only changed the default collation for future columns that will be added to this table; no collation was changed for existing columns.

Table options

Other attributes that influence the table's behavior may be specified using the **Table options** dialog:

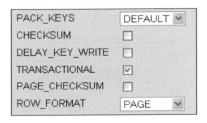

The options are:

- **PACK_KEYS**: Setting this attribute results in a smaller index. This can be read faster but takes more time to update. Available for the MyISAM storage engine.
- **CHECKSUM**: This makes MySQL compute a checksum for each row. This results in slower updates, but finding of corrupted tables becomes easier. Available for MyISAM only.
- **DELAY_KEY_WRITE**: This instructs MySQL not to write the index updates immediately, but to queue them for writing later. This improves performance but there is a negative trade-off — the index might need to be rebuilt in case of a server failure (refer to http://dev.mysql.com/doc/refman/5.1/en/miscellaneous-optimization-tips.html). Available for MyISAM only.
- **TRANSACTIONAL, PAGE_CHECKSUM**: Applies to the Aria storage engine, previously known as Maria. The **TRANSACTIONAL** option marks this table as being transactional; however, the exact meaning of this option varies as future versions of this storage engine will gain more transactional features. **PAGE_CHECKSUM** computes a checksum on all index pages. Currently documented at http://kb.askmonty.org/en/aria-storage-engine.
- **ROW_FORMAT**: To the storage engines that support this feature (MyISAM, InnoDB, PBXT, and Aria), a choice of row format is presented. The default value being the current state of this table's row format.
- **AUTO_INCREMENT**: This changes the auto-increment value. It is shown only if the table's primary key has the auto-increment attribute.

Emptying or deleting a table

Emptying a table (erasing its data) and deleting a table (erasing its data and the table's structure) can be done with the **Empty the table (TRUNCATE)** and **Delete the table (DROP)** links located in the **Delete data or table** section.

Renaming, moving, and copying tables

The **Rename** operation is the easiest to understand—the table simply changes its name and stays in the same database.

The **Move** operation (shown in the following screenshot) manipulates a table in two ways—changes its name and also the database in which it is stored.

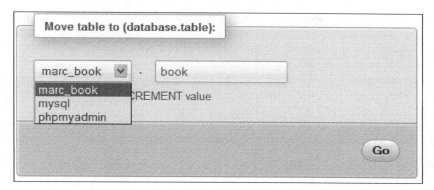

Moving a table is not directly supported by MySQL. So, phpMyAdmin has to create the table in the target database, copy the data, and then finally drop the source table. This could take a long time depending on the table's size.

The **Copy** operation leaves the original table intact and copies its structure or data (or both) to another table, possibly in another database. Here, the **book-copy** table will be an exact copy of the book source table. After the copy, we remain in the Table view for the book table, unless we selected **Switch to copied table** option, in which case we are moved to the Table view of the newly created table.

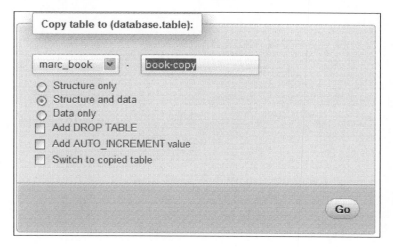

The **Structure only** copy is done to create a test table with the same structure but without the data.

Appending data to a table

The **Copy** dialog may also be used to append (add) data from one table to another. Both tables must have the same structure. This operation is achieved by entering the table to which we want to copy the data and choosing **Data only**.

For example, book data is coming from various sources (various publishers) in the form of one table per publisher and we want to aggregate all the data to one place. For MyISAM, a similar result can be obtained by using the Merge storage engine (which is a collection of identical MyISAM tables). However, if the table is InnoDB, we need to rely on phpMyAdmin's **Copy** feature.

Performing other table operations

On the table **Operations** interface, other dialogs may appear. The referential integrity verification dialog will be covered in *Chapter 10*. Partition maintenance will be examined in *Chapter 17*.

Multi-table operations

In the Database view, there is a checkbox next to each table name and a drop-down menu under the table list. This enables us to quickly choose some tables and perform an operation on all those tables at once. Here, we select the **book-copy** and the **book** tables, and choose the **Check table** operation for the selected tables as shown in the following screenshot:

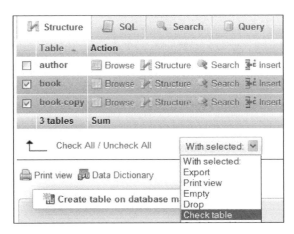

We could also quickly select or deselect all the checkboxes with **Check All / Uncheck All** option.

Repairing an "in use" table

The multi-table mode is the only method (unless we know the exact SQL query to type) for repairing a corrupted table. Such tables may be shown with the **in use** flag in the database list. Users seeking help in the support forums for phpMyAdmin often receive this tip from experienced phpMyAdmin users.

Database operations

The **Operations** tab in the `Database` view gives access to a panel that enables us to perform operations on a database taken as a whole as shown in the following screenshot:

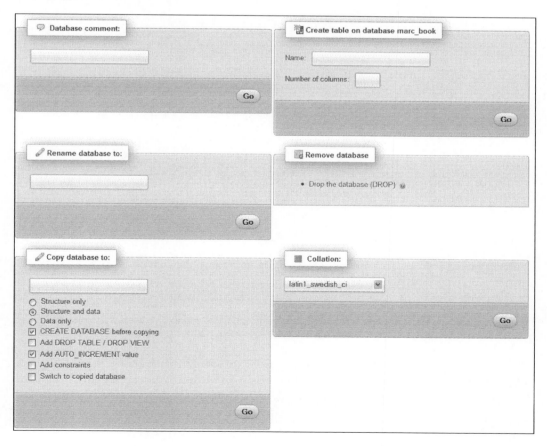

Renaming a database

A **Rename database to** dialog is available. Although this operation is not directly supported by MySQL, phpMyAdmin does it indirectly by creating a new database, renaming each table (thus sending it to the new database), and dropping the original database.

Copying a database

It is also possible to do a complete copy of a database, even if MySQL itself does not support this operation natively. The options are similar to those already explained for the table copy.

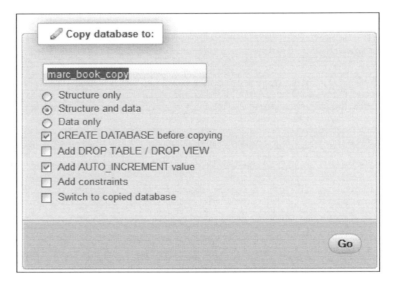

Summary

This chapter covered the operations we can perform on entire tables or databases. It also looked at table maintenance operations for table repair and optimization, changing various table attributes, table movements (including renaming and moving to another database), and multi-table operations.

In the next chapter, we will begin to examine advanced features that rely on the phpMyAdmin configuration storage, such as the relational system.

10
Benefiting from the Relational System

The relational system allows users to work more closely with phpMyAdmin, as we will see in the following chapters. This chapter explains how to define inter-table relations.

Relational MySQL

When application developers use PHP and MySQL to build web interfaces or other data manipulation applications, they usually establish relations between tables using the underlying SQL queries. Examples of this would be queries to "get an invoice and all its items" and "get all books by an author".

In the earlier versions of phpMyAdmin, the relational data structure (how tables relate to each other) was not stored within MySQL. Tables were programmatically joined by the applications to generate meaningful results.

This was considered a shortcoming of MySQL by phpMyAdmin developers and users. Therefore, the team started to build an infrastructure to support relations for MyISAM tables, which is now called the phpMyAdmin configuration storage. The infrastructure evolved to support a growing array of special features such as query bookmarks and MIME-based transformations.

Now-a-days, relations between tables are normally defined natively with the FOREIGN KEY feature of the InnoDB and PBXT storage engines. phpMyAdmin supports both this type of relations and those defined for MyISAM.

InnoDB and PBXT

InnoDB (http://www.innodb.com) is a MySQL storage engine developed by Innobase Oy, a subsidiary of Oracle. Prior to MySQL 5.5, this storage engine may not be available as it must be activated by a system administrator; however, it's the default storage engine in version 5.5.

The PrimeBase XT storage engine or PBXT (http://www.primebase.org) is developed by PrimeBase Technologies. The minimum MySQL required version is 5.1, as this version supports the pluggable storage engine API that is used by PBXT and other third parties to offer alternative storage engines. This transactional storage engine is newer than InnoDB. It is usually installed after downloading it from their website and then going through a compilation step. For some operating systems, a precompiled binary is available—please visit the aforementioned website for download and installation instructions.

When considering the relational aspect, here are the benefits of using the InnoDB or PBXT storage engine for a table:

They support referential integrity based on foreign keys, which are the keys in a foreign (or reference) table. By contrast, using only phpMyAdmin's internal relations (discussed later) brings no automatic referential integrity verification.

The exported structure for InnoDB and PBXT tables contains the defined relations. Therefore, they are easily imported back for better cross-server interoperability.

The foreign key feature of these storage engines can effectively replace the part of phpMyAdmin's configuration storage that deals with relations. We will see how phpMyAdmin interfaces with the InnoDB and PBXT foreign key system.

 The other parts of phpMyAdmin's configuration storage (for example, bookmarks) have no equivalent in InnoDB, PBXT, or MySQL. Hence, they are still required to access the complete phpMyAdmin feature set. However, in MySQL 5.x, views are supported, and have similarities with phpMyAdmin's bookmarks.

Defining relations with the relation view

After the installation of the phpMyAdmin configuration storage, there are more options available in the Database view and the Table view. We will now examine the **Relation view** link in the **Structure** page of the Table view.

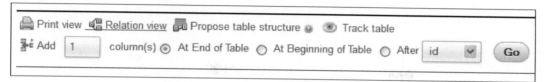

This view is used to:

- Define the relations of the current table with the other tables
- Choose the display column

Our goal here is to create a relation between the book table (which contains the author ID) and the author table (which describes each author by an ID). We start on the Table view for the book table, go to **Structure**, and click on the **Relation view** link.

Defining internal relations

If the book table is in MyISAM format, we see the following screen (otherwise, the display would be different, as explained in the *Defining foreign key relations* section later):

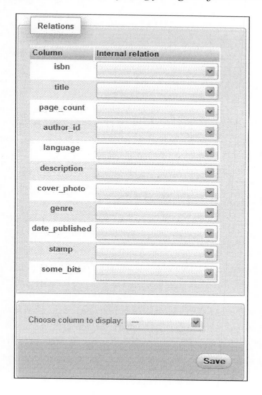

This screen allows us to create **Internal relation** (stored in the `pma_relation` table) as MySQL itself does not have any relational notion for `MyISAM` tables. The empty drop-down list next to each column indicates that there are no relations (links) to any foreign table.

Defining the relation

We can relate each column of the `book` table to a column in another table (or in the same table because self-referencing relations are sometimes necessary). The interface finds both the unique and the non-unique keys in all the tables of the same database, and presents the keys in drop-down lists. (Creating internal relations to other databases from the interface is not currently supported.) The appropriate choice for the **author_id** column is to select the corresponding **id** column from the `author` table.

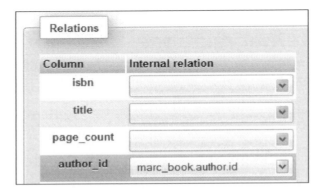

We then click on **Save**, and the definition is saved in phpMyAdmin's configuration storage. To remove the relation, we would just come back to the screen, select the empty choice, and click on **Save**.

Defining the display column

The primary key of our `author` table is the `id`, which is a unique number that we made up for key purposes. The author's name is the natural way to refer to an author. It would be interesting to see the author's name when browsing the `book` table. This is the purpose of the display column. We should normally define a display column for each table that participates in a relation as a foreign table.

We will see how this information is displayed in the *Benefiting from the defined relations* section. We now go to the **Relation view** for the `author` table (which is the foreign table in this case) and specify the display column. We choose **name** as the display column and click on **Save**, as shown in the following screenshot:

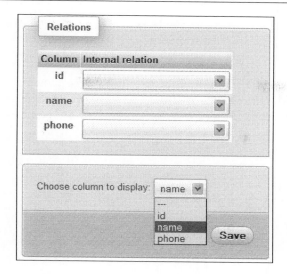

 phpMyAdmin offers to define only one display column for a table, and this column is used in all the relations where this table is used as a foreign table.

The definition of this relation is now done. Although we did not relate any of the columns in the author table to another table, it can be done. For example, we could have a country code in this table and could create a relation to the country code of a country table.

For now, we will see what happens if our tables are under the control of the InnoDB or PBXT storage engine.

Foreign key relations

The InnoDB and PBXT storage engines offer us a native foreign key system.

 At your choice, the exercises in this section can be accomplished with either InnoDB or PBXT storage engines. InnoDB has been chosen in the text.

For this exercise, our book and author tables must be under the InnoDB storage engine. We can do this from the **Operations** page in the Table view.

Another step is necessary in order to see the consequences of a missing index during the exercise. We go back to the **Structure** for the book table and remove the combined index we created on **author_id** and **language** columns.

The foreign key system in InnoDB maintains integrity between the related tables. Hence, we cannot add a non-existent author ID to the book table. In addition, actions are programmable when DELETE or UPDATE operations are performed on the master table (in our case, book).

Opening the book table on its **Structure** page and entering the **Relation view**, now displays a different page:

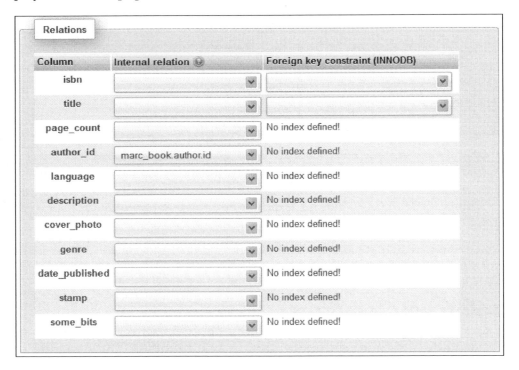

This page provides us the following information:

- There is an internal relation defined for **author_id** to the author table.
- No InnoDB relations are defined yet.
- We will be able to remove the internal relation, when the same relation has been defined in InnoDB. Indeed, hovering over the question mark next to **Internal relations** displays the following message: **An internal relation is not necessary when a corresponding FOREIGN KEY relation exists**. So, it will be better to remove it.

In the possible choices for the related key, we see the keys defined in all the `InnoDB` tables of the same database. (Creating a cross-database relation is currently not supported in phpMyAdmin.) The keys defined in the current table are also shown, as self-referring relations are possible. Let us remove the internal relation for the **author_id** column and click on **Save**. Our goal is to add an `InnoDB`-type relation for the **author_id** column, but it's not possible as the **No index defined!** message appears on this line. This is because foreign key definitions in `InnoDB` or `PBXT` can be done only if both the columns have indexes.

 Other conditions regarding constraints are explained in the MySQL manual. Please refer to `http://dev.mysql.com/doc/refman/5.1/en/innodb-foreign-key-constraints.html`.

Thus, we come back to the **Structure** page for the book table and add an ordinary (non-unique) index to the **author_id** column producing the following screen:

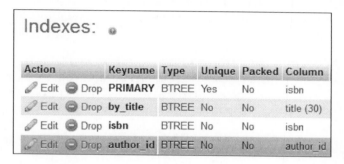

In the **Relation view**, we can try again to add the relation we wanted; it works this time!

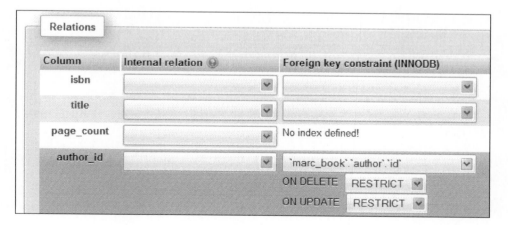

We can also set some actions with the **ON DELETE** and **ON UPDATE** options. For example, **ON DELETE CASCADE** would make MySQL automatically delete all the rows in the related (foreign) table when the corresponding row is deleted from the parent table. This would be useful, for example, when the parent table is `invoices`, and the foreign table is `invoice-items`. These options are supported natively by MySQL, so deleting outside of phpMyAdmin would cause the delete cascade.

 If we have not done so already, we should define the display column for the `author` table, as explained in the *Defining the display column* section.

Foreign keys without phpMyAdmin configuration storage

We see the **Relation view** link on the **Structure** page of an `InnoDB` or `PBXT` table, even when the configuration storage is not installed. This would bring us to a screen where we could define the foreign keys, in this case for the `book` table.

Note that, if we choose this, the display column for the linked table (in this case `author`) cannot be defined, as it belongs to phpMyAdmin's configuration storage. Thus, we would lose the benefit of seeing the associated description of the foreign key.

Defining relations with the Designer

The Ajax-based **Designer** offers a visually-driven way of managing relations (both internal and foreign key-based), and defining the display column for each table. It can also act as:

- A menu to access the structure of existing tables and to access the table creation page
- A PDF schema manager, if we want a PDF schema encompassing all our tables

On the **Designer** workspace, we can work on the relations for all tables on the same panel. On the other hand, the **Relation view** shows the relations for only a single table at a time.

We access this feature from the `Database` view by clicking on the **Designer** menu tab.

If this menu tab does not appear, it's because we are yet to install the phpMyAdmin configuration storage as described in *Chapter 1*.

Over viewing the interface

The **Designer** page contains the main workspace where the tables can be seen. This workspace will dynamically grow and shrink, depending on the position of our tables. The following screenshot demonstrates the **Designer** interface containing our three tables and the relations between them:

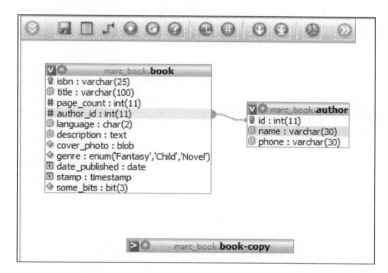

A top menu contains icons whose description is revealed by hovering the mouse over them. The following table gives a summary of the goals for the top menu's icons:

Icon	Description
Show/Hide left menu	To display or hide the left hand menu.
Save position	Saves the current state of the workspace.
Create table	Quits the **Designer** and enters a dialog to create a table; we should take care of saving the position of tables before clicking on this.
Create relation	Puts the **Designer** in a relation-creating mode.
Choose column to display	Specifies which column represents a table.
Reload	Refreshes the table's information in case their structure has changed outside of the **Designer**.

Icon	Description
Help	Displays an explanation about selecting the relations.
Angular links/Direct links	Specifies the shape of relation links.
Snap to grid	Influences the behavior of table movements, relative to an imaginary grid.
Small/Big All	Hides or displays the list of columns for every table.
Toggle small/big	Reverses the display mode of columns for every table, as this mode can be chosen for each table with its corner icon **V** or **>**.
Import/Export	Displays a dialog to import from an existing PDF schema definition or to export to it.
Move Menu	The top menu can move to right and back again.

A side menu appears when clicking on the **Show/Hide left menu** icon. Its purpose is to present the complete list of tables, so that you can decide which table appears on the workspace, and to enable access to the **Structure** page of a specific table. In this example, we choose to remove the **book-copy** table from the workspace as shown in the following screenshot:

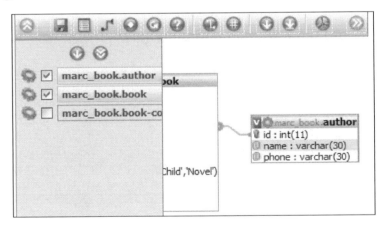

If we want to remove it permanently, we click on the **Save position** top icon. This icon also saves the current position of our tables on the workspace.

Tables can be moved on the workspace by dragging their title bars, and the list of columns for a table can be made visible/invisible with the help of upper-left icon of each table. In this list of columns, small icons show us the data type (numeric, text, and date), and also tell us whether this column is a primary key.

Defining relations

As we have already defined a relation with the **Relation view**, we will first see how to remove it. The **Designer** does not permit a change in a relation. However, the **Designer** allows the relation to be removed and defined.

The question mark icon displays a panel that explains where to click, in order to select a relation for subsequent deletion.

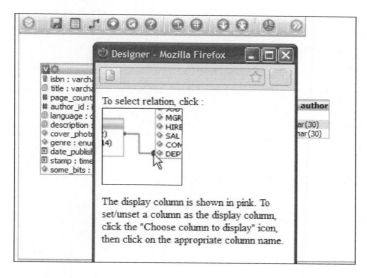

Let us click on the relation line to select it. We get a confirmation panel on which we click on **Delete**.

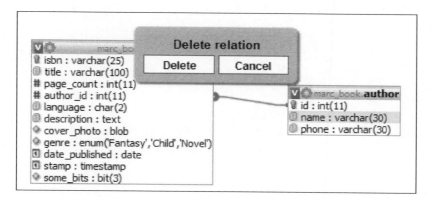

We can then proceed to recreate it. To do this, we start by clicking on the **Create relation** icon:

The cursor then takes the form of a short message saying **Select referenced key**. In our case, the referenced key is the **id** column of the **author** table; so we bring the cursor on this column and click on it. A validation is done, ensuring that we chose a primary or unique key.

Next, having changed the cursor to **Select foreign key**, we bring it to the author_id column of the book table and click on it again. This confirms the creation of the relation. Currently, the interface does not permit the creation of compound keys (having more than one column).

Defining foreign key relations

The procedure to delete or define a relation between InnoDB or PBXT tables is the same as that for internal relations. The only exception is that at the time of creation, a different confirmation panel appears enabling us to specify the on delete and on update actions.

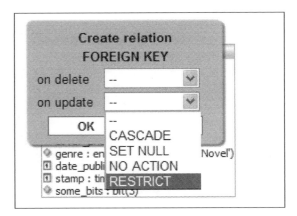

Defining the display column

On the workspace, the `name` column in `author` table has a special background color. This indicates that this column serves as the display column. We can simply click on the **Choose column to display** icon, and drag the short message **Choose column to display** onto another column—for example, the `phone` column. This changes the display column to this column. If we were to drag the message to an existing display column, we would have removed the definition of this column as the display column for the table.

Exporting for PDF schema

In Chapter 15, we will see how to produce a PDF schema for a subset of our database. We can import the coordinates of tables from such a schema into the **Designer**'s workspace, and conversely export them to the PDF schema. The **Import/ export coordinates** icon is available for that purpose.

Benefiting from the defined relations

In this section, we will look at the benefits of the defined relations that we can currently test. Other benefits will be described in *Chapter 12* and *Chapter 15*. Additional benefits of the phpMyAdmin configuration storage will appear in *Chapter 14*, *Chapter 16*, and *Chapter 18*.

These benefits are available for both internal and foreign key relations.

Foreign key information

Let us browse the `book` table. We see that the values of the related key (**author_id**) are now links. Moving the cursor over any **author_id** value reveals the author's name (as defined by the display column of the `author` table).

Clicking on the **author_id** brings us to the relevant table — author — for this specific author:

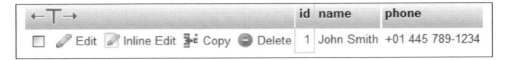

Instead of viewing the keys, we might prefer to see the display column for all the rows. Going back to the book table, we can select the **Relational display column** display option and click on **Go**. This produces a screen similar to the following screenshot:

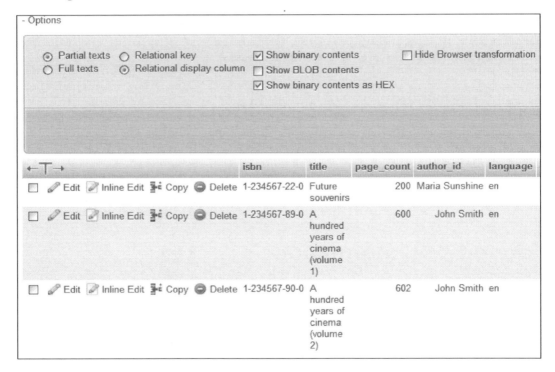

We now switch back to viewing the keys by selecting **Relational key** and clicking on **Go**.

The drop-down list of foreign keys

Displaying the book table, in **Insert** mode (or in **Edit** mode), there is now a drop-down list of the possible keys for each column that has a defined relation. The list contains the keys and the description (display column) in both orders — key to the display column as well as display column to the key. This enables us to use the keyboard and type the first letter of either the key or the display column.

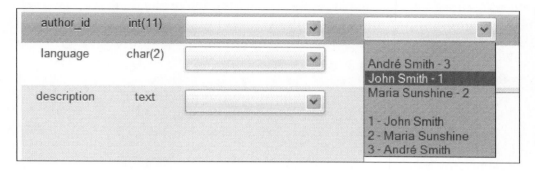

 Only the key (in this case **1**) will be stored in the book table. The display column is shown only to assist us.

By default, this drop-down list will appear if there are a maximum of 100 rows in the foreign table. This is controlled by the following parameter:

```
$cfg['ForeignKeyMaxLimit'] = 100;
```

For foreign tables bigger than that, a distinct window appears — the foreign-table window (refer to the next section) that can be browsed.

We might prefer to see information differently in the drop-down list. Here, **John Smith** is the content and **1** is the ID. The default display is controlled by the following line of code:

```
$cfg['ForeignKeyDropdownOrder'] = array( 'content-id', 'id-content' );
```

We can use one or both of the strings — content-id and id-content — in the defining array and in the order we prefer. Thus, defining $cfg['ForeignKeyDropdownOrder'] to array('id-content') would produce a list with only those choices:

```
1 - John Smith
2 - Maria Sunshine
3 - André Smith
```

The browseable foreign-table window

Our current author table has very few entries. Thus, to illustrate this mechanism, we will set the $cfg['ForeignKeyMaxLimit']$ to an artificially low number, 1. Now in the **Insert** mode for the book table, we see a small table-shaped icon and a **Browse foreign values** link for **author_id** column. This icon opens another window, which will present the values of the author table and a **Search** input field. On the left, the values are sorted by key value (here, the **id** column), and on the right, they are sorted by description.

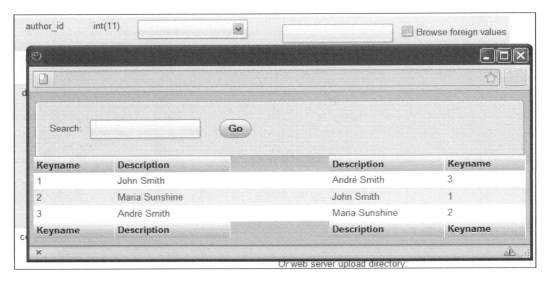

Choosing one of the values (by clicking either a key value or a description) closes this window and brings the value back to the **author_id** column.

Referential integrity checks

We discussed the **Operations** page and its **Table maintenance** section in Chapter 9. For this exercise, we suppose that both the book and author tables are not under the control of the InnoDB or PBXT storage engine. If we have defined an internal relation for the author table, a new choice appears for the book table—**Check referential integrity**.

A link (**author_id -> author.id**) appears for each defined relation, and clicking on it starts verification. For each row, the presence of the corresponding key in the foreign table is verified and errors, if any, are reported. If the resulting page reports zero rows, it is good news!

This operation exists because for tables under the storage engines that do not support foreign key natively, neither MySQL nor phpMyAdmin enforces referential integrity. It is perfectly possible, for example, to insert data in the book table with invalid values for **author_id** column.

Automatic updates of metadata

phpMyAdmin keeps the metadata for internal relations synchronized with every change that is made to the tables via phpMyAdmin. For example, renaming a column that is part of a relation would make phpMyAdmin rename this column in the metadata for the relation. This guarantees that an internal relation continues to function, even after a column's name is changed. The same thing happens when a column or table is dropped.

> Metadata should be maintained manually in case a change in the structure is done from outside phpMyAdmin.

Column commenting

Prior to MySQL 4.1, the MySQL structure itself did not support the addition of comments to a column. Nevertheless, thanks to phpMyAdmin's metadata, we could comment on columns. However, since MySQL 4.1, native column commenting has been supported. The good news is that for any MySQL version, column commenting in phpMyAdmin is always accessed via the **Structure** page by editing the structure of each column. In the following example, we need to comment on three columns of the book table. Hence, we choose them and click on the pencil icon near the **With selected** choice.

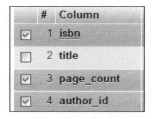

To obtain the next panel, as seen here, we are working in vertical mode. This mode was covered in *Chapter 5*. We enter the comments as shown in the following screenshot, and then click on **Save**:

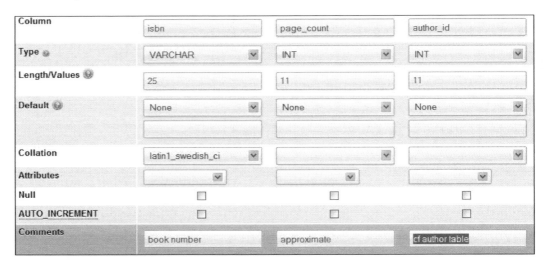

These comments appear at various places, for example, in the export file (refer to *Chapter 6*), on the PDF relational schema (refer to *Chapter 15*), and in browse mode, as shown in the following screenshot:

If we do not want the comments to appear in browse mode, we can set `$cfg['ShowBrowseComments']` to FALSE. (It is TRUE by default.)

Column comments also appear as a tool tip in the **Structure** page, and column names are underlined with dashes. To deactivate this behavior, we can set `$cfg['ShowPropertyComments']` to FALSE. (This one is also TRUE by default.)

Automatically migrating column comments

Whenever phpMyAdmin detects that column comments have been stored in its metadata, it automatically migrates these column comments to the native MySQL column comments.

Summary

This chapter covered how to define relations between both InnoDB and non-InnoDB tables. It also examined the modified behavior of phpMyAdmin (when relations are present) and foreign keys. Finally, it covered the **Designer** feature, column commenting, and how to obtain information from the table.

The next chapter will cover the means of entering SQL commands, which are useful when the phpMyAdmin's interface is not sufficient to accomplish what we need.

11
Entering SQL Statements

This chapter explains how we can enter our own SQL statements (queries) into phpMyAdmin, and how we can keep a history of those queries. Traditionally, one would interact with a MySQL server via the "mysql" command-line client by entering SQL statements and watching the server's response. Official MySQL training still involves directly typing statements to such a client.

The SQL query box

phpMyAdmin allows us to accomplish many database operations via its graphical interface. However, there will be times when we have to rely on SQL query input to achieve operations that are not directly supported by the interface. Following are two examples of such queries:

```
SELECT department, AVG(salary) FROM employees GROUP BY department
HAVING years_experience > 10;

SELECT FROM_DAYS(TO_DAYS(CURDATE()) +30);
```

To enter such queries, the SQL query box is available from a number of places within phpMyAdmin.

The Database view

We encounter our first SQL query box when going to the **SQL** menu available in the Database view.

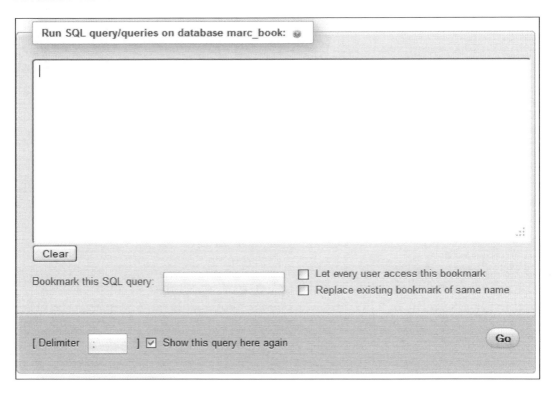

This box is simple—we type in some valid (hopefully) MySQL statement and click on **Go**. Under the query text area, there are bookmark-related choices (explained later in *Chapter 14*). Usually, we don't have to change the standard SQL delimiter, which is a semicolon. However, there is a **Delimiter** dialog in case we need it (refer to *Chapter 17*).

For a default query to appear in this box, we can set it with the $cfg['DefaultQueryDatabase'] configuration directive, which is empty by default. We could put a query such as SHOW TABLES FROM @DATABASE@ in this directive. The @DATABASE@ placeholder in this query would be replaced by the current database name, resulting in SHOW TABLES FROM `marc_book` in the query box.

The Table view

A slightly different box is available in the `Table` view of the `book` table from the SQL menu.

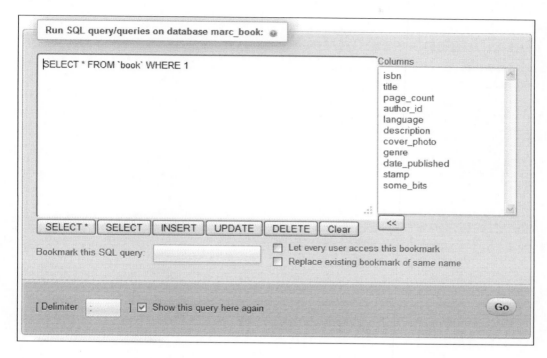

The box already has a default query as seen in the previous screenshot. This default query is generated from the `$cfg['DefaultQueryTable']` configuration directive, which contains `SELECT * FROM @TABLE@ WHERE 1`. Here, the `@TABLE@` is replaced by the current table name. Another placeholder available in `$cfg['DefaultQueryTable']` is `@FIELDS@`. This placeholder would be replaced by the complete column's list of this table, thus producing the following query:

```
SELECT `isbn`, `title`, `page_count`, `author_id`, `language`,
`description`, `cover_photo`, `genre`, `date_published`, `stamp`,
`some_bits` FROM `book` WHERE 1.
```

`WHERE 1` is a condition that is always true. Therefore, the query can be executed as it is. We can replace **1** with the condition we want, or we can type a completely different query.

Because this SQL box appears in the `Table` view, the table name is known; therefore, phpMyAdmin shows buttons below the query box, which permit to quickly create common SQL queries which contain this table name. Most of the queries generated by these buttons contain the full column list.

The Columns selector

The **Columns** selector is a way to speed up query generation. By choosing a column and clicking on the arrows **<<**, this column name is copied at the current cursor position in the query box. Here, we select the **author_id** column, remove the digit **1**, and click on **<<**. Then we add the condition **= 2** as shown in the following screenshot:

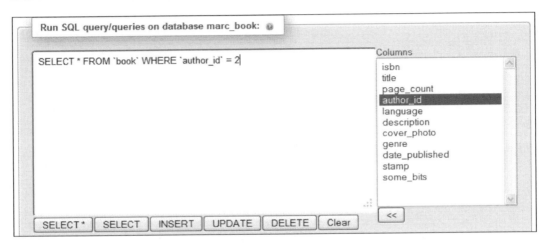

The **Show this query here again** option (checked by default) ensures that the query stays in the box after its execution if we are still on the same page. This can be seen more easily for a query like an UPDATE or DELETE, which affects a table, but does not produce a separate results page.

Clicking into the query box

We might want to change the behavior of a click inside the query box with the `$cfg['TextareaAutoSelect']` configuration directive. Its default value is FALSE, which means that no automatic selection of the contents is done upon a click. Should you change this directive to TRUE, the first click inside this box will select all its contents. (This is a way to quickly copy the contents elsewhere or delete them from the box.) The next click would put the cursor at the click position.

The Query window

In *Chapter 3*, we discussed the purpose of this window, and the procedure for changing some parameters (such as dimensions). This window can easily be opened from the navigation panel using the **SQL** icon or the **Query window** link, as shown in the following screenshot, and is very convenient for entering a query and testing it:

The following screenshot shows the Query window that appears over the main panel:

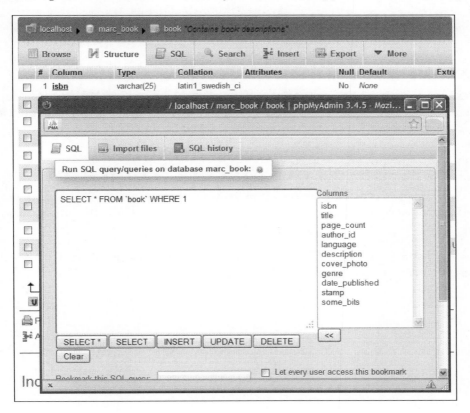

The window seen in the screenshot contains the same **Columns** selector and **<<** button as that used in a `Table` view context. This distinct Query window is a feature supported only on JavaScript-enabled browsers.

Query window options

The **SQL** tab is the default active tab in this window. This comes from the configuration directive `$cfg['QueryWindowDefTab']`, which contains `sql` by default.

If we want another tab to be the default active tab, we can replace `sql` with `files` or `history`. Another value, `full`, shows the contents of all the three tabs at once.

In the Query window, we see a checkbox for the **Do not overwrite this query from outside the window** choice. Normally, this checkbox is selected. If we deselect it, the changes we make while generating queries are reflected in the Query window. This is called **synchronization**. For example, choosing a different database or table from the navigation or main panel would update the Query window accordingly. However, if we start to type a query directly in this window, the checkbox will get checked in order to protect its contents and remove synchronization. This way, the query composed here will be locked and protected.

Session-based SQL history

This feature collects all the successful SQL queries we execute as PHP session data, and modifies the Query window to make them available. This default type of history is temporary, as `$cfg['QueryHistoryDB']` is set to `FALSE` by default.

Database-based SQL history (permanent)

As we installed the phpMyAdmin configuration storage (refer to *Chapter 1*), a more powerful history mechanism is available. We should now enable this mechanism by setting `$cfg['QueryHistoryDB']` to `TRUE`.

After we try some queries from one of the query boxes, a history is built, visible only from the Query window as shown in the following screenshot:

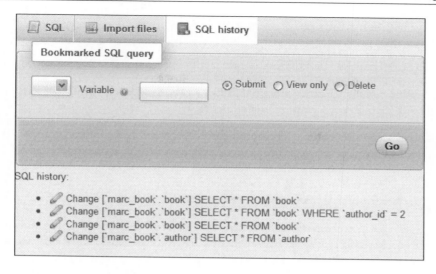

We see (in the reverse order) the last successful queries and the database on which they were made. Queries typed only from the query box are kept in this history, along with queries generated by phpMyAdmin (such as those generated by clicking on **Browse**).

They are clickable for immediate execution, and the **Change** icon is available to insert a recorded query into the query box for editing.

The number of queries that will be kept is controlled by $cfg['QueryHistoryMax'], which is set to 25 by default. This limit is not kept for performance reasons, but as a practical limit in order to achieve a visually unencumbered view. Extra queries are eliminated at login time in a process traditionally called **garbage collection**. The queries are stored in the table configured in $cfg['Servers'][$i]['history'].

Editing queries

On the results page of a successful query, a header containing the executed query appears as shown in the following screenshot:

Clicking on **Edit** opens the Query window's **SQL** tab, with this query ready to be modified. This happens because of the following default setting for this parameter:

```
$cfg['EditInWindow'] = TRUE;
```

When it is set to FALSE, a click on **Edit** will not open the Query window; instead, the query will appear inside the query box of the **SQL** page.

Clicking on **Inline** replaces the displayed query by a text area where it's possible to edit and submit this query, without leaving the current results page.

Multi-statement queries

In PHP and MySQL programming, we can send only one query at a time using the `mysql_query()` function call. phpMyAdmin allows us to send many queries in one transmission, using a semicolon as a separator. Suppose we type the following query in the query box:

```
INSERT INTO author VALUES (100,'Paul Smith','111-2222');
INSERT INTO author VALUES (101,'Melanie Smith','222-3333');
UPDATE author SET phone='444-5555' WHERE name LIKE '%Smith%';
```

We will receive the following results screen:

INSERT INTO author VALUES (100,'Paul Smith','111-2222');# 1 row affected.

INSERT INTO author VALUES (101,'Melanie Smith','222-3333');# 1 row affected.

UPDATE author SET phone='444-5555' WHERE name LIKE '%Smith%';# 4 rows affected.

We see the number of affected rows through comments because `$cfg['VerboseMultiSubmit']` is set to TRUE.

Let us send the same list of queries again and watch the results:

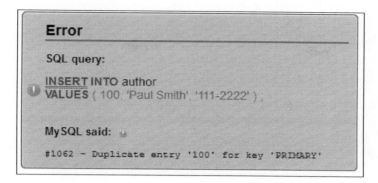

It is normal to receive a **Duplicate entry** error message that says the value **100** exists already. We are seeing the results of the first **INSERT** statement; but what happens to the next one? Execution stops at the first error because $cfg['IgnoreMultiSubmitErrors'] is set to FALSE telling phpMyAdmin not to ignore errors in multiple statements. If it is set to TRUE, the program successively tries all the statements, and we see two **Duplicate entry** errors.

This feature would not work as expected, if we tried more than one SELECT statement. We would see the results of only the last SELECT statement.

Pretty printing (syntax highlighting)

By default, phpMyAdmin parses and highlights the various elements of any MySQL statement it processes. This is controlled by $cfg['SQP']['fmtType'], which is set to 'html' by default. This mode uses a specific color for each different element (a reserved word, a variable, a comment, and so on) as described in the $cfg['SQP']['fmtColor'] array located in the theme-specific layout.inc.php file.

Setting fmtType to 'text' would remove all color formatting, inserting line breaks at logical points inside a MySQL statement. Finally, setting fmtType to 'none' removes every kind of formatting, leaving our syntax intact.

The SQL Validator

Each time phpMyAdmin transmits a query, the MySQL server interprets it and provides feedback. The syntax of the query must follow MySQL rules, which are not the same as the SQL Standard. However, conforming to SQL Standard ensures that our queries are usable on other SQL implementations.

A free external service, the **Mimer SQL Validator**, is available to us, thanks to Mimer Information Technology AB. It validates our query according to the Core SQL-99 rules and generates a report. The Validator is available directly from phpMyAdmin, and its home page is located at http://developer.mimer.com/validator/index.htm.

 For statistical purposes, this service anonymously stores on its server, the queries it receives. When storing the queries, it replaces database, table, and column names with generic names. Strings and numbers that are part of the query are replaced with generic values so as to protect the original information.

System requirements

This Validator is available as a SOAP service. Our PHP server must have XML, PCRE, and SOAP support. SOAP support is offered by either a PHP extension or by a PEAR module. If we choose the PEAR way, the following command (executed on the server by the system administrator) installs the modules we need:

```
pear install Net_Socket Net_URL HTTP_Request Mail_Mime Net_DIME SOAP
```

If we have problems with this command due to some of the modules being in a beta state, we can execute the following command, which installs SOAP and other dependent modules:

```
pear -d preferred_state=beta install -a SOAP
```

Making the Validator available

Some parameters must be configured in config.inc.php. Setting $cfg['SQLQuery']['Validate'] to TRUE enables the **Validate SQL** link.

We should also enable the Validator itself (as other validators might be available on future phpMyAdmin versions). This is done by setting $cfg['SQLValidator'] ['use'] to TRUE.

The Validator is accessed with an anonymous Validator account by default, as configured using the following commands:

```
$cfg['SQLValidator']['username'] = '';
$cfg['SQLValidator']['password'] = '';
```

Instead, if Mimer Information Technology has provided us with an account, we can use that account information here.

Validator results

There are two kinds of reports returned by the Validator—one if the query conforms to the standard, and the other if it does not conform.

Standard-conforming queries

We will try a simple query: SELECT COUNT(*) FROM book. As usual, we enter this query in the query box and send it. On the results page, we now see an additional link—**Validate SQL** as shown in the following screenshot:

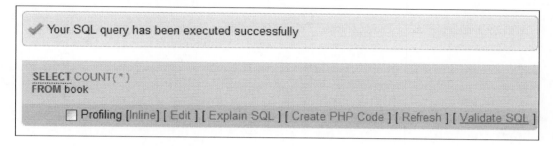

Clicking on **Validate SQL** produces a report as shown in the following screenshot:

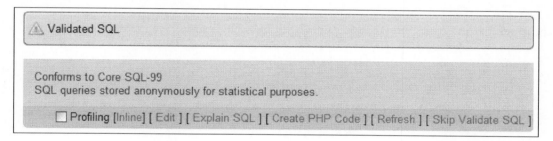

We have the option of clicking on **Skip Validate SQL** to see our original query.

Non standard-conforming queries

Let us try another query, which works correctly in MySQL: SELECT * FROM book WHERE language = 'en'. Sending it to the Validator produces a report as shown in the following screenshot:

Each time the Validator finds a problem, it adds a message such as {error: 1} at the point of the error and adds a footnote in the report. In this query, the **language** column name is non-standard. Hence, the Validator tells us that it was expecting an identifier at this point. Another non-standard error is reported about the use of a LIMIT clause, which was added to the query by phpMyAdmin.

Another case is that of the backquote. If we just click on **Browse** for the book table, phpMyAdmin generates SELECT * FROM `book`, enclosing the table name with backquote. This is MySQL's way of protecting identifiers, which might contain special characters, such as spaces, international characters, or reserved words. However, sending this query to the Validator shows us that the backquotes do not conform to standard SQL. We may even get two errors, one for each backquote.

Summary

This chapter helped us understand the purpose of query boxes and showed us where to find them. It also gave us an overview of how to use the column selector, the Query window options, how to get a history of the typed commands, multi-statement queries, and finally, how to use the SQL Validator.

The next chapter will show how to produce multi-table queries without typing much, thanks to phpMyAdmin's query generator.

12
Generating Multi-table Queries

The **Search** pages in the `Database` or `Table` view are intended for single-table lookups. This chapter covers the multi-table **Query by example** (**QBE**) feature available in the `Database` view.

Many phpMyAdmin users work in the `Table` view, table by table, and thus tend to overlook the multi-table query generator, which is a wonderful feature for fine-tuning queries. The query generator is useful not only in multi-table situations but also in single-table situations. It enables us to specify multiple criteria for a column, a feature that the **Search** page in the `Table` view does not possess.

 The examples in this chapter assume that a multi-user installation of the phpMyAdmin configuration storage has been made (refer to *Chapter 1*), and that the `book-copy` table created during an exercise of *Chapter 9* is still there in the `marc_book` database.

To open the page for this feature, we go to the `Database` view for a specific database (the query generator supports working on only one database at a time) and click on **Query**.

The following screenshot shows the initial QBE page. It contains the following elements:

- A **visual builder** link (covered at the end of this chapter)
- Criteria columns
- An interface to add criteria rows
- An interface to add criteria columns
- A table selector

- The query area
- Buttons to update or to execute the query

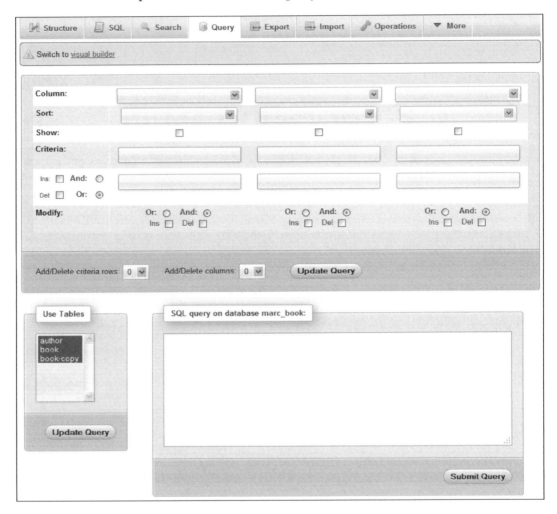

Choosing tables

The initial selection includes all tables. Consequently, the **Column** selector contains a great number of columns. For our example, we will work only with the **author** and the **book** tables. Hence, we select only these from the **Use Tables** selector.

We then click on the **Update Query** button. This refreshes the screen and reduces the number of columns available in the **Column** selector. We can always change the selected tables later, using our browser's mechanism for multiple choices in drop-down menus (usually control click).

Exploring column criteria

Three criteria columns are provided by default. This section discusses the options we have for editing their criteria. These include options for selecting columns, sorting individual columns, entering conditions for individual columns, and so on.

Column selector: Single column or all columns

The **Column** selector contains all the individual columns for the selected tables, plus a special choice ending with an asterisk (*) for each table, which means that all the columns are selected.

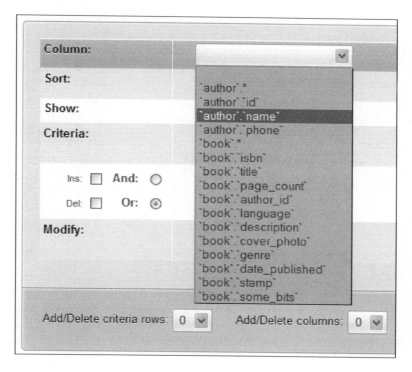

To display all the columns in the author table, we would choose `` `author`.* `` and check the **Show** checkbox, without entering anything in the **Sort** and the **Criteria** boxes. In our case, we select `` `author`.`name` ``, as we want to enter some criteria for the author's name.

Sorting columns

For each selected individual column, we can specify a sort (in **Ascending** or **Descending** order), or let this line remain intact (no sorting, which is the default behavior). If we choose more than one sorted column, the sorting will be carried out from left to right.

 When we ask for a column to be sorted, we normally check the **Show** checkbox. But this is not necessary, as we might want to do just the sorting operation without displaying this column.

Showing a column

We check the **Show** checkbox so that we can see the column in the results. Sometimes, we may just want to apply a criterion on a column, and not include it in the resulting page. Here, we add the phone column, ask for it to be sorted, and choose to show both the name and the phone number. We also ask for a sort on the name in the ascending order. The sort will be done first by name, and then by the phone number if the names are identical. This is because the name is in a column criterion to the left of the phone column, and thus has a higher priority.

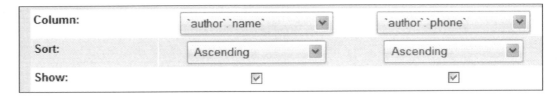

Column:	`` `author`.`name` ``	`` `author`.`phone` ``
Sort:	Ascending	Ascending
Show:	☑	☑

Updating the query

At any point, we can click on the **Update Query** button to see the progress of our generated query. We have to click it at least once before executing the query. For now, let us click it and see the query generated in the query area. In the following examples, we will click on the **Update Query** button after each modification.

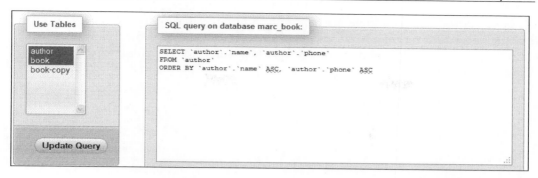

We have selected two tables, but have not yet chosen any column from the **book** table. Hence, this table is not mentioned in the generated query.

Adding conditions to the criteria box

In the **Criteria** box, we can enter a condition (respecting the SQL WHERE clause's syntax) for each of the corresponding columns. By default, we have two criteria rows. To find all the authors with **Smith** in their names, we use a **LIKE** criterion (**LIKE '%SMITH%'**) and click on **Update Query**.

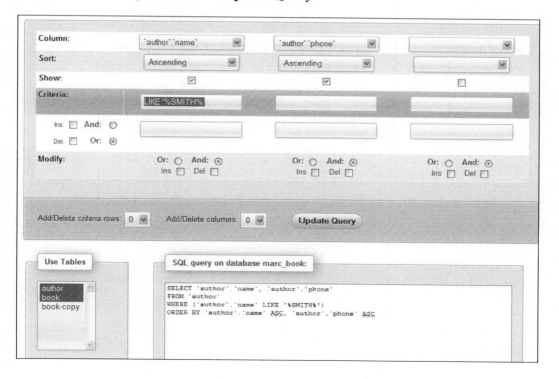

We have another line available to enter an additional criterion. Let us say we want to find the author **Maria Sunshine** as well. This time, we use an = condition. The two condition rows will be joined by the **Or** operator, selected by default from the left side of the interface.

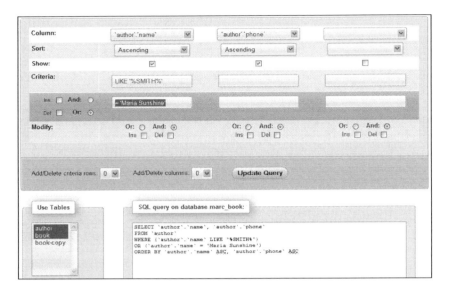

To better demonstrate that the **Or** operator links both the criteria rows, let us now add a condition, **LIKE '%8%'**, on the phone number as shown in the following screenshot:

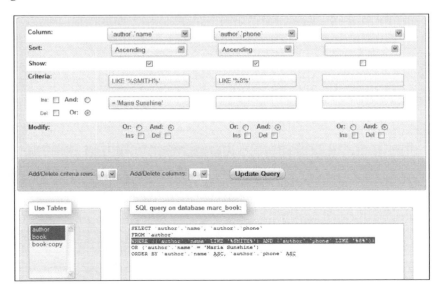

By examining the positioning of the **AND** and **OR** operators, we can see that the first row of the conditions is linked by the **AND** (because **AND** is chosen under the **name** column) operator, and the second row of conditions is linked to the rest by the **OR** operator. The condition that we have just added (**LIKE '%8%'**) is not meant to find anyone, because we changed the phone number of all the authors with the name "Smith" to "444-5555" (in *Chapter 11*).

If we want another criterion on the same column, we just add a criteria row.

Adjusting the number of criteria rows

The number of criteria rows can be changed in two ways. First, we can select the **Ins** checkbox under **Criteria** to add one criteria row (after clicking on **Update Query**). As this checkbox can add only one criteria row at a time, we will uncheck it and use the **Add/Delete criteria rows** dialog instead. In this dialog, we choose to add two rows.

Another click on the **Update Query** button produces the following screen:

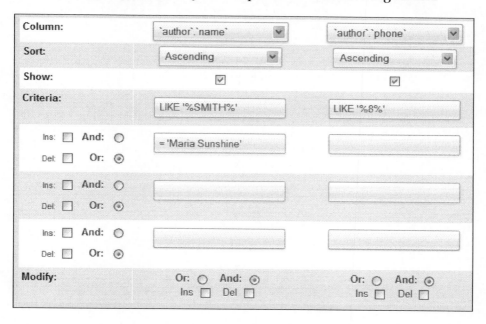

Now, you can see that there are two additional criteria rows (which are empty at the moment). We can also remove criteria rows. This can be done by ticking the **Del** checkbox beside the row(s) we want to remove. Let us remove the two rows we have just added, as we don't need them now. The **Update Query** button refreshes the page with the specified adjustment.

Adjusting the number of criteria columns

Using a similar mechanism, we can add or delete columns by checking the **Ins** or **Del** checkboxes under each column in the **Modify** dialog, or the **Add/Delete columns** dialog. We already had one unused column (not shown on the previous images). Here, we have added one column using the **Ins** checkbox located under the unused column (this time, we will need it):

Generating automatic joins (internal relations)

phpMyAdmin can generate the joins between the tables in the query it builds, provided internal relations have been defined. Let us now populate our two unused columns with the **title** and the **genre** columns from our **book** table, and see what happens when we update the query.

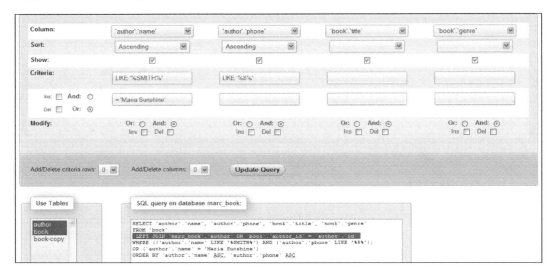

There are now two additional criteria columns that relate to the `book`.`title` and the `book`.`genre` columns respectively. phpMyAdmin used its knowledge of the relations defined between the tables to generate a **LEFT JOIN** clause (highlighted in the preceding screenshot) on the **author_id** key column. A shortcoming of the current version is that only the internal relations, and not the InnoDB relations, are examined.

[There may be more than two tables involved in a join.]

Executing the query

Clicking on the **Submit Query** button sends the query for execution. In the following screenshot, you can see the complete generated query in the upper part, and the resulting data row in the lower part:

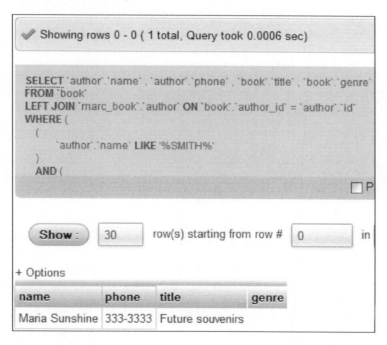

There is no easy way (except by using the browser's **Back** button) to come back to the query generation page once we have submitted the query. *Chapter 14* discusses how to save the generated query for later execution.

The visual builder

Starting with version 3.4, another method for query building is offered. It leverages the **Designer** interface that might be more familiar to users, by combining query generation to it. We can open this interface by clicking on the **Switch to visual builder** link, which produces an initial screen, shown in the following screenshot:

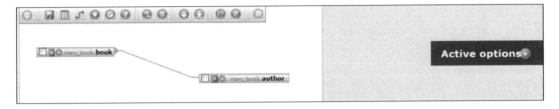

We should now open the list of columns for all tables by clicking on the **Small/Big All** icon.

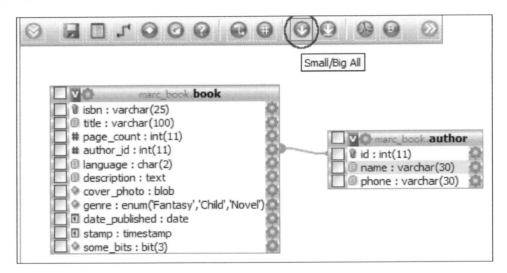

Each column has a left-side checkbox and a right-side options icon. The checkbox is used to indicate which column we want to be part of the results; while the option icon permits to open a panel where we will specify the criterion we want to apply to this column. For example, should we want to select books of more than 200 pages, we would click on the options icon next to **page_count** column and fill the criterion dialog, as depicted in the following screenshot:

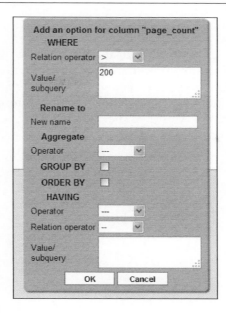

Clicking on **OK** saves this query option; it's now available under the **Active options** dialog at the right-side, should we need to review the option or remove it.

To build the query, we use the **Build Query** icon, producing a screen shown in the following screenshot:

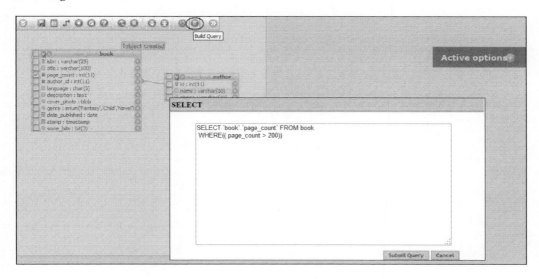

At this point, we either refine the query with additional options or click on **Submit Query** to obtain the results.

Summary

This chapter covered various aspects including opening the query generator, choosing tables, entering column criteria, sorting and showing columns, and altering the number of criteria rows or columns. We also learnt how to use the AND and OR operators to define relations between the rows and columns, and how to use automatic joins between tables. The **Designer**-integrated visual query builder was covered as well.

The next chapter will show you how to synchronize data between servers and how to manage replication.

13

Synchronizing Data and Supporting Replication

In this chapter, we will cover two features that were released in phpMyAdmin 3.3.0. The first feature is the ability to synchronize databases, and was asked for by developers who work on more than one server. The second feature permits the management of MySQL replication, which is used in environments where performance and data security are important. These features are somewhat related because we usually need to synchronize the database to a slave server when setting it up in a replication process.

Synchronizing data and structure

In earlier phpMyAdmin versions, it was possible to achieve some synchronization of the structure and data between two databases on the same server or on different servers, but this required manual operations. It was (and still is) possible to export structure and/or data from one database and import in another one. We can even visually compare the structure of two tables and adjust them according to our needs. However, comparing the two databases to ascertain what needs to be imported had to be done with the developer's own eyeballs. Moreover, differences in structure between the databases were not taken into account, possibly resulting in errors when a column was missing in the target table.

The **synchronize** feature of phpMyAdmin permits much flexibility, by taking care of the initial comparison process and, of course, by performing the synchronization itself. We will first discuss the reasons for synchronizing, and then examine and experiment with all the steps involved.

Goals of synchronization

Although the reasons for wanting to synchronize two databases may be many, we can group them into the following categories.

Moving between the development and production servers

A sound database development strategy includes performing development and testing on a server that is distinct from the production one. If having a separate development server is not an option, having at least a distinct development database is encouraged. Over time, differences in structure between test and production environments build up, and this is normal. For example, a column may be added in the test version, or character column may be enlarged. The synchronize feature permits us to first see the differences and then apply them to production if they make sense.

Moving data sometimes needs to be done the other way around, for example, to populate a test database with real production data in order to measure performance.

Collaboration between database designers

Due to the easy manner in which a MySQL test server can be put in place, the situation might arise where each member of a development team has his own server (or his own copy of the database) in which he develops some aspect of a project. When the time comes to reconcile everyone's changes for the same table, the synchronize feature is invaluable.

Preparing for replication

MySQL supports asynchronous replication between a master server and one or many slave servers. This data replication is termed "asynchronous" because the connection between master and slaves does not need to be permanent. However, to put a replication process in action (and assuming that the master already contains some data), one needs to copy all the data over to the slaves. A suggestion to accomplish this copy is given in the MySQL manual that can found at `http://dev.mysql.com/doc/refman/5.1/en/replication-howto.html`, and is mentioned as follows:

"If you already have data on your master and you want to use it to synchronize your slave, you will need to create a data snapshot. You can create a snapshot using `mysqldump` (...)"

However, this requires using a command-line tool that is not always possible depending on the hosting options. Besides, some parts of the database may already exist on the slave; therefore, the synchronize feature comes in handy because it's integrated into phpMyAdmin, and also because it takes care of the comparison phase.

Over viewing the synchronization process

The important principle is that synchronization is done from a source database to a target database. During this operation, the source database remains unchanged. It's up to us to correctly identify which database is the source and which one is the target (and will be possibly modified).

The whole process is subdivided into steps which can be stopped at any stage:

- Server and database choice
- Comparison
- Full or selective synchronization

We could elect to stop the process for one of the following reasons:

- We don't have the necessary credentials to connect to one of the servers
- We see discrepancies between two databases and are not ready to synchronize because further research needs to be done
- We notice after the comparison phase that the target database is adequately synchronized

Before performing synchronization, we will put the necessary elements in place.

Preparing for the synchronization exercise

As we will play with only the author and book tables, this exercise will assume that there are no other tables in the marc_book database. We start by copying the marc_book database to marc_book_dev (refer to *Chapter 9* for the exact method for doing this).Then we open the marc_book_dev database and perform the following actions:

- Delete the book table
- Delete one row of the author table
- Change the type of the name column from VARCHAR(30) to VARCHAR(29)
- Delete the phone column from the author table

Chapter 5 covers how to perform the previous actions.

Choosing source and target servers and databases

The initial Synchronize page is displayed via the **Synchronize** menu tab in `Server` view. Please note that this is the only place where this menu is available.

The first panel permits us to connect to servers (if needed) and to pick the correct database. If the `$cfg['AllowArbitraryServer']` parameter is set to its default value of `false`, the following panel appears:

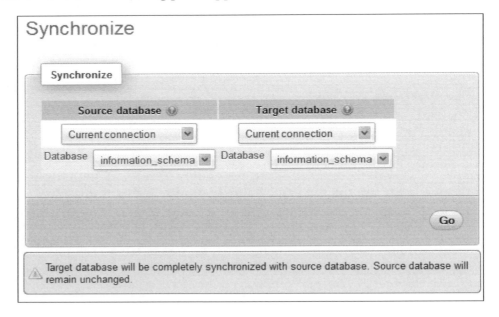

This means that we can only use the servers already defined in `config.inc.php`. If arbitrary servers are allowed, we see a different panel, shown in the following screenshot:

For both the source and target databases, we can select the server location. By default, the selector is placed on **Enter manually** and we can enter its hostname, port, socket name, username, password, and database name. In most cases, the port should be left to the default 3306 and the socket name should be left empty. Notice that we are currently connected to a MySQL server (via the normal login panel) and this panel could permit us to connect to two more servers.

Another choice for server location is **Current connection**. This refers to the server on which we are connected for normal phpMyAdmin operations; its name is displayed at the top of the main panel. Should we choose this, a JavaScript-enabled browser hides all choices except for the database name (connection credentials are unnecessary in this situation) and a selector becomes available, showing all of the databases to which we have access.

It's perfectly possible to pick the same server on both the source and target sides; however, we would at least choose a source database different to the target one in this case. Another common case is to pick the current server and some database as the source, and a remote server with the same database as the target, assuming that the remote server is the production one and that both servers hold a database with the same name.

For this exercise, let us pick **Current connection** for both source and target servers; we can then choose marc_book as the source database and marc_book_dev as the target one, as shown in the following screenshot:

After clicking on **Go**, phpMyAdmin attempts to connect to the servers if needed. At this point, a connection error message may be displayed. However, the connection should hopefully succeed and the program will start comparing both databases and then show us the results.

Analyzing comparison results

The comparison results panel contains three sections. The first section displays the structure and data differences, and contains icons that will be used to initiate a selective synchronization:

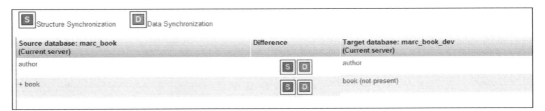

As depicted in the upper part, the red **S** icon triggers structure synchronization, whereas the green **D** icon is for data synchronization. Then, for each table, we get a rundown of the differences. The central **Difference** column would be empty in the case of identical structure and data for the corresponding table. Here we see a red **S** and a green **D** for both tables, but the reason is not the same for each table.

The middle part shows the actions that are scheduled as part of the synchronization process (there are currently none, as can be seen in the following screenshot):

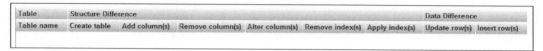

The lower part contains a checkbox (**Would you like to delete all the previous rows from target tables?**) and two action buttons. We will see their purpose in the following sections:

Please note that the book table has a plus sign (**+**) next to it on the **Source** side, to show that this table is in the source database but not in the target database. We even see a **not present** comment for this table on the **Target** side. If a table was in the target database but not in the source one, it would be marked with a minus sign (-) on the **Target** side.

At this point, we can decide that we are satisfied with the comparison and don't want to proceed further; in this case, we would just have to continue in phpMyAdmin by picking a database and resuming our work. We also have the opportunity of synchronizing the databases in one sweep (**complete synchronization**) or to make changes in a more granular way (**selective synchronization**). Let us examine both methods.

Performing a complete synchronization

If we don't want to ask ourselves too many questions and just need a complete synchronization, we click on **Synchronize Databases**. Note that in this case, we don't have to use any red **S** or green **D** icons.

 If one of the target tables contains some rows that are not present in the corresponding source table, these will remain in the target tables, unless we tick the **Would you like to delete...** checkbox. This is a safety net to avoid unintended loss of data. However, we should select this option if we want an exact synchronization.

After clicking, we obtain the following message: **Target database has been synchronized with source database**. In the lower part of the screen, we see the queries that had to be executed in order to achieve this operation. We also get a visual confirmation that the databases are now synchronized:

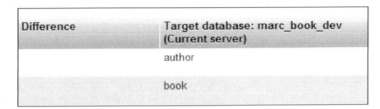

Difference	Target database: marc_book_dev (Current server)
	author
	book

Performing a selective synchronization

If we prefer to be more cautious and receive a preliminary feedback on the actions that are about to be done, we can synchronize selected tables. This section assumes that the databases are in the same state as at the end of the *Preparing for the synchronization exercise* section, covered previously in this chapter.

If we click on the red **S** icon on the line describing the author table, this **S** icon turns to grey and the middle part of the screen is updated with the actions to be done, as shown in the following screenshot:

Table	Structure Difference						Data Difference	
Table name	Create table	Add column(s)	Remove column(s)	Alter column(s)	Remove index(s)	Apply index(s)	Update row(s)	Insert row(s)
author	--	1	0	1	0	0	--	--

No real action on the data has been done yet! We still can change our mind by clicking on the same icon which would turn back to red, removing the proposed changes as depicted in the middle part of the screen.

Now we click on the green **D** icon and see another line of proposed changes show up, as shown in the following screenshot:

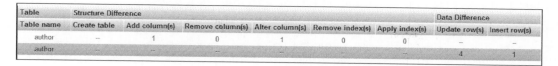

Table	Structure Difference						Data Difference	
Table name	Create table	Add column(s)	Remove column(s)	Alter column(s)	Remove index(s)	Apply index(s)	Update row(s)	Insert row(s)
author	--	1	0	1	0	0	--	--
author	--	--	--	--	--	--	4	1

A row in the author table needs to be inserted because there is one less author in the target database. Altogether four rows need to be updated, because we removed the phone column in the same table.

We can now click on **Apply Selected Changes** button. The **Would you like to delete...** checkbox does not apply to this operation.

We now see that the upper part of the screen proposes fewer changes to make:

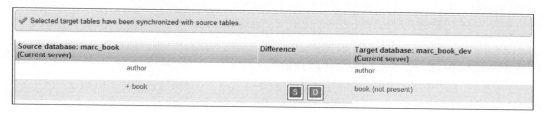

Selected target tables have been synchronized with source tables.			
Source database: marc_book (Current server)		Difference	**Target database: marc_book_dev** (Current server)
	author		author
	+ book	[S] [D]	book (not present)

We can go on by selecting structure or data changes and then applying them in the order we deem appropriate.

This concludes the section describing the synchronization feature. We continue with coverage of replication support.

Supporting MySQL replication

In the *Preparing for replication* section, we saw an overview of MySQL replication. In this section, we cover the following topics:

- How we can use phpMyAdmin to configure replication
- How to prepare a test environment containing one master server and two slave servers
- How to send commands to control the servers
- How to obtain information on replication for servers, databases, and tables

phpMyAdmin's interface offers a **Replication** page; however, other pages contain either information about replication or links to control replication actions. We will point to each appropriate location when covering the related subject.

How to use this section depends on how many servers we have at our disposal. If we have at least two servers and want to configure them via phpMyAdmin in a master/slave relationship, we can follow the *Configuring replication* section. If instead we only have one server to play with, then we should take advice from the *Setting up a test environment* section to install many instances of the MySQL server on the same machine.

The Replication menu

In `Server` view, the **Replication** menu is only shown to privileged users, such as the MySQL root user. When a server is already configured as a master server or a slave server (or both), the **Replication** page is used to display status information and provide links that send commands.

Configuring replication

For this exercise, we assume that the server does not currently occupy the role of master or slave server. phpMyAdmin cannot directly configure all aspects of MySQL replication. The reason is that, contrary to manipulating database structure and data by sending queries to the MySQL server, replication configuration consists (in part) of command lines stored in a MySQL configuration file, often named `my.cnf`. phpMyAdmin, being a web application, does not have access to this file. This is how the MySQL server's developers intended the configuration to be—at a configuration file level.

The best that phpMyAdmin can do in this situation is to guide us by generating (on screen) the proper command lines in reaction to our preferences, then it's up to us to copy these lines where they need to go and to restart the server(s). phpMyAdmin cannot even read the current replication configuration lines; it can only deduce server status via some `SHOW` commands.

Let us enter the **Replication** menu and see what happens:

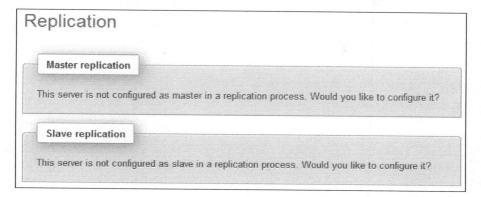

Master server configuration

Now we choose to configure the server as a master by clicking on the appropriate **configure** link. The panel that appears gives us a thorough advice:

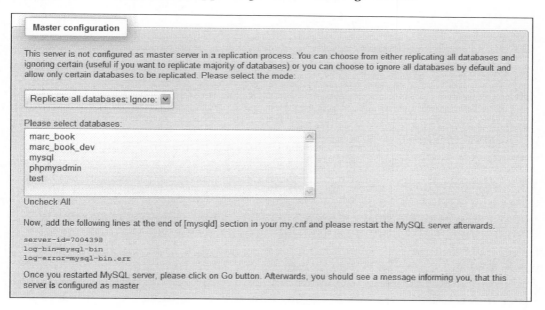

The first paragraph confirms that this server is not configured as a master in a replication process. We want to achieve this configuration, but first we need to think about the kind of replication we want. Should all databases be replicated, except for some of them? Or do we want the opposite? A convenient drop-down list offers us these choices:

- **Replicate all databases; Ignore:**
- **Ignore all databases; Replicate:**

The first choice (which is the default) implies that, in general, all databases are replicated; we don't even have to enumerate them in the configuration file. In this case, the databases selector is used to specify which database we want to exclude from the replication process. Let us pick up the **mysql** database and see what happens in our JavaScript-enabled browser:

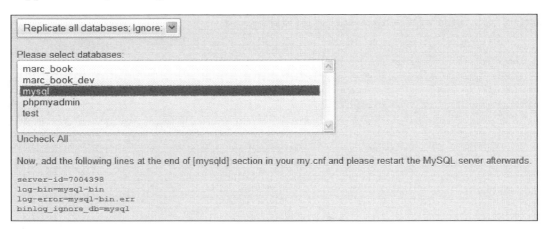

We notice that a line appeared, stating `binlog_ignore_db=mysql`. This is a MySQL server instruction (not a SQL statement) that tells the server to ignore sending transactions about this database to the binary log. Let us examine the meaning of the other lines. The `server-id` is a unique ID generated by phpMyAdmin; each server that participates in replication must have a unique server ID. Therefore, we either track the server IDs by hand, ensuring their uniqueness, or we simply use the number randomly generated by phpMyAdmin. We also see the `log-bin` and `log-error` instructions; in fact, binary logging is mandatory in order for any replication to occur.

We could add other database names to the list by using *Ctrl + Click* or *Command + Click*, depending on our workstation's OS. However, all that phpMyAdmin does is to generate correct lines; to make them operational, we still need to follow the given advice and paste these lines at the end of the `[mysqld]` section of our MySQL configuration file. We should then restart the MySQL server process—the way to do this depends on our environment.

After our server has been restarted, we go back to the **Replication** menu; at this point, we see a different panel regarding the master:

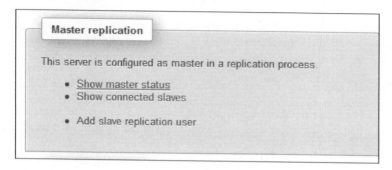

We can use the **Show master status** link to get some information about the master, including the current binary log name and position, and information on which databases to replicate or to ignore, as specified previously.

The **Show connected slaves** link would report nothing currently, as no slave is yet connected to this master.

Now would be the time to use the **Add slave replication user** link, because this master needs to have a separate account dedicated to replication. The slaves will use this account created on the master to connect to it. Clicking on this link displays the following panel, in which a user account, **replic**, is being created with a password of our choosing:

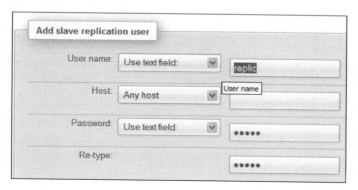

After clicking on **Go**, phpMyAdmin takes care of creating this user with the correct permissions set.

Slave server configuration

Now, on the machine that will act as a slave server in the replication process, we start phpMyAdmin. In the **Replication** menu, we click on **configure** in the following dialog:

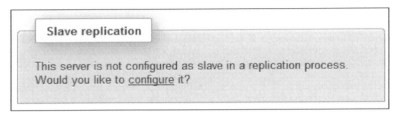

The slave server configuration panel appears, as shown in the following screenshot:

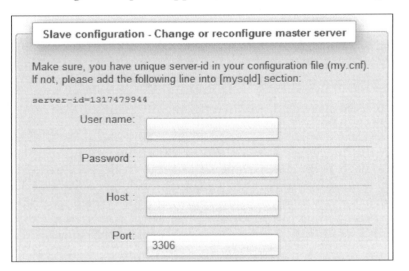

As with the master configuration, we get a suggestion about having a unique server ID in the configuration file for the slave, and we should follow this advice.

In this panel, we enter the username and password of the dedicated replication account we created on the master. We also have to indicate the hostname and port number corresponding to the master server. After filling this panel and clicking on **Go**, phpMyAdmin sends the appropriate CHANGE MASTER command to the slave, which puts this server in slave mode.

Setting up a test environment

The replication process occurs between at least two instances of the MySQL server. In production, this normally implies a minimum of two physical servers to procure these benefits:

- Better performance
- Increased redundancy

However, due to MySQL's configurable port number (the default being 3306), data directory, and socket, it's possible to have more than one MySQL instance on the same server. This setup can be configured manually, or via an installation system such as the MySQL Sandbox. This is an open source project located at `http://mysqlsandbox.net`. With this tool, we can set up one or many MySQL servers very quickly. By using the powerful `make_replication_sandbox` Linux shell command, we can install an environment that consists of one master server and two slave servers. Each server can be started or stopped individually.

The following exercises assume that the MySQL Sandbox has been installed on your server and that phpMyAdmin's `config.inc.php` contains a reference to these Sandbox servers, as shown in the following code block (please adjust the socket names to your own environment):

```
$i++;
$cfg['Servers'][$i]['auth_type']  = 'cookie';
$cfg['Servers'][$i]['host']       = 'localhost';
$cfg['Servers'][$i]['socket']     = '/tmp/mysql_sandbox25562.sock';
$cfg['Servers'][$i]['verbose']    = 'master';

$i++;
$cfg['Servers'][$i]['auth_type']  = 'cookie';
$cfg['Servers'][$i]['host']       = 'localhost';
$cfg['Servers'][$i]['socket']     = '/tmp/mysql_sandbox25563.sock';
$cfg['Servers'][$i]['verbose']    = 'slave1';

$i++;
$cfg['Servers'][$i]['auth_type']  = 'cookie';
$cfg['Servers'][$i]['host']       = 'localhost';
$cfg['Servers'][$i]['socket']     = '/tmp/mysql_sandbox25564.sock';
$cfg['Servers'][$i]['verbose']    = 'slave2';
```

Here, we use the `$cfg['Servers'][$i]['verbose']` directive to give a unique name to each instance, as the real server name is `localhost` for all of these instances. Each Sandbox server initially contains two databases: `mysql` and `test`.

Controlling a slave server

Here we will assume that the Sandbox testing environment has been set. However, the explanations are useful for all situations in which we have a slave server. After connecting to a slave and once again opening the **Replication** menu, we see:

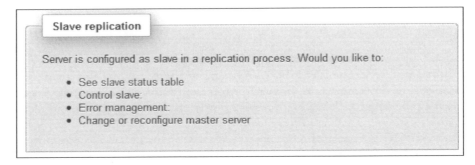

The following options are available:

- The **See slave status table** link permits us to receive information about all the system variables related to replication for this slave server.

- The **Control slave:** link reveals more options; some of them can toggle between the stop and start condition:

  ○ The **Full stop** option is used to stop both the IO thread (the part of the MySQL server responsible for receiving updates from the master and writing them to the slave's relay log) and the SQL thread (which reads the updates from the relay log and executes them)

  ○ The **Reset slave** option stops the slave, sends a RESET SLAVE command that causes it to forget its replication position in the master's binary log, and then restarts the slave

  ○ The **SQL Thread Stop only** option and **IO Thread Stop only** option are used to stop just the respective thread

- The **Error management:** link permits to tell the slave server to skip some of the events (updates) sent from the master. For more details, please refer to http://dev.mysql.com/doc/refman/5.1/en/set-global-sql-slave-skip-counter.html.

- The **Change or reconfigure master server** link could be used to specify that this slave server should now receive updates from a different master.

Obtaining replication information

Apart from the **Replication** menu, other screens in phpMyAdmin inform us about replication-related items. These screens are not found with the other replication dialogs; rather they are scattered on various pages, where they display replication information in the context of the respective pages.

Gathering replication status

By entering the **Status** panel in `Server` view, we first get a brief message, for example:

"This MySQL server works as master in replication process. For further information about replication status on the server, please visit the replication section."

There are a few **Replication** links on this page that show us the status variables of either the master or slave servers, and some links to get information about how many slave hosts are connected and the status of replication in general.

Replicated databases

On the master server, having a look at the **Databases** menu in `Server` view shows us that some databases can potentially be replicated, with a green checkmark in the **Master replication** column:

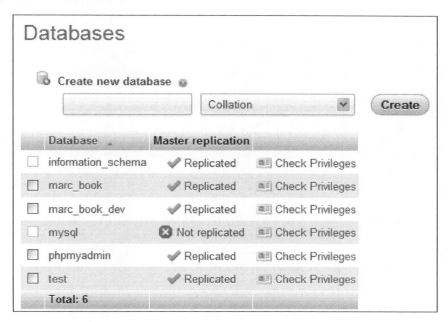

This is because this server is configured with a binary log and these databases are not excluded from replication.

As we have the following line of code in the [mysqld] section within the master's configuration file, we can exclude from the binary log all transactions that affect the mysql database:

```
binlog_ignore_db=mysql
```

Therefore, the output of the **Databases** page shows a red icon next to the mysql database.

If this is a slave server, a **Server replication** column is shown.

 Note that a slave server can itself have a binary log; therefore, in this case, both **Master replication** and **Slave replication** columns are shown. This means that this slave could in turn be a master server for another slave server.

Replicated tables

Let us suppose that on the master server, we create a table named employee in the test database. At this point, replication does its magic and we can have a look at the test database on a slave server:

Here, the **Replication** column is shown as a reminder. We should not modify this table on the slave server directly, because its existence is for replication purpose only. If we decide to alter it directly, our changes will be done only in this table, introducing inconsistencies between the master and this slave, which is not a good idea.

Summary

In this chapter, we learnt how to synchronize both the structure and data from one database to another, on the same server or on different servers. We covered the goals of synchronization and how to perform a complete or selective synchronization. We then examined how to use phpMyAdmin to guide us into replication setup, including a master and a slave server; how to prepare a test environment using the MySQL Sandbox, and how to control the slave servers.

The next chapter will show you how to keep permanent bookmarks of your queries.

14
Using Query Bookmarks

This chapter covers query bookmarks—one of the features of the phpMyAdmin configuration storage. Being able to label queries, and recall them by label, can be a real time saver. Bookmarks are queries that have the following properties:

- Stored permanently
- Viewable
- Erasable
- Related to one database
- Recorded only as a consequence of a user's action
- Labeled
- Private by default (only available to the user creating them) but possibly public

A bookmark can also have a variable part, as explained in the *Passing a parameter to a bookmark* section later in this chapter.

There is no bookmark page for managing bookmarks. Instead, the various actions for bookmarks are available on specific pages, such as results pages or query box pages.

Comparing bookmark and query history features

In *Chapter 11*, we learned about the SQL history feature, which automatically stores queries (temporarily or permanently). There are similarities between queries stored in the history and bookmarks. After all both features are intended to store queries for later execution. However, there are important differences regarding the way the queries are stored and the action that triggers the recording of a query.

Storing of queries in the history is automatic; whereas a query is saved as a bookmark via an explicit request from the user. Also, there is a configurable limit (refer to *Chapter 11*) on the number of queries stored in the permanent history; however, the number of bookmarks is not limited. Finally, the history feature presents the queries in the reverse order of the time they were sent. However, bookmarks are shown by label (not showing the query text directly).

To summarize, the automatic query history is useful when we neither plan to recall a query, nor wish to remember which queries we typed. This contrasts with the bookmark facility where we intentionally ask the system to remember a query, and even give it a name (label). Therefore, we can do more with bookmarks than with the query history, but both features have their own importance.

Creating bookmarks

There are two instances when it is possible to create a bookmark—after a query is executed (in which case we don't need to plan ahead for its creation), and before sending the query to the MySQL server for execution. Both of these options are explored in the following sections.

Creating a bookmark after a successful query

Initial bookmark creation is made possible by the **Bookmark this SQL query** button. This button appears only after executing a query that generates a result (when at least one row is found); so this method for creating bookmarks only stores SELECT statements. For example, a complex query produced by the multi-table query generator (as seen in *Chapter 12*) could be stored as a bookmark in this way, provided that it finds some results.

Let us see an example. In the **Search** page for the book table, we select the columns that we want in the results, and enter the search values as shown in the following screenshot:

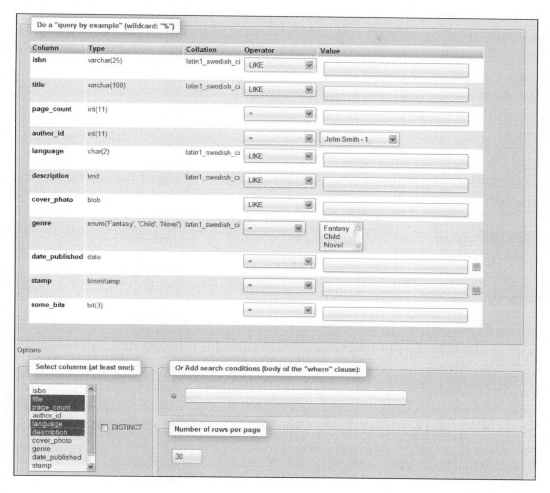

After clicking on **Go**, we see that the results page shows a bookmark dialog. We enter only a label, **books for author 1**, for this bookmark, and then click on **Bookmark this SQL query** to save this query as a bookmark. Bookmarks are saved in the table defined by `$cfg['Servers'][$i]['bookmarktable']`.

This bookmark dialog can be seen on any page that contains results. As a test, we could just click on **Browse** for a table to get results, and then store this query as a bookmark. However, it does not make much sense to store (in a bookmark) a query that can easily be made with one click.

Storing a bookmark before sending a query

We have seen that it's easy to create a bookmark after the execution of a SELECT statement that generates results. Sometimes, we may want to store a bookmark even if a query does not find any results. This may be the case if the data to which the query refers is not yet present, or if the query is a statement other than SELECT. To achieve this, we have the **Bookmark this SQL query** dialog available in the **SQL** tab of the Database view, Table view, and the Query window.

We now go to the **SQL** page of the book table, enter a query to retrieve French books, and directly put the **books in French** bookmark label in the **Bookmark this SQL query** dialog. If this bookmark label has been used previously, a new bookmark with the same name will be created, unless we check the **Replace existing bookmark of same name** checkbox. Bookmarks carry an internal identifying number, as well as a label chosen by the user.

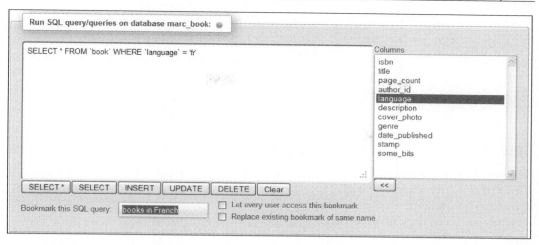

On clicking on **Go**, the query is executed and stored as a bookmark. It does not matter if the query does not find anything. This is how we can generate bookmarks for non-SELECT queries such as UPDATE, DELETE, CREATE TABLE, and so on.

 This technique can also be used for a SELECT statement that either returns results or does not return results.

Making bookmarks public

All bookmarks we create are private by default. When a bookmark is created, the username, which we are logged in as, is stored with the bookmark. Let us suppose that we check the **Let every user access this bookmark** checkbox as shown in the following screenshot:

This would have the following effect:

- All users having access to the same database (the current one) will have access to the bookmark.
- A user's ability to see meaningful results from the bookmark depends on the privileges they have on the tables referenced in the bookmark.

- Any user will be able to delete the bookmark.
- Users will be permitted to change the bookmark's query, by storing this bookmark before sending a query and using the **Replace existing bookmark of same name** option.

Public bookmarks are shown with a **(shared)** suffix when recalled.

The default initial query for a table

In the previous examples, we chose bookmark labels according to our preferences. However, by convention, if a private bookmark has the same name as a table, it will be executed when **Browse** is clicked for this table. Thus, instead of seeing the normal **Browse** results of this table, we will see the bookmark's results.

Suppose that we are interested in viewing (by default, in the **Browse** mode) all books with a page count lower than 300. We first generate the appropriate query, which can be done easily from the **Search** page, and then we use **book** as a bookmark label on the results page.

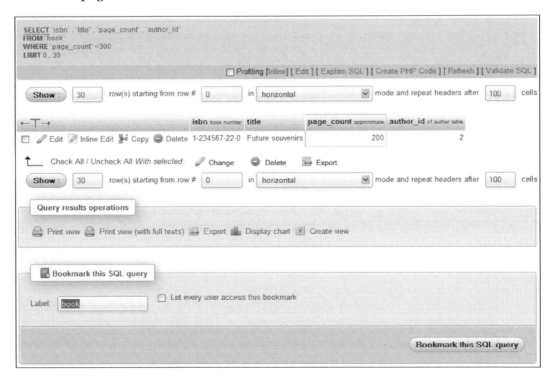

Following this action, every time the user, who created this bookmark, browses the book table, he sees the following screenshot:

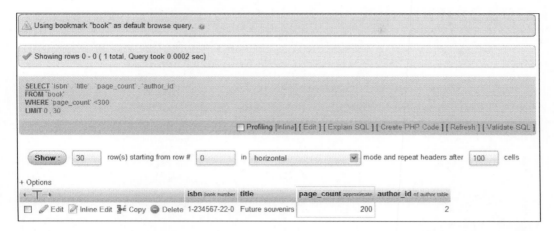

Multi-query bookmarks

A single bookmark can also store more than one query (separated by a semicolon). This is mostly useful for non-SELECT queries. As an example, let us assume that we need to clean data about authors by removing an invalid area code from the phone numbers on a regular basis. This operation would always be followed by a display of the author table.

To accomplish this goal, we store a bookmark (before sending it for execution) that contains these queries:

```
update author set phone = replace(phone,'(123)', '(456)');
select * from author;
```

In the bookmark, we could put many data modification statements such as INSERT, UPDATE, or DELETE, followed optionally by one SELECT statement. Stacking a lot of SELECT statements would not yield the intended result because we would only see the data fetched by the last SELECT statement.

Recalling bookmarks from the bookmarks list

Any created bookmarks can be found on the following pages:

- The Table view: **SQL** page of any table from **marc_book**
- The Query window: The **SQL-History** tab
- The Database view: **SQL** page of the **marc_book** database

Three choices are available when recalling a bookmark—**Submit**, **View only**, and **Delete**. (**Submit** being the default).

Executing bookmarks

Choosing a bookmark and hitting **Go** executes the stored query and displays its results. The page resulting from a bookmark execution does not have another dialog to create a bookmark, as this would be superfluous.

 The results we get are not necessarily the same as when we created the bookmark. They reflect the current contents of the database. Only the query is stored as a bookmark.

Manipulating bookmarks

Sometimes, we may just want to ascertain the contents of a bookmark. This is done by choosing a bookmark and selecting **View only**. The query is then displayed and we have the opportunity of reworking its contents. By doing so, we would be editing a copy of the original bookmarked query. To keep this new, edited query, we can save it as a bookmark. Again, this will create another bookmark even if we choose the same bookmark label, unless we explicitly ask for the original bookmark to be replaced.

A bookmark can be erased with the **Delete** option. There is no confirmation dialog to confirm the deletion of the bookmark. We should now proceed with the deletion of our **book** bookmark.

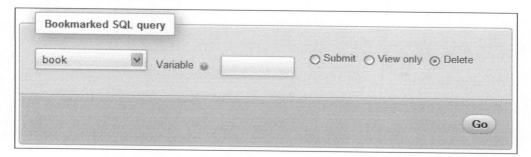

Passing a parameter to a bookmark

If we look again at the first bookmark we created (finding all books for **author 1**), we realize that although it's useful, it's limited to finding just one author—always the same one.

Special query syntax enables the passing of parameters to bookmarks. This syntax uses the fact that SQL comments enclosed within /* and */ are ignored by MySQL. If the /* [VARIABLE] */ construct exists somewhere in the query, it will be expanded at execution time with the value provided when recalling the bookmark.

Creating a parameterized bookmark

Let us say we want to find all the books for a given author when we don't know the author's id. We first enter the following query:

```
SELECT author.name, author.id, book.title
FROM book, author
WHERE book.author_id = author.id
/* AND author.name LIKE '%[VARIABLE]%' */
```

The part between the comment characters (/* */) will be expanded later, and the tags will be removed. We label this query as a bookmark named **find author by name** (before executing it) and then click on **Go**. The first execution of the query just stores the bookmark while retrieving all books by all the authors, as this time we haven't passed a parameter to the query.

In this example, we have two conditions in the WHERE clause, of which one contains the special syntax. If our only criterion in the WHERE clause needs a parameter, we can use a syntax such as /* WHERE author_id = [VARIABLE] */.

Passing the parameter value

To test the bookmark, we recall it as usual and enter a value in the **Variable** dialog.

When we click on **Go**, we see the expanded query, and the author Smith's books.

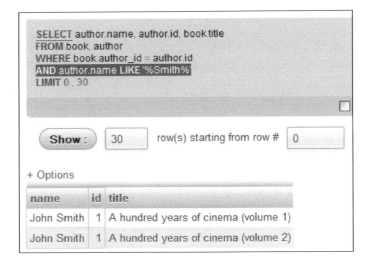

Summary

In this chapter, we saw an overview of how to record bookmarks (after or before sending a query), how to manipulate them, and how some bookmarks can be made public. The chapter also introduced us to the default initial query for **Browse** mode. It also covered passing parameters to bookmarks.

The next chapter will explain how to produce documentation that explains the structure of your databases via the tools offered by phpMyAdmin.

15
Documenting the System

Producing and maintaining good documentation about data structure is crucial for a project's success, especially when it's a team project. Indeed, being able to show the current data dictionary and proposed column changes to the other team members provides a valuable means of communication. Moreover, a graphical display of the inter-table relations quickly demonstrates the inner workings of the database. Fortunately, phpMyAdmin has documentation features that take care of these things.

Producing structure reports

From the **Structure** page of either the `Database` or the `Table` view, the **Print view** link is available for producing reports about our database's structure. Moreover, a **Data Dictionary** link in `Database` view produces a different report. These are detailed in the following sections.

Creating a printable report

When phpMyAdmin generates results, there is always a **Print view** link that can be used to generate a printable report of the data. The **Print view** feature can also be used to produce basic structure documentation. This is done in two steps. The first click on **Print view** displays a report on the screen, with a **Print** button at the end of the page. This **Print** button later generates a report formatted for the printer.

The database print view

Clicking on **Print view** on the **Structure** page for a database generates a list of tables. This list contains the number of rows, storage engine, size, comments, and the creation date for each table, as shown in the following screenshot:

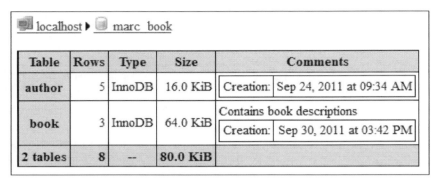

The selective database print view

Sometimes, we prefer to get a report for a subset of the tables. This can be done from the **Structure** page for a database by selecting the tables we want, and then choosing **Print view** from the drop-down menu as shown in the following screenshot:

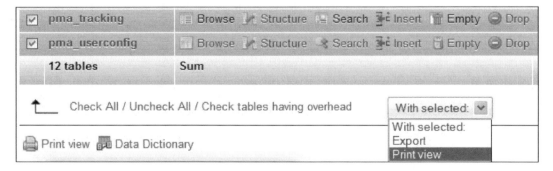

The table print view

There is also a **Print view** link on the **Structure** page for each table. Clicking on this link produces information about columns and indexes for the table, as shown in the following example:

book

Table comments: Contains book descriptions

Column	Type	Null	Default	Comments	MIME
isbn	varchar(25)	No		book number	
title	varchar(100)	No			
page_count	int(11)	No		approximate	
author_id	int(11)	No		cf author table	
language	char(2)	No	en		
description	text	No			
cover_photo	longblob	No			
genre	enum('Fantasy', 'Child', 'Novel')	No	Fantasy		
date_published	datetime	No			
stamp	timestamp	No	0000-00-00 00:00:00		
some_bits	bit(3)	No			

Indexes: ●

Keyname	Type	Unique	Packed	Column	Cardinality	Collation	Null	Comment
PRIMARY	BTREE	Yes	No	isbn	2	A		
by_title	BTREE	No	No	title (30)	2	A		
isbn	BTREE	No	No	isbn	2	A		
author_id	BTREE	No	No	author_id	2	A		

Preparing a complete report with the data dictionary

A more complete report about the tables and columns in a database is available from the **Structure** page of the `Database` view. We just have to click on **Data dictionary** link to get this report, which is partially shown in the following screenshot:

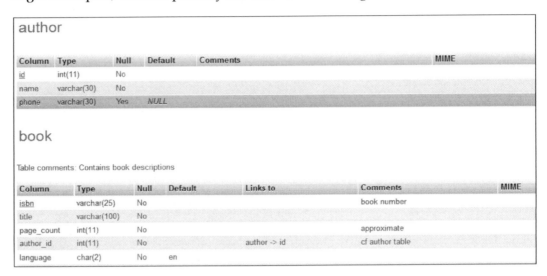

The **MIME** column is empty until we add MIME-related information to some columns (as explained in *Chapter 16*).

Generating relational schemas

In *Chapter 10*, we defined relations between the `book` and `author` tables. These relations were used for various foreign key functions (for example, getting a list of possible values in **Insert** mode). We will now examine a feature that enables us to generate a custom-made relational schema for our tables in the popular PDF format and other formats as well. This feature requires that the phpMyAdmin configuration storage be properly installed and configured.

Adding a third table to our model

To get a more complete schema, we will now add another table, country, to our database. The following block of code displays the contents of its export file:

```
CREATE TABLE IF NOT EXISTS `country` (
  `code` char(2) NOT NULL,
  `description` varchar(50) NOT NULL,
  PRIMARY KEY (`code`)
) ENGINE=MyISAM DEFAULT CHARSET=latin1;

INSERT INTO `country` (`code`, `description`) VALUES
('ca', 'Canada'),
('uk', 'United Kingdom');
```

We will now link this table to the author table. First, in the **Relation view** for the country table, we specify the column that we want to display, and then click on **Save**.

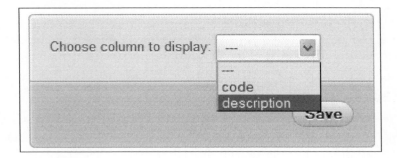

We then add a **country_code** column (same type and size as that of the code column in the country table) to the author table, and in the **Relation view**, we link it to the newly-created country table.

 We must remember to click on **Save** for the relation to be recorded.

For this example, it's not necessary to enter any country data for an author, as we are interested only in the relational schema.

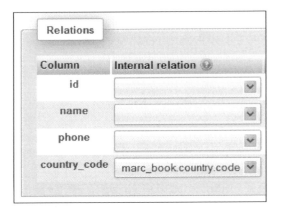

Producing schema pages

Each relational schema is called a **page**. We can create or edit a page by clicking on **Edit or export relational schema** in the **Operations** page of the `Database` view.

Page planning

A relational schema cannot span multiple databases. But even working with just one database, the number of tables might be large. Representing the various table relations in a clear way could be a challenge. This is why we may use many pages, each showing some tables and their relations.

We must also take into account the dimensions of the final output. Printing on letter-size paper gives us less space to show all of our tables and still have a legible schema.

Creating a new page

As there are no existing pages, we need to create one. As our most important table is `book`, we will also name this page **book**.

We will choose which tables we wish to see in the relational schema. We could choose each table individually. However, for a good start, checking the appropriate **Automatic layout** checkbox is recommended. Doing this puts all the related tables from our database onto the list of tables to be included in the schema. It then generates appropriate coordinates so that the tables will appear in a spiral layout, starting from the center of the schema. These coordinates are expressed in millimeters, with (0, 0) being located at the upper-left corner. We then click on **Go**:

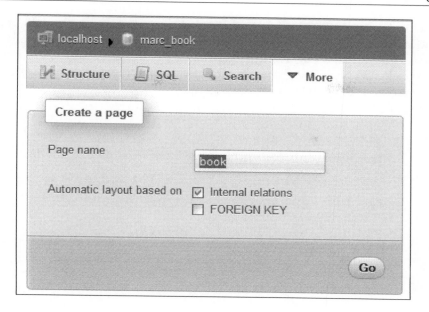

Editing a page

We now get a page with three different sections. The first one is the page menu, where we choose the page on which we want to work (from the drop-down menu). We can also delete the chosen page. We could also eventually create a second schema (page).

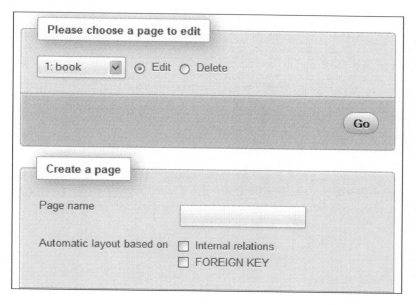

The next section is the table placement portion. We can now see the benefit of the **Automatic layout** feature — we already have our three tables selected, with the **X** and **Y** coordinate columns filled in. We can add a table (on the last line), delete a table (using the checkbox), and change the coordinates (which represent the position of the upper-left corner of each table on the schema):

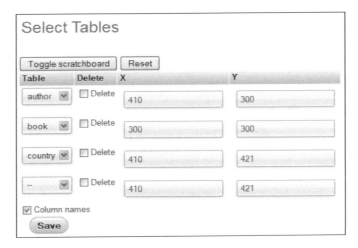

To help set exact coordinates, a visual editor is available for JavaScript-enabled browsers. The editor appears when the **Toggle scratchboard** button is clicked once. It will disappear when this button is clicked again. We can drag and drop tables on the scratchboard, and the coordinates will change accordingly. The appearance of the tables on the scratchboard provides a rough guide to the final PDF output. Some people prefer to see only the table names (without every column name) on the scratchboard. This can be done by deselecting the **Column names** checkbox and then clicking on **Save**. The following image shows an example of this scratchboard:

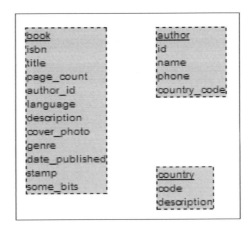

When we are satisfied with the layout, we must click on **Save**.

Exporting a page for display

The last section of the screen is the report generation dialog. Now that we have created a page, the **Display relational schema** shows a dialog as seen in the following screenshot:

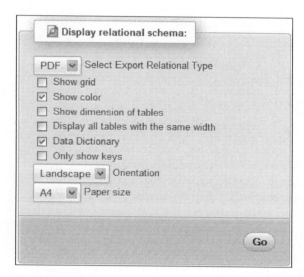

The available options are:

Option	Description
Select Export Relational Type	Permits to choose the file format to export to (PDF, SVG, DIA, Visio, or EPS).
Show grid	The schema will have a grid layer with the coordinates displayed. Useful when designing and testing the schema.
Show color	The links, table names, and special columns (primary keys and display columns) will be in color.
Show dimension of tables	The visual dimension of each table in the table title (for example, **32x30**) will be displayed. This is useful when designing and testing the schema.
Display all tables with the same width	All tables will be displayed using the same width. (Normally, the width adjusts itself according to the length of the table and column names.)

Option	Description
Data Dictionary	The data dictionary, which was covered earlier in this chapter, will be included at the beginning of the report.
Only show keys	Does not show the columns on which there are no indexes defined.
Orientation	Here, we choose the printed orientation of the report
Paper size	Changing this option will influence the schema and the scratchboard dimensions.

In `config.inc.php`, the following parameters define the available paper sizes and the default choice:

```
$cfg['PDFPageSizes'] = array('A3', 'A4', 'A5', 'letter', 'legal');
$cfg['PDFDefaultPageSize']   = 'A4';
```

The following screenshot shows the last page of the generated report (the schema page) in PDF format. The first four pages contain the data dictionary along with an additional feature.

Arrows point in the direction of the corresponding foreign table. If **Show color** checkbox has been ticked, the primary keys are shown in red and the display columns in blue, as shown in the following screenshot:

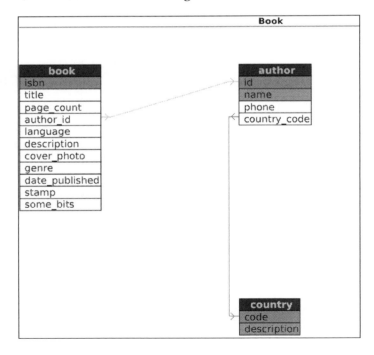

The following screenshot provides another example generated from the same book table's PDF page definition. This time the grid is shown, but not the colors:

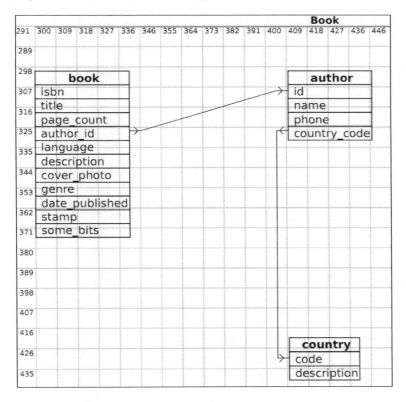

Changing the font in PDF schema

All the text we see in the PDF schema is drawn using a specific font. phpMyAdmin uses the DejaVuSans font (http://dejavu.sourceforge.net), which covers a wide range of characters.

For actual PDF generation, phpMyAdmin relies on the tcpdf library (http://tcpdf.sourceforge.net). This library has two ways of using fonts— embedded and not embedded. Embedding fonts will produce a bigger PDF file because the whole font is included in the PDF file. This is the default option chosen by phpMyAdmin because the library does not depend on the presence of a specific TrueType font in the client operating system.

The fonts are located in libraries/tcpdf/fonts under the main phpMyAdmin directory.

To use a different font file, we must first add it to the library (tools are present in the original `tcpdf` kit and a tutorial is available on the `http://www.fpdf.org` website) and then modify phpMyAdmin's `libraries/schema/ Pdf_Relation_Schema. class.php` source code.

Laying out a schema with the Designer feature

The **Designer** feature (available in the `Database` view) offers a more refined way of moving the tables on screen, as the column links follow the table movements. Therefore, an interface exists between the tables' coordinates, as saved by the **Designer**, and the coordinates for the schema. Let us enter the **Designer** and click on the small PDF logo.

This brings us to a panel where we can choose the (existing) schema name and the action we want to perform—in our case, to export the **Designer** coordinates to the schema definition. We could also use the **New page name** dialog, entering a page name, and then clicking on **Go** to create an empty page. From here, we can subsequently export the coordinates saved from the **Designer** workspace:

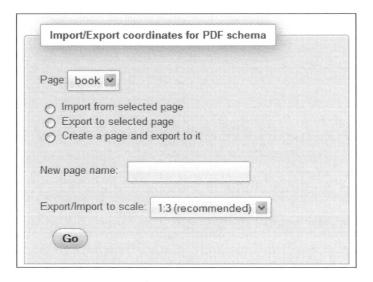

 There is a difference in the span of tables managed by the **Designer** and by the **Edit or export relational schema** feature. The **Designer** manipulates, by default, every table of a database, whereas the **Edit or export relational schema** panel offers us a choice of tables, enabling us to represent a subset of the relations if there are many tables.

Summary

This chapter covered the documentation features offered by phpMyAdmin—the print view for a database or a table and the data dictionary for a complete column list. The chapter also covered relational schemas. In particular, it focused on how to create, modify, and export a schema page, and how to use the visual editor (scratchboard).

The next chapter will explain how to apply transformations to data, in order to customize the data format at view time.

16
Transforming Data using MIME

In this chapter, we will cover a powerful phpMyAdmin feature—its ability to transform a column's contents during a table browse, based on specific rules called transformations. Normally, browsing a table shows only the original data that resides in it. However, MIME-based transformations permit the alteration of the display format.

Note that this kind of transformation does not have the same effect as a permanent data change, such as one made via the UPDATE statement. The transformed data is not written back to the MySQL server; it is just sent to the browser for display purposes.

Browsing data without transformations

Normally, the exact contents of each row are displayed, except that:

- The **TEXT** and **CHARACTER** columns might be truncated, according to $cfg['LimitChars'], and depending on whether we have chosen to see **Full Texts** or not

- **BLOB** and geometry-related columns might be replaced by a message such as **[BLOB - 1.5 KB]**

We will use the term **cell** to indicate a specific column of a specific row. The cell containing the cover photograph for the "Future souvenirs" book (a **BLOB** column) is currently displayed as cryptic data such as **‰PNG\r\n\Z\n\0\0\0\rIHDR\0** or as a message stating the **BLOB** column's size. It would be interesting to see a thumbnail (shown in the following screenshot) of the picture directly in phpMyAdmin and possibly the full-size picture itself. This will be made possible with proper transformation.

isbn book number	title	page_count approximate	author_id cf author table	language	description	cover_photo
1-234567-22-0	Future souvenirs	200	2	en		

Switching display options

In **Browse** mode, the **Options** link reveals a slider that contains, among other choices, a **Hide Browser transformation** checkbox. We can use it whenever we want to switch between viewing the real data of a cell and its transformed version.

Enabling transformations

We define **transformation** as a mechanism by which all the cells related to a column are transformed at browse time, using the metadata defined for this column. Only the cells visible on the current results page are transformed.

The use of this feature is controlled by the `$cfg['BrowseMIME']` directive in `config.inc.php`. The default value of this directive is TRUE, meaning that transformations are enabled. However, the phpMyAdmin configuration storage must be in place (refer to *Chapter 1*) as the metadata necessary for the transformation is not available in the official MySQL table structure. It's an addition made especially for phpMyAdmin.

The transformation logic itself is coded in PHP scripts, stored in `libraries/transformations`, and is called using a plugin architecture. In the documentation section on phpMyAdmin's home site (currently at `http://www.phpmyadmin.net/ home_page/docs.php`), there is a link pointing to additional information for developers who would like to learn the internal structure of the plugins in order to code their own transformation.

Configuring settings for MIME columns

If we go to the `Table` view of the **Structure** page for the `book` table and click on the **Change** link for the **cover_photo** column, we see three additional attributes (provided the transformations feature is enabled):

- **MIME type**
- **Browser transformation**
- **Transformation options**

This is shown in the following screenshot:

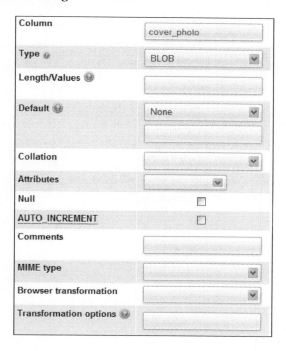

For a specific column, it's possible to indicate only one type of transformation. Here, the column is a **BLOB**. Hence, it can hold any kind of data. In order for phpMyAdmin to interpret and act correctly on the data, the transformation system must be informed of the data format and the intended results. Accordingly, we have to ensure that we upload data that always follows the same file format.

We will first learn the purpose of these attributes and then try some possibilities in the *Examples of transformation* section, later in this chapter.

Selecting the MIME type

The MIME specification (http://en.wikipedia.org/wiki/MIME) has been chosen as a metadata attribute to categorize the kind of data that a column holds. **Multipurpose Internet Mail Extensions (MIME)**, originally designed to extend mail, are now used to describe content types for other protocols as well. In the context of phpMyAdmin, the current possible values are:

- **image/jpeg**
- **image/png**
- **text/plain**
- **application/octetstream**

The **text/plain** type can be chosen for a column containing any kind of text (for example, XHTML or XML text). In the *Examples of transformations* section, you will see which MIME type you are required to choose to achieve a specific effect.

Browser transformations

This is where we set the exact transformation to be done. More than one transformation may be supported per MIME type. For example, for the **image/jpeg** MIME type, we have two transformations available: **image/jpeg: inline** for a clickable thumbnail of the image, and **image/jpeg: link** to display just a link.

The following screenshot shows the list of the available transformations:

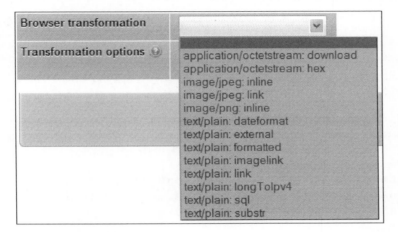

A more complete transformation explanation and a list of the possible options are available on clicking the question mark icon next to **Transformation options**, and then clicking on the **transformation descriptions** link that appears.

Assigning values to transformation options

In the *Examples of transformations* section, we will see that some transformations accept options. For example, we can indicate the width and height in pixels for a transformation that generates an image. A comma is used to separate the values in the options list, and some options may need to be enclosed within quotes.

Some options have a default value, and we must be careful to respect the documented order for options. For example, if there are two options, and we only want to specify a value for the second option, we can use empty quotes as a placeholder for the first option, to let the system use its default value.

Requirements for image generation

Normal thumbnail generation requires that some components exist on the web server, and that a parameter in `config.inc.php` be correctly configured.

Configuring GD2 library availability verification

phpMyAdmin uses some internal functions to create the thumbnails. These functions need the GD2 library to be present on our PHP server.

phpMyAdmin can detect the presence of the correct GD2 library, but this detection takes some time. It also takes place not once per session, but almost every time an action is taken in phpMyAdmin.

Setting the `$cfg['GD2Available']` parameter in `config.inc.php` to its default value `'auto'` indicates that the detection of the library's presence and version is needed.

If we know that the GD2 library is available, setting `$cfg['GD2Available']` to `yes` will make execution quicker. If the GD2 library is not available, you are recommended to set this parameter to `no`.

To find out which GD2 library we have on the server, we can go to phpMyAdmin's home page and click on **Show PHP information**. If this link is not present, we need to set the `$cfg['ShowPhpInfo']` parameter to `true`. We then look for a section titled **gd** and verify which version is identified. In the following screenshot, all is fine as we can see that the GD version is 2.X with JPEG and PNG support:

gd	
GD Support	enabled
GD Version	bundled (2.0.34 compatible)
FreeType Support	enabled
FreeType Linkage	with freetype
FreeType Version	2.3.12
GIF Read Support	enabled
GIF Create Support	enabled
JPEG Support	enabled
libJPEG Version	8
PNG Support	enabled
libPNG Version	1.2.43
WBMP Support	enabled
XBM Support	enabled

Asserting support of JPEG and PNG libraries

The PHP component in our web server needs to have support for the JPEG and PNG images if we want to generate thumbnails for these types of images. For more details, please refer to `http://php.net/manual/en/ref.image.php`.

Evaluating the impact of memory limits

On some servers, the default value in `php.ini` for `memory_limit` is 8M, meaning 8 MiB. This is too low for correct image manipulation, because the GD functions used to produce the final images need working memory. For example, in one test, a value of 11M in `memory_limit` was needed to generate the thumbnail from a 300 KiB JPEG image. Also, if multiple rows are viewed at once, more working memory will be needed.

Examples of transformations

We will now discuss a few transformation examples. Typical option values are shown, and it's recommended to tweak them until we have achieved the desired results. Depending on the phpMyAdmin version, more transformations may be available.

Clickable thumbnail (JPEG or PNG)

We will start by changing our **cover_photo** column type from **BLOB** to **LONGBLOB** to ensure that we can upload photographs bigger than 65 KiB in size. We then enter the attributes shown in the following screenshot:

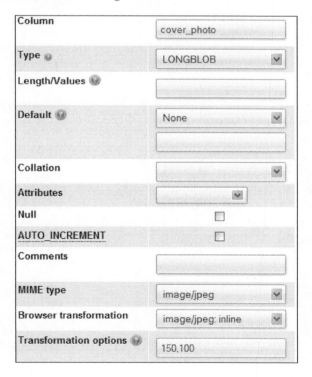

Here, the options are presented in the form of width and height. If we omit the options, the default values are 100 and 100. The thumbnail generation code preserves the original aspect ratio of the image. Therefore, the values entered are the maximum width and height of the generated image. We then upload a .jpeg file in a cell (using instructions from *Chapter 5*). As a result, we get the following screen in **Browse** mode for this table:

isbn book number	title	page_count approximate	author_id cf author table	language	description	cover_photo
1-234567-22-0	Future souvenirs	200	2	en		

This thumbnail can be clicked to reveal a full-size photograph.

> The thumbnail is not stored anywhere, but generated each time we go into **Browse** mode for this set of rows. On a double Xeon 3.2 GHz server, we commonly experience a generation rate of six JPEG images per second. No caching of these thumbnails is offered by phpMyAdmin.

For a .png file, we have to use **image/png** in the **MIME type** dialog, and **image/png: inline** in the **Browse transformation** dialog.

Adding links to an image

To provide a link without the thumbnail, we use the **image/jpeg: link** transformation. There are no transformation options. This link can be used to view the photograph (by left-clicking on the link) and then possibly download it (by right-clicking on the photograph itself).

isbn book number	title	page_count approximate	author_id cf author table	language	description	cover_photo
1-234567-22-0	Future souvenirs	200	2	en		[BLOB]

Date formatting

We have a column named **date_published** in our book table; let us change its type to **DATETIME**. Then, we set its MIME type to **text/plain** and the browser transformation to **text/plain: dateformat**. The next step is to edit the row for the "Future souvenirs" book, and enter **2003-01-01 14:56:00** in the **date_published** column. When we browse the table, we now see that the column has been formatted. Hovering the mouse over it reveals the unformatted original contents, as shown in the following screenshot:

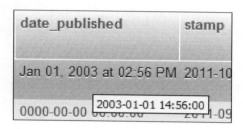

This transformation accepts two options. The first is the number of hours (zero by default) that will be added to the original value. Adding number of hours can be useful if we store all time values based on **Coordinated Universal Time (UTC)**, but want to display them for a specific zone (for example, UTC+5). The second option is the time format we want to use, specified using any PHP `strftime` parameters (more details at `http://php.net/strftime`). So, if we put **'0','Year: %Y'** in the **Transformation options**, we will get the following output:

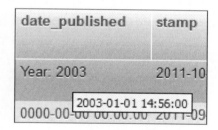

Links from text

Suppose that we have put a complete URL—`http://domain.com/abc.pdf`—in the **description** column in our book table. The text of the link will be displayed while browsing the table, but we would not be able to click it. We will now see the use of the **text/plain** MIME type in such a situation.

text/plain: link

If we use a **text/plain** MIME type and a **text/plain: link** browser transformation in the scenario just mentioned, we will still see the text for the link, and it will be clickable.

isbn book number	title	page_count approximate	author_id cf author table	language	description
1-234567-22-0	Future souvenirs	200	2	en	http://domain.com /abc.pdf

If all the documents that we want to point to are located at a common URL prefix, we can put this prefix (for example, `http://domain.com/`) in the first transformation option, within the enclosing quotes. Then, we would only need to put the last part of the URL (`abc.pdf`) in each cell.

A second transformation option is available for setting a title. This would be displayed in the **Browse** mode instead of the URL contents, but a click would nonetheless bring us to the intended URL.

If we use only the second transformation option, we have to use quotes as the value of the first option. It could be done as `''`,`'this is the title'`.

text/plain: imagelink

text/plain: imagelink transformation is similar to the previous one, except that in the cell, we place a URL that points to an image. This image will be fetched and displayed in the cell along with the link text. The image could be anywhere on the web, including our local server.

Here, we have the following three options available:

- The common URL prefix (such as the one for `text/plain: link`)
- The width of the image in pixels (default: 100)
- The height (default: 50)

For our test URL, you should enter the following options:

```
'','100','123'
```

If the text for the link is too long, the transformation does not occur. By default, the **Partial texts** display option is selected.

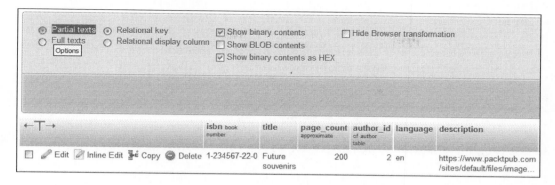

In this case, we can switch to **Full texts** to reveal the complete link. We can then see the complete image.

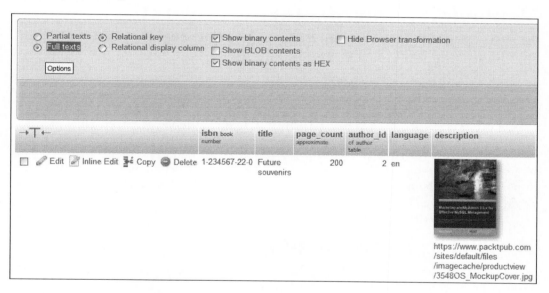

Other transformations, such as image/jpeg: inline and image/png: inline, specify the exact MIME type of the image. In these cases, phpMyAdmin uses GD2 library functions for the thumbnail generation. However, the link contained in a text/plain: imagelink transformation may refer to any browser-supported image type. Therefore, phpMyAdmin just displays a resized image with an HTML img tag, and width and height attributes set according to the size options defined in the transformation. To see the original image, we can click on either the link or the thumbnail.

Preserving the original formatting

Normally, when displaying text, phpMyAdmin escapes special characters. For example, if we entered **This book is good** in the **description** column for one book, we would normally see **This book is good** when browsing the table. However, if we used the transformation **text/plain: formatted** for this column, we would get the following output while browsing:

This book is **good**

In this example, the results are correct. However, other HTML tags entered in the column could produce surprising results (including invalid HTML pages). For example, as phpMyAdmin presents results using HTML tables, a non-escaped `</table>` tag in the column would ruin the output.

Displaying parts of a text

The `text/plain: substr` transformation is available for displaying only a portion of the text. The following are the options:

- Where to start in the text (default: 0)
- How many characters (default: all of the remaining text)
- What to display as a suffix to show that truncation has occurred; the default is to display ellipses (...)

Remember that `$cfg['LimitChars']` is doing a character truncation for every non-numeric column. Hence, `text/plain: substr` is a mechanism for fine-tuning this column by column.

Displaying a download link

Let us say we want to store a small audio comment about each book inside MySQL. We add a new column to the `book` table, with the name **audio_contents**, and type **MEDIUMBLOB**. We set its **MIME type** to **application/octetstream** and choose the **application/octetstream: download** transformation. In the **Transformation options**, we insert **'comment.wav'**.

This MIME type and extension will inform our browser about the incoming data, and the browser should open the appropriate player. To insert a comment, we first record it in a `.wav` format, and then upload the contents of the file into the **audio_contents** column for one of the books. When browsing our table, we can see a link **comment.wav** for our audio comment:

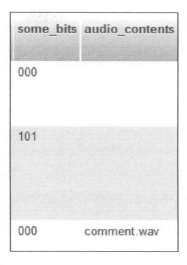

some_bits	audio_contents
000	
101	
000	comment.wav

Hexadecimal representation

Characters are stored in MySQL (and in computers in general) as numeric data, and converted into something meaningful for the screen or printer. Users sometimes cut and paste data from another application to phpMyAdmin, leading to unexpected results if the characters are not directly supported by MySQL. A case that was reported in phpMyAdmin's help forum involved special quotation marks entered in a Microsoft Word document and pasted to phpMyAdmin. It helps to be able to see the exact hexadecimal codes, and this can be done by using the `application/octetstream: hex` transformation.

In the following example, this transformation will be applied to the **title** column of our `book` table. When browsing the row containing the **Future souvenirs** title, we can see the following screen:

isbn book number	title
1-234567-22-0	46 75 74 75 72 65 20 73 6f 75 76 65 6e 69 72 73

As we know which character set this column is encoded with, we can compare its contents with a chart describing each character. For instance, http://en.wikipedia.org/wiki/Latin1 describes the Latin1 character set.

SQL pretty printing

The term **pretty printing** (http://en.wikipedia.org/wiki/Pretty_printing) refers to a way of "beautifying" source code (in our case, SQL statements). In the phpMyAdmin configuration storage, the pma_bookmark.query and pma_history.sqlquery columns contain SQL statements. With the text/plain: sql transformation defined for these columns, these SQL statements will be displayed in color with syntax highlighting when the table is browsed.

IP address

An IP (v4) address can be encoded into a long integer (for example, via the PHP iptolong() function), and stored into a MySQL UNSIGNED INT column. To convert it back to the familiar dotted string (for example, 127.0.0.1), you can use the text/plain: longToIpv4 transformation.

Transforming data via external applications

The transformations that have been described previously are implemented directly from within phpMyAdmin. However, some transformations are better executed via existing external applications.

The text/plain: external transformation enables us to send a cell's data to another application that will be started on the web server, capture this application's output, and display this output in the cell's position.

 This feature is supported only on a Linux or UNIX server (under Microsoft Windows, output and error redirection cannot be easily captured by the PHP process). Furthermore, PHP should not be running in safe mode. Hence, the feature may not be available on hosted servers.

For security reasons, the exact path and name of the application cannot be set from within phpMyAdmin as a transformation option. The application names are set directly inside one of the phpMyAdmin scripts.

First, in the phpMyAdmin installation directory, we edit the text_plain__external.inc.php file in libraries/transformations/, and find the following section:

```
$allowed_programs        = array();
//$allowed_programs[0] = '/usr/local/bin/tidy';
//$allowed_programs[1] = '/usr/local/bin/validate';
```

No external application is configured by default, and we have to explicitly add our own.

 The names of the transformation scripts are constructed using the following format—the MIME type, a double underscore, and then a part indicating which transformation should take place.

Every program that is allowed, along with its complete path, must be described here with an index number starting from 0. Then we save the modifications to this script and put it back on the server if needed. The remaining setup is completed from the panel where we choose the options for the other browser transformations.

Of course, we will now choose **text/plain: external** in the transformations menu.

As the first option, we place the application number (for example, 0 would be for the tidy application). The second option holds the parameters we need to pass to this application. If we want phpMyAdmin to apply the `htmlspecialchars()` function to the results, we put **1** as the third parameter—this is the default. We could put a **0** there to avoid protecting the output with `htmlspecialchars()`.

If we want to avoid reformatting the cell's lines, we put **1** as the fourth parameter. This will use the NOWRAP modifier, and is done by default.

External application example: In-cell sort

This example shows how to sort the text contents of a single cell. We start by modifying the `text_plain__external.inc.php` script, as mentioned in the previous section, to add the sort program:

```
$allowed_programs[0] = '/bin/sort';
```

Note that our new program bears the index number 0.

We then add a **TEXT** column whose name is **keywords** to our book table. Finally, we fill in the MIME-related information, entering **'0','-r'** as the transformation options, as shown in the following screenshot:

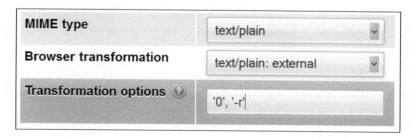

The **'0'** here refers to the index number for sort, and the **'-r'** is a parameter for sort, which makes the program sort in the reverse order.

Next, we edit the row for the book "A hundred years of cinema (volume 1)", entering some keywords in no particular order (as seen in the following screenshot) and hitting **Go** in order to save the changes:

To test the effects of the external program, we browse our table and see the sorted in-cell keywords:

Notice that the keywords are displayed in reverse sorted order.

Summary

In this chapter, we learnt how to improve the browsing experience by transforming data using various methods. In particular, we saw how to display an overview of thumbnail and full-size images from .jpeg and .png **BLOB** columns, how to generate links, format dates, display only parts of texts, and how to execute external programs to reformat cell contents.

The next chapter will cover phpMyAdmin's support for the MySQL features that are new in versions 5.0 and 5.1.

17
Supporting Features Added in MySQL 5

MySQL 5.0 introduced a number of new features that calmed down a number of developers and industry observers who were claiming that MySQL was inferior to competitors' products. Views, stored procedures, triggers, a standard information_schema, and (more recently) a profiling mechanism are now present in the MySQL spectrum. These features are covered in this chapter.

Among the new features of MySQL 5.1, the ones that relate to a web interface (for example, partitioning and events) are supported in phpMyAdmin and are covered in this chapter as well.

Supporting views

MySQL 5.0 introduced support for named and updatable views (more details are available at http://dev.mysql.com/doc/refman/5.5/en/views.html). A view is a derived table (consider it a virtual table) whose definition is stored in the database. A SELECT statement done on one or more tables (or even on views), can be stored as a view and can also be queried.

Views can be used to:

- Limit the visibility of columns (for example, do not show salary information)
- Limit the visibility of rows (for example, do not show data for specific world regions)
- Hide a changed table structure (so that legacy applications can continue to work)

Instead of defining cumbersome column-specific privileges on many tables, it's easier to prepare a view containing a limited set of columns from these tables. We can then grant permissions on the view as a whole.

To activate support for views on a server after an upgrade from a pre-5.0 version, the administrator has to execute the `mysql_upgrade` program, as described in the MySQL manual (`http://dev.mysql.com/doc/refman/5.0/en/upgrading-from-previous-series.html`).

 Each user must have the appropriate SHOW_VIEW or CREATE_VIEW privilege to be able to see or manipulate views. These privileges exist at the global (server), database, and table levels.

Creating a view implies that the user has privileges on the tables involved, or at least a privilege such as SELECT or UPDATE on all the columns mentioned in the view.

Creating a view from results

We can take advantage of phpMyAdmin's **Search** (at the table level) or **Query** (at the database level) features to build a rather complex query, execute it, and then easily create a view from the results. We will see how this is done.

We mentioned that a view can be used to limit the visibility of columns (and, in fact, of tables). Let us say that the number of pages in a book is highly classified information. We open the `book` table, click on **Search**, and choose a subset of the columns that does not include the **page_count** column (we might have to open the **Options** slider).

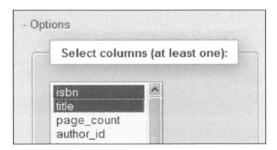

Clicking on **Go** produces a results page, where we see a **CREATE VIEW** link in the **Query results operations** section. We use this link to access the view creation panel, which already has the underlying query in the **AS** box. We need to choose a name for this view (here, we use **book_public_info**), and we can optionally set different column names for it (here, we use **number, title**), as shown in the following screenshot:

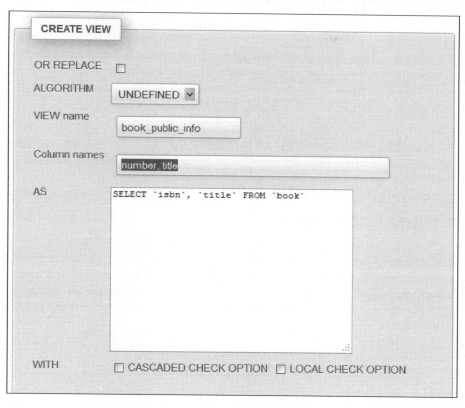

The other options can influence the view's behavior, and have been explained in the MySQL manual (http://dev.mysql.com/doc/refman/5.5/en/create-view.html). The LOCAL CHECK OPTION clause influences the behavior of the updateable views (this is explained in the MySQL manual at the page cited previously).

Clicking on **Go** generates the view we asked for. At this point, the view has been created. If we refresh our browser's page and then access the `marc_book` database, we will see the following screenshot:

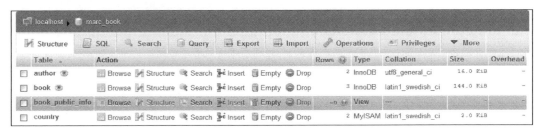

In the main panel, we see the information on the newly-created view. The number of rows for the view currently indicates **~0** (more on this in the *Controlling row counting for improved performance* section, later in this chapter), and **View** is indicated in the **Type** column. There is no collation or size associated with a view.

Main panel and views

As a view has similarities with a table, its name is available along with the names of the ordinary tables. On clicking the view name, a panel similar to the one seen for tables is displayed, but with fewer menu tabs than seen in a normal table. Indeed, some operations do not make sense on a view, for example, **Import**. This is because a view does not actually contain data. However, other actions, such as **Browse**, are perfectly acceptable.

Let us browse the view shown in the following screenshot:

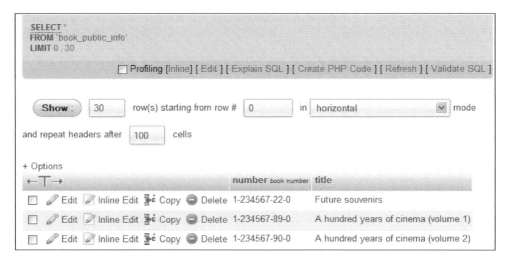

We notice that, in the generated SQL query, we do not see our original CREATE VIEW statement. The reason is that we are selecting from the view using a SELECT statement, hiding the fact that we are pulling data from a view. However, exporting the view's structure would show how MySQL internally stored our view:

```
CREATE ALGORITHM=UNDEFINED DEFINER=`root`@`%` SQL SECURITY DEFINER
   VIEW `book_public_info` AS
select `book`.`isbn` AS `number`,`book`.`title` AS `title` from
   `book`;
```

The main panel's menu may look similar to that of a table. However, when necessary, phpMyAdmin generates the appropriate syntax for handling views.

> To perform actions on existing views, a user needs to have the appropriate privilege at the view level, but not necessarily any privilege on the tables involved in this view. This is how we can achieve column and table hiding.

Controlling row counting for improved performance

phpMyAdmin has a configuration parameter, $cfg['MaxExactCountViews'], that controls the row-counting phase of phpMyAdmin. Sometimes, a view comprises many huge tables, and browsing it would make a large number of virtual rows appear. Therefore, the default value of 0 for this parameter ensures that no row counting happens for views. In this case, we will see rather strange results when browsing a view: **Showing rows 0 - -1 (0 total, Query took 0.0006 sec)**. This is more acceptable than slowing down a server.

Nonetheless, if we prefer to see a more exact row count for views, we can put a larger value in this parameter, which acts as an upper limit for the row counting phase.

Supporting routines—stored procedures and functions

It took a while before phpMyAdmin started to include support for stored procedures and functions. The reason is that these are blocks of code (like a sub-program) that are kept as a part of the database. phpMyAdmin, being a web interface, is more oriented towards operations that are performed quickly using a mouse.

Nonetheless, phpMyAdmin has a few features that permit a developer to create such routines, save them, recall them to make some modifications, and delete them.

Procedures are accessed by a CALL statement to which we can pass parameters (more details at http://dev.mysql.com/doc/refman/5.5/en/call.html). On the other hand, functions are accessed from SQL statements (for example, SELECT), and are similar to other MySQL internal functions, thus returning a value.

The CREATE ROUTINE and ALTER ROUTINE privileges are needed to be able to create, see, and delete a stored procedure or function. The EXECUTE privilege is needed to run the routine, although the privilege is normally granted automatically to the routine's creator.

Creating a stored procedure

We will create a procedure to change the page count for a specific book, by adding a specific number of pages. The book's ISBN and the number of pages to be added will be the input parameters to this procedure. We are using the SQL query box (refer to *Chapter 11*) to enter this procedure.

Changing the delimiter

The standard SQL delimiter is the semicolon, and this character will be used inside our procedure to delimit SQL statements. However, the CREATE PROCEDURE statement is by itself a SQL statement; hence, we must come up with a way to indicate to the MySQL parser where this statement ends. The query box has a **Delimiter** input box, which contains a semicolon by default. Therefore, we change it to another string, which, by convention, is a double slash "//".

Entering the procedure

We then enter the procedure's code in the main query box:

```
CREATE PROCEDURE `add_page`(IN param_isbn VARCHAR(25),
   IN param_pages INT, OUT param_message VARCHAR(100))
BEGIN
  IF param_pages > 100 THEN
    SET param_message = 'the number of pages is too big';
  ELSE
    UPDATE book SET page_count = page_count + param_pages WHERE
       isbn=param_isbn;
    SET param_message = 'success';
  END IF;
END
//
```

On clicking **Go**, we get a success message if the syntax is correct. If it is not, well it's time to revise our typing abilities or debug our syntax. Unfortunately, MySQL does not come with a procedure debugger.

Testing the procedure

Again, in the query box, we test our procedure by entering the following statements. Here, we are using a SQL variable, @message, which will receive the contents of the OUT parameter param_message:

```
call add_page('1-234567-22-0', 4, @message);
SELECT @message;
```

If all went well, we should see that the **@message** variable contains **success**.

We can then verify whether the page count for this book has increased. We also need to test the problematic case:

```
call add_page('1-234567-22-0', 101, @message);
SELECT @message;
```

This procedure is now available for calling (for example) from your PHP scripts using the mysqli extension, which is the one recommended to access all the functionalities provided by MySQL 4.1 and above.

Manipulating procedures and functions

A procedure is stored inside a database, and is not tied to a specific table. Therefore, the interface for manipulating procedures and functions can be found at the database level, on the **Structure** page under the **Routines** slider, which appears if at least one routine is already defined.

The first icon brings this procedure's text into a query box for editing. The second icon would be used to delete this procedure. When editing the procedure, we notice that the text has been somewhat modified.

```
DROP PROCEDURE `add_page`//
CREATE DEFINER=`marc`@`%` PROCEDURE `add_page`(IN param_isbn
VARCHAR(25), IN param_pages INT, OUT param_message VARCHAR(100))
BEGIN
  IF param_pages > 100 THEN
    SET param_message = 'the number of pages is too big';
  ELSE
    UPDATE book SET page_count = page_count + param_pages WHERE
      isbn=param_isbn;
    SET param_message = 'success';
  END IF;
END
```

First, a DROP PROCEDURE statement appears. This is normal because MySQL does not offer a statement that would permit changing the body of a procedure. Therefore, we have to delete a procedure every time we want to change it. It's true that the ALTER PROCEDURE statement exists, but it can only change the procedure's characteristics, for example, by adding a comment. Then, a DEFINER clause is shown. It was generated at creation time, and indicates who created this procedure.

At this point, we make any changes we need to the code, and click on **Go** to save this procedure.

It might be tempting to open the book table on its **Structure** page and look for a list of procedures that manipulate this table, such as our add_page() procedure. However, all procedures are stored at the database level, and there is no direct link between the code itself (UPDATE book) and the place where the procedure is stored.

Manually creating a function

Functions are similar to stored procedures. However, a function may return just one value, whereas a stored procedure can have more than one OUT parameter. On the other hand, using a stored function from within a SELECT statement may seem more natural as it avoids the need for an intermediate SQL variable to hold the value of an OUT parameter.

What is the goal of functions? As an example, a function can be used to calculate the total cost of an order, including tax and shipping. Putting this logic inside the database instead of at the application level helps to document the application-database interface. It also avoids duplicating business logic in every application that needs to deal with this logic.

We should not confuse MySQL 5.0 functions with **UDF (User-Defined Functions)**, which existed prior to MySQL 5.0. A UDF consists of code written in C or C++, compiled into a shared object, and referenced with a CREATE FUNCTION statement and the SONAME keyword.

phpMyAdmin's treatment of functions is, in many ways, similar to what we have covered in procedures:

- A query box in which to enter a function
- The use of a delimiter
- A mechanism to manipulate a function that is already defined

Let us define a function that retrieves the country name, based on its code. I prefer to use a param_ prefix to clearly identify the parameters inside the function's definition and a var_ prefix for local variables. We will use our trusty SQL query box to enter the function's code, again indicating to this box to use // as the delimiter.

```
CREATE FUNCTION get_country_name(param_country_code CHAR(2))
  RETURNS VARCHAR(50)
  READS SQL DATA
BEGIN
  DECLARE var_country_name VARCHAR(50) DEFAULT 'not found';
  SELECT description
```

```
      FROM country
      WHERE code = param_country_code
      INTO var_country_name;
   RETURN var_country_name;
END
//
```

We should note that our newly-created function can be seen on the database's **Structure** page, along with its friend, the add_page procedure:

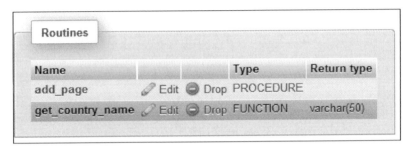

Testing the function

To test the function we just created, enter the following query in a query box (refer to *Chapter 11*):

```
SELECT CONCAT('ca->', get_country_name('ca'), ', zz->',

get_country_name('zz')) as test;
```

This will produce the following result:

```
ca->Canada, zz->not found
```

Exporting stored procedures and functions

When exporting a database, procedures and functions appear in an SQL export. This is because the **Add CREATE PROCEDURE / FUNCTION / EVENT** checkbox is selected by default in the **Object creation options** dialog of the **Export** page (it can be seen in the **Custom** export mode). Here is the part of the export file related to procedures and functions:

```
DELIMITER $$
--
-- Procedures
--
CREATE DEFINER=`marc`@`%` PROCEDURE `add_page`(IN param_isbn
```

```
          VARCHAR(25), IN param_pages INT, OUT param_message VARCHAR(100))
BEGIN
    IF param_pages > 100 THEN
        SET param_message = 'the number of pages is too big';
    ELSE
        UPDATE book SET page_count = page_count + param_pages WHERE
            isbn=param_isbn;
        SET param_message = 'success';
    END IF;
END$$


--
-- Functions
--
CREATE DEFINER=`marc`@`%` FUNCTION `get_country_name`
(param_country_code CHAR(2)) RETURNS varchar(50) CHARSET latin1
    READS SQL DATA
BEGIN
    DECLARE var_country_name VARCHAR(50) DEFAULT 'not found';
    SELECT description into var_country_name FROM country WHERE
        code = param_country_code;
    RETURN var_country_name;
END$$

DELIMITER ;
```

Executing code with triggers

Triggers are code that we associate with a table to be executed when certain actions occur, for example, after a new INSERT statement in the book table. The action does not need to happen within phpMyAdmin.

Contrary to routines that are related to an entire database and are visible on the database's **Structure** page, triggers for each table are accessed from this specific table's **Structure** page.

> Prior to MySQL 5.1.6, we needed the SUPER privilege to create and delete triggers. In version 5.1.6, a TRIGGER table-level privilege was added to the privilege system. Hence, a user no longer needs the powerful SUPER privilege for these tasks.

In order to perform the following exercise, we will need a new INT column—total_page_count—in our author table.

The idea here is that every time a book is created, its page count will be added to the total page count of the books from this author. Some people may advocate that it would be better not to keep a separate column for the total here, and instead compute the total every time we need it. In fact, a design decision must be made when dealing with this situation in the real world. Do we need to retrieve the total page count very quickly, for example, for web purposes? what is the response time to compute this value from a production table with thousands of rows? Anyway, since I need it as an example, the design decision is easy to make here.

Let us not forget that following its addition to the table's structure, the total_page_count column should initially be seeded with the correct total. (However, this is not the purpose of our trigger.)

Manually creating a trigger

The current phpMyAdmin version does not have an interface for trigger creation. Therefore, we enter the trigger definition in a query box taking special care to enter // in the delimiter box:

```
CREATE TRIGGER after_book_insert AFTER INSERT ON book
FOR EACH ROW
BEGIN
  UPDATE author
  SET total_page_count = total_page_count + NEW.page_count
  WHERE id = NEW.author_id;
END
//
```

Later, the **Structure** page for our book table reveals a new **Triggers** section that can be used the same way as routines, to edit or delete a trigger, as shown in the following screenshot:

Triggers				
Name			Time	Event
after_book_insert	Change	Drop	AFTER	INSERT

Testing the trigger

Contrary to testing stored procedures or functions, there is neither a CALL sequence nor a function inside a SELECT statement to execute the trigger. Any time the defined operation (a book INSERT) happens, the code will execute (in our case, after the insertion). Therefore, we simply have to insert a new book to see that the author. total_page_count column is updated.

Of course, a completely automatic management of this column would involve creating AFTER UPDATE and AFTER DELETE triggers on the book table.

Using information_schema

In the SQL:2003 Standard, access to the data dictionary (or database metadata) is provided by a structure called information_schema. As this is part of the Standard, and already exists in other database systems, the decision to implement this feature into MySQL was a very good one.

> MySQL has added some information that is not part of the standard, for example, INFORMATION_SCHEMA.COLUMNS.COLUMN_TYPE. Be aware of the fact that if you use this information in a software project, it might not be portable to other SQL implementations.

A phpMyAdmin user sees the information_schema as a normal database containing views. These views describe many aspects of the structure of the databases hosted on this server. The following screenshot shows a subset of what can be seen (and in fact, the only possible operation on this database is SELECT):

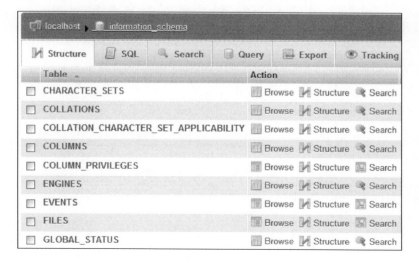

Internally, phpMyAdmin can call the `information_schema`, instead of the corresponding `SHOW` statements to retrieve metadata. This behavior is controlled by the `$cfg['Servers'][$i]['DisableIS']` directive. Some `SELECT` operations involving a `WHERE` clause on `information_schema` are really slow (many minutes of wait time) when the server hosts hundreds of databases or tables, and this is yet to be fixed by the MySQL team; this is why this directive is set to `true` by default, thus avoiding the use of `information_schema`.

The `$cfg['Servers'][$i]['hide_db']` parameter can be used to hide this "database" to users who might be confused by the sudden appearance of a database that they know nothing about. It will probably depend on their level of expertise in MySQL. On a multi-user installation of phpMyAdmin, we cannot please everyone about this parameter's value.

Partitioning

User-defined partitioning (refer to http://dev.mysql.com/doc/refman/5.1/en/partitioning.html) is offered in MySQL 5.1. It allows us to "distribute portions of individual tables across a file system according to rules which you can set largely as needed". Using this feature in phpMyAdmin requires knowledge of its syntax as there are many partition types. Also, for each partition type, the number of partitions and the values associated with each partition are too random to be easily represented on a web interface.

Creating a table with partitions

Let us try it by creating a table named `test` with one column **id**. On the table creation panel, if connected to a MySQL 5.1 server, phpMyAdmin shows a **PARTITION definition** dialog, as shown in the following screenshot:

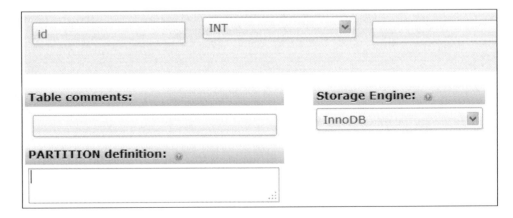

Here, we enter a PARTITION BY RANGE clause, which will create partitions on the
id column:

```
PARTITION BY RANGE (id) (
   PARTITION p0 VALUES LESS THAN (1000),
   PARTITION p1 VALUES LESS THAN (2000),
   PARTITION p2 VALUES LESS THAN (30000)
);
```

Maintaining partitions

For a table on which a partition has been defined, the **Operations** page displays a
Partition maintenance dialog where we can:

- Choose a partition and then request an action, such as **Rebuild**
- Remove the partitioning

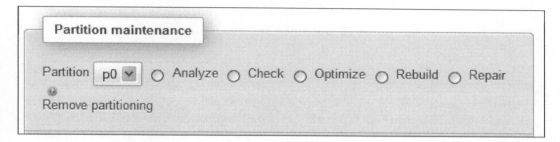

Exporting a partition definition

Finally, exporting this test table in SQL mode produces statements with embedded
comments that a MySQL 5.1 server would recognize and interpret in order to
recreate the same partitions:

```
CREATE TABLE `test` (
   `id` int(11) NOT NULL
) ENGINE=MyISAM DEFAULT CHARSET=latin1
/*!50100 PARTITION BY RANGE (id)
(PARTITION p0 VALUES LESS THAN (1000) ENGINE = MyISAM,
   PARTITION p1 VALUES LESS THAN (2000) ENGINE = MyISAM,
   PARTITION p2 VALUES LESS THAN (3000) ENGINE = MyISAM) */;
```

Exploring the event scheduler

The **Event Scheduler** (http://dev.mysql.com/doc/refman/5.1/en/events.
html), another new feature of MySQL 5.1, permits the creation of tasks that will run automatically according to a schedule. The schedule is quite flexible and permits, for example, a statement to be run every ten seconds, starting from midnight of May 18, 2011. These can be one-time events or recurring ones.

Activating the scheduler

We should first verify whether the scheduler is active on our server. If not, we need to activate it. Otherwise, nothing will happen! We will start by entering the following statement in the query box:

```
SHOW VARIABLES LIKE 'event%';
```

Next, we look in the results for a variable named event_scheduler. If this variable is set to OFF, we need to ask the system administrator (or someone with the SUPER privilege) to execute the following statement:

```
SET GLOBAL event_scheduler = ON;
```

Granting EVENT permission

Every user who wants to create or drop an event needs the EVENT privilege, either globally or on the database on which he or she plans to add the event. Please refer to *Chapter 19* for details about granting such privileges.

Creating an event

The current phpMyAdmin version does not have an interface on which we could choose the various parts of the CREATE EVENT statement. Therefore, the only method left is to use the SQL query box to enter the statement and to understand its syntax! Here, we will use a totally fictitious example:

```
CREATE EVENT add_page_count
  ON SCHEDULE
    EVERY 1 MINUTE
  DO
    UPDATE author set total_page_count = total_page_count + 1
      WHERE id = 1;
```

You can now get some amusement by browsing the author table once in a while, and see the counter incrementing for author 1.

Manipulating events

Events are related to a single database, which is why you see an **Events** slider on the **Structure** page for the marc_book database. Activating it reveals the following panel:

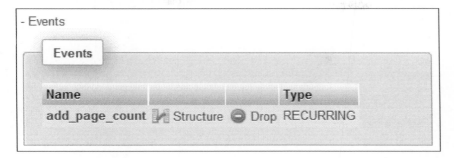

Indeed, this is a recurring event. We can use the first icon to edit the event (which will have the effect of deleting and recreating the event), and the second icon to remove it.

Exporting

It's possible to generate event-related statements at the end of an SQL database export file by selecting the **Add CREATE PROCEDURE / FUNCTION / EVENT** option. Please remember that some events may have an expiration time. Hence, they may have vanished between the time you create them and the time you attempt to export them, unless the ON COMPLETION PRESERVE clause was used when creating the event.

Summary

MySQL 5.0's new features helped the product to comply with standards. Even though phpMyAdmin has limited support for these features (especially lacking a syntax-oriented editor), it has a basic set of features to work with views, routines, triggers, and information_schema. phpMyAdmin also supports MySQL 5.1 partitions and events.

The next chapter covers the use of the tracking feature that permits the recording of changes made to a MySQL database via phpMyAdmin.

18
Tracking Changes

This chapter will examine how we can use the change-tracking mechanism, in order to record structure and data changes done from the phpMyAdmin interface and to obtain reports about such changes.

Understanding the goals of the tracking system

Each software application has its own idea of what changes are important to track for its users. This section describes tracking systems that exist in other applications, and compares them to the one offered by phpMyAdmin.

Tracking in other software applications

Having access to historic data that displays all of the changes made to an information system is a feature that is taken for granted in many software products. The "undo" feature of any serious word-processing software is an example of being able to go back in time, albeit one step at the time. A more complex example would be the history feature of MediaWiki (the core software of Wikipedia). It enables us to go back to any state of a given page, to see the changes between any two versions, and even to mark any older version as the current one. Tracking information includes the author (or IP address), the date and time of change, and a comment.

In MySQL itself, the logging system (binlog) records all changes made to the database; however, in this case, the goal is two-fold:

- To allow master-slave synchronization
- To enable restoration via the mysqlbinlog command-line utility

Tracking in phpMyAdmin

phpMyAdmin's tracking system allows the user to specify which table is going to be tracked, so it can be called an **opt-in system**. By default, no table is tracked unless a developer elects to do so; and when a developer activates tracking for a table, changes start to be recorded even if performed by someone else. Only the changes done via phpMyAdmin are recorded.

Furthermore, for a given table, we can indicate which statements we are interested in tracking. The list of statements is divided into two groups: data definition and data manipulation.

Suppose that a team is working on a project that involves making changes to the structure of tables. With tracking activated and assuming that each developer logs in to MySQL with his or her own account, we now have access to historic data, including information about which developer dropped some critical column! Of course, this tracking is not tamper-proof; after all, it's stored in a MySQL table so the security of this tracking information depends on who has access to the tracking table.

Prerequisites

The phpMyAdmin configuration storage holds all metadata for the tracking mechanism. If we have implemented this storage a while ago (for a previous phpMyAdmin version, such as 3.1 or older), we can use `scripts/create_tables.sql` from the current phpMyAdmin version to upgrade the configuration storage with the missing tables (in our case, the `pma_tracking` table). The reason for this is that the script creates this table in a prudent way by using the `CREATE TABLE IF NOT EXISTS` `pma_tracking` statement, thus ensuring that it won't be created if the table is already present.

> In phpMyAdmin 3.3.3, the type of the `data_sql` column in `pma_tracking` was changed from `TEXT` to `LONGTEXT` in the `create_tables.sql` script. Therefore, it's important to make this change manually in our own `pma_tracking` table, if we ran this script prior to version 3.3.3.

Configuring a basic tracking mechanism

In `config.inc.php`, for a specific MySQL server's configuration, the `$cfg['Servers'][$i]['tracking']` should contain the name of the tracking table; the suggested name is `pma_tracking` to match the default value inside `scripts/create_tables.sql`.

 If this directive is left blank, no tracking is possible on this server (we won't see any **Tracking** menu).

By default, tracking must be activated per table. If we prefer that the tracking mechanism be switched on automatically for all future tables and views, the `$cfg['Servers'][$i]['tracking_version_auto_create']` can be set to TRUE. Please note that this is only for future tables and views—we still need to activate tracking for existing tables.

The advantage of using automatic creation is that we don't have to think about it; tracking is done from the birth of a table. An inconvenient side effect of this is that we don't have the possibility of choosing which statements will be tracked; these will be taken from the default list (refer to the *Choosing the statements to be tracked* section later in this chapter).

Other configuration directives will be discussed in the section that relates to them.

Principles

This section defines important principles on which the tracking mechanism is based: versioning, snapshot, and the archiving issues of tracking information.

Versioning

Using version numbers is something we are familiar with; for example, this book describes phpMyAdmin version 3.4.x. However, at this point we must understand exactly why we use version numbers.

A good reference on software versioning is located in Wikipedia at `http://en.wikipedia.org/wiki/Software_versioning`. This article mentions that version names can be used, but version numbers are more common. More importantly, it states that version numbers "correspond to new developments in the software".

If we apply this principle to database development, the decision that a table is ripe for a new version should be made by the development team when a significant change is about to occur on this table. How significant the change has to be in order to trigger a new version is a matter of interpretation within the team. At least one of these decisions is easy to make: version 1 always represents the moment where we first switch on the tracking for a particular table.

In the situation where data manipulation statements are tracked, we should note also that the change can be relative to data itself, not necessarily to the structure.

 phpMyAdmin's tracking system uses only positive integers as version numbers; it's not possible to use a decimal point as in "1.1".

Taking a snapshot of the current structure

Every time we create a new version, the tracking system takes a snapshot of the current structure and indexes of the table, and creates a new entry in the tracking system. In this entry are stored the database name, table name, version number, date of creation, and the complete structure information.

 This tracking snapshot does not contain a table's data! Therefore, the tracking system does not replace a backup system.

During the lifespan of this table after the snapshot has been taken, all tracked statements are stored alongside this snapshot. Therefore, a table tracking version consists of the snapshot in addition to all of the changes made after this snapshot was taken, until a new version is started.

Understanding archiving issues

When a table is dropped, its tracking information survives, unless we decide to suppress it. The impact of this will be discussed later in the *Deleting tracking information* section.

Initiating tracking for one table

In this section, we will use the **Tracking** menu in Table view to start collecting the changes that occur for the author table. So we open the author table and then click on **Tracking**, which produces the following screen:

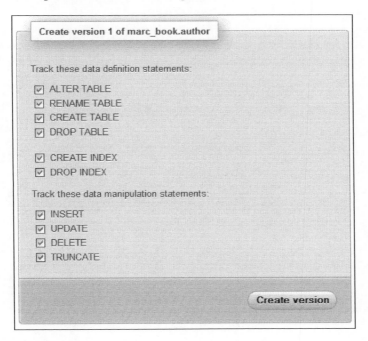

This panel tells us that we are about to create version 1 of the table; this is what we expected. We are offered a choice of data definition and data manipulation statements; for now we will leave all of them marked, and will click on **Create version** button. The next section explains how we can specify which statements are to appear in the panel shown above.

After version 1 is created, the following confirmation panel is shown:

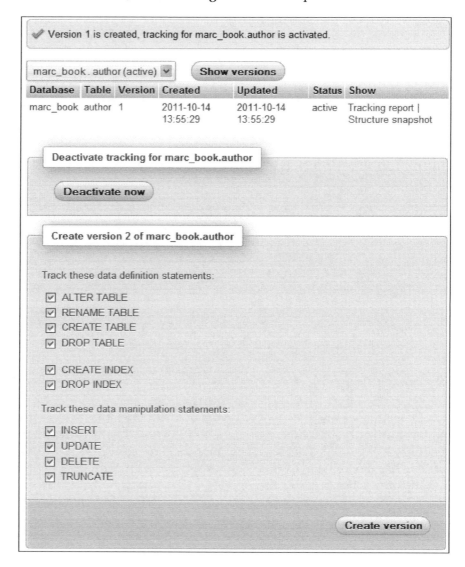

We notice that two distinct actions took place:

- The creation of version 1 itself
- The activation of tracking for this table

Indeed, one or many versions of a table may exist, each one containing a snapshot from some point in time and the changes since this snapshot; but this is independent of the fact that tracking is active for a table and changes are being recorded.

In this panel, we see sub-panels that will be covered in the *Choosing the statements to be tracked* and *Deactivating and activating tracking* sections.

Choosing the statements to be tracked

`$cfg['Servers'][$i]['tracking_default_statements']` contains a string that consists of comma-separated statements. These are the ones that are offered in the panel where we can choose which statements we want to track. The default list of statements is defined as follows; please note the presence of dot characters that permit the concatenation of strings in PHP:

```
$cfg['Servers'][$i]['tracking_default_statements'] =
    'CREATE TABLE,ALTER TABLE,DROP TABLE,RENAME TABLE,' .
    'CREATE INDEX,DROP INDEX,' .
    'INSERT,UPDATE,DELETE,TRUNCATE,REPLACE,' .
    'CREATE VIEW,ALTER VIEW,DROP VIEW,' .
    'CREATE DATABASE,ALTER DATABASE,DROP DATABASE';
```

Testing the tracking mechanism

We are now ready to verify that this tracking system really works! As the system is supposed to track ALTER TABLE statement, we will make a slight structure change and see what happens. We go to the **Structure** panel for table **author**, select the **name** column, and increase its size from **30** to **40** characters (refer to *Chapter 5* for the detailed steps).

We get a message, as shown in the following screenshot:

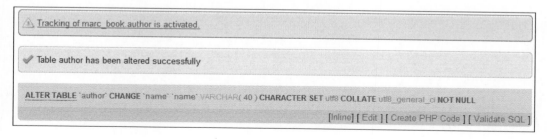

We will perform another action, this time related to data itself—changing the phone number of author **John Smith** to **111-2222**.

To ensure that these actions were recorded by the tracking system, let us compile a report.

Tracking report

Going back to the **Tracking** panel (still in `Table` view for **author**) we click on **Tracking report** for version 1, which produces a report as shown in the following screenshot:

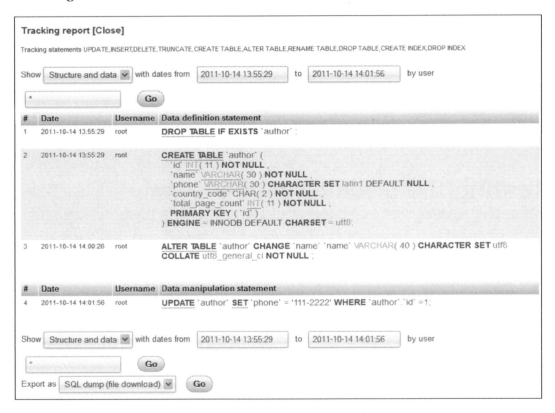

In fact, the report is prefixed to the main tracking information; we could click on **Close** and be back to where we were previously.

We can see that under the **Tracking report** header, a list of the statements that are tracked is shown. Then we have a selector to determine if we want to see on the report the statements corresponding to:

- **Structure and data**
- **Structure only**
- **Data only**

We can also specify the range of dates and times for which we want to produce the report. It's also possible to indicate which users we want to report on (an asterisk represents all users).

The main part of the report consists of the statements themselves; here we see four statements. The first statement is a DROP TABLE statement, which would be useful to create this table anew should we need to export this version and import it back. The second statement (CREATE TABLE) contains the snapshot that was taken when version 1 was initiated. Then we see the ALTER TABLE and UPDATE statements that correspond to the actions we performed as a test.

How to export a structure will be covered in the *Exporting a version* section later in this chapter.

Determining tracking status

Let us cover all of the places in the interface where we can ascertain the tracking activity for a table. First, in Table view, we can see a message positioned under the menu tabs, stating that tracking is activated for this table, as shown in the following screenshot:

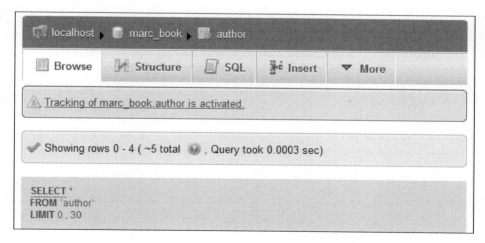

In the **Tracking** panel itself, a **Status** column tells us that tracking is either **active** or **not active** for the latest version. In fact, when we create another version for the table, we will see that only the current version can have an active tracking status, as previous versions now only contain historical data.

Database	Table	Version	Created	Updated	Status
marc_book	author	1	2011-10-14 13:55:29	2011-10-14 14:01:56	active

In `Database` view, each table that is tracked by the system (with an active or not active status) is shown with the icon of an eye either in color or grayed out, depending upon its status. In the following example, the eye is in color:

This eye icon is clickable and brings us to the **Tracking** panel for this specific table.

Finally, in `Database` view, the **Tracking** menu provides us with an overview of all the tables. First the tracked tables are presented, then the untracked ones. For either category, we have links to see more information or to start tracking:

For the tracked tables, the following table gives a breakdown of the information presented, along with the available links:

Title or link	Description
Database	In which database the table is located
Table	Which table is tracked
Last version	The latest tracked version; it's interesting to see how many versions exist for this table
Created	When was this version created
Updated	When was the last tracked statement stored for this table
Status	Active or not active
Action	The **Drop** link can be used to remove all tracking (refer to the *Deleting tracking information* section later in this chapter)
Show | Versions	Enters `Table` view for this table, and displays the tracking versions
Show | Tracking report	Enters `Table` view for this table, and displays the tracking report
Show | Structure snapshot	Enters `Table` view for this table, and displays the structure snapshot (refer to the *Structure snapshot* section later in this chapter)

For the untracked tables, a **Track table** link allows us to enter `Table` view for this table, directly in the **Tracking** panel, hence creating version 1 in order to start the tracking mechanism.

Deactivating and activating tracking

From the **Tracking** page of a specific table, the **Deactivate now** button (which acts as a toggle, and changes to **Activate now**) is the one to use if we wish to stop (temporarily or permanently) further storing of the tracked statements. Past statements that were stored remain untouched in the tracking data related to the current version.

Structure snapshot

In the **Tracking** panel of `Table` view, the **Structure snapshot** link displays the past state of the table at the time this version was created. The panel shows both the stored SQL code and a visual representation in the familiar phpMyAdmin **Structure** panel format.

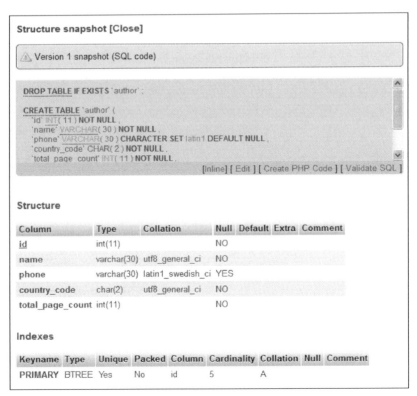

Exporting a version

As the complete SQL code at the time of creation for a specific version has been stored along with all of the tracked statements that occurred since that moment, we might want to reuse them in their executable form. At the bottom of the **Tracking report** panel, an **Export as** dialog is available, offering three variants for exporting. If we choose **SQL dump (file download)** menu option, then all of the statements stored for this version are transferred in a file that we can save to our workstation. For the author table, this would produce a file containing the following lines:

```
# Tracking report for table `author`
# 2011-10-14 14:24:12

DROP TABLE IF EXISTS `author`;

CREATE TABLE `author` (
  `id` int(11) NOT NULL,
  `name` varchar(30) NOT NULL,
  `phone` varchar(30) CHARACTER SET latin1 DEFAULT NULL,
  `country_code` char(2) NOT NULL,
  `total_page_count` int(11) NOT NULL,
  PRIMARY KEY (`id`)
) ENGINE=InnoDB DEFAULT CHARSET=utf8;
ALTER TABLE `author` CHANGE `name` `name` VARCHAR(40) CHARACTER SET
utf8 COLLATE utf8_general_ci NOT NULL;
UPDATE `author` SET `phone` = '111-2222' WHERE `author`.`id` = 1;
```

If, instead, we pick the **SQL dump** choice, the statements appear on screen in a text area; from this point we could cut and paste the SQL code or click on **Go** to run it. As a measure of precaution, extra statements are generated on top of the code; these handle the creation of another database in which the table would be created. Of course the user must have the rights to create this database.

Finally, the **SQL execution** choice permits to directly execute the stored statements in the current database. However, a warning message is issued as these statements might reflect an older state of the table; we might not want to revert to this old state. Also, the first statement is, by default, a DROP TABLE, which may or may not succeed depending on whether some foreign key constraint blocks the deletion of the table.

Creating a new version

As previously discussed, we can decide to mark a new milestone for a certain table; in other words, we can start a new version. We will now create a new version as an exercise.

In the **Tracking** panel for the `author` table, we see the dialog for creating **version 2** (as the highest one is currently version 1):

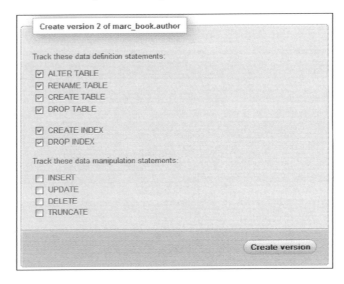

We notice that each version can track its own set of statements; versions are independent from each other in this matter. Here, we have decided that version 2 will track only data-definition statements. We now see something interesting relative to the status of these versions, as shown in the following screenshot:

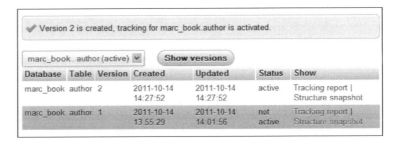

Indeed, version 1 was automatically marked as **not active**; it went into some kind of historical status. We can also have a look at version 2's snapshot, which reflects that the **name** column is a **VARCHAR(40)**.

Quickly accessing tracking information

When we are in the **Tracking** panel for one table, a shortcut dialog allows us to go directly to the **Tracking** panel of any other tracked table.

To explore this feature, let us now create version 1 of the book table. After this is done, we examine the drop-down list next to **Show versions** button, as shown in the following screenshot:

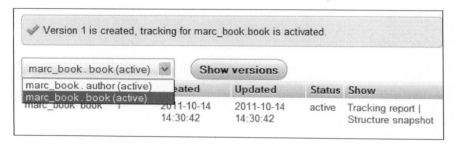

This list is similar to what we would see in the **Tracking** panel for database marc_book when looking at the **Tracked tables** portion, but without the need to go back to this panel.

Deleting tracking information

A feature of the tracking system that might not be evident is that tracking information for all versions of a table, and thus for its whole lifespan, is still kept when the corresponding table is dropped. The reason is to keep the history information intact should we happen to create a table with the same name later on.

Let us do a copy of the author table (refer to *Chapter 9* if needed), and name it author_copy. We then activate tracking on this new table. The last operation is to drop this author_copy table. Even if we no longer see it in the normal list of tables, it's different in the **Tracking** panel for database marc_book.

Tracked tables

Database	Table	Last version	Created	Updated	Status	Action	Show
marc_book	author	2	2011-10-14 14:27:52	2011-10-14 14:27:52	active	⊖ Drop	Versions | Tracking report | Structure snapshot
marc_book	author_copy	1	2011-10-14 14:33:37	2011-10-14 14:33:50	active	⊖ Drop	Versions | Tracking report | Structure snapshot
marc_book	book	1	2011-10-14 14:30:42	2011-10-14 14:30:42	active	⊖ Drop	Versions | Tracking report | Structure snapshot

Delete tracking data for this table

At this point we can go back in time, sort of, and see the tracking report and snapshot for the versions of this deleted table. If we really want to remove all evidence of the table ever having existed, then we can use the **Drop** link to destroy the tracking data also (after clicking on **OK** in the subsequent confirmation panel).

Summary

In this chapter, we saw an overview of the benefits given by the statements' tracking feature, and then we covered all of the panels involved in the creation and maintenance of versions for tables.

The next chapter covers administration of a MySQL server, focusing on the management of user accounts and privileges.

19
Administrating the MySQL Server

This chapter discusses how a system administrator can use the phpMyAdmin server-management features for day-to-day user account maintenance, server verification, and server protection. The subject of how non-administrators can obtain server information from phpMyAdmin is also covered.

Server administration is mostly done via the `Server` view, which is accessed via the menu tabs available on phpMyAdmin's home page.

Managing users and their privileges

The **Privileges** page (visible only if we are logged in as a privileged user) contains dialogs to manage MySQL user accounts. It also contains dialogs to manage privileges on global, database, and table levels. This page is hierarchical. When editing a user's privileges, we can see the global privileges as well as the database-specific privileges. Then, when viewing database-specific privileges for a user, we can view and edit this user's privileges for any table within this database.

The user overview

The first page displayed when we enter the **Privileges** page is called **User overview**. This shows all user accounts and a summary of their global privileges, as shown in the following screenshot:

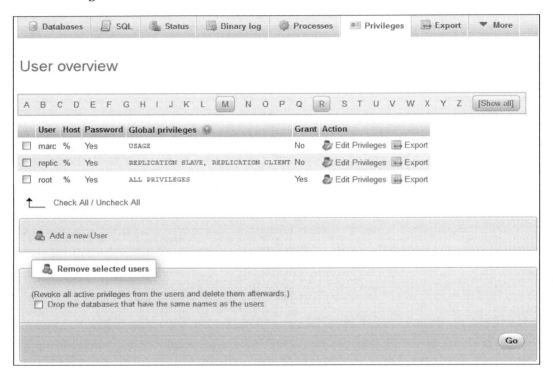

From this page, we can:

- Edit a user's privileges, via the **Edit Privileges** link for this user
- Export a user's privileges definition, via the **Export** link for this user
- Use the checkboxes to remove users, via the **Remove selected users** dialog
- Access the page where the **Add a new User** dialog is available

The displayed users' list has columns with the following characteristics:

Column	Characteristic
User	The user account we are defining.
Host	The machine name or IP address, from which this user account will be connecting to the MySQL server. A % value here indicates all hosts.
Password	Contains **Yes** if a password is defined and **No** if it isn't. The password itself cannot be seen from phpMyAdmin's interface or by directly looking at the `mysql.user` table, as it is encrypted with a one-way hashing algorithm.
Global privileges	A list of the user's global privileges.
Grant	Contains **Yes** if the user can grant his/her privileges to others.
Action	Contains a link to edit this user's privileges or export them.

Exporting privileges

This feature can be useful when we need to create a user with the same password and privileges on another MySQL server. Clicking on **Export** for user **marc** produces the following panel:

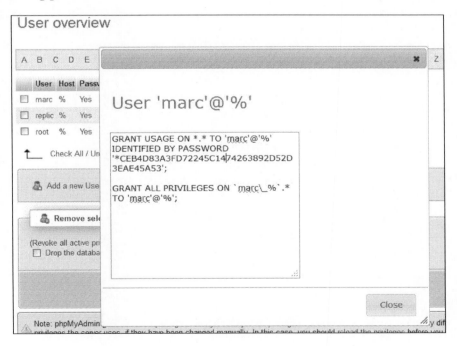

Then it's only a matter of selecting these **GRANT** statements and pasting them in the SQL box of another phpMyAdmin window, where we have logged in on another MySQL server.

Privileges reload

At the bottom of **User overview** page, this message is displayed:

```
Note: phpMyAdmin gets the users' privileges directly from MySQL's
privilege tables. The content of these tables may differ from the
privileges the server uses, if they have been changed manually. In
this case, you should reload the privileges before you continue.
```

Here, the text **reload the privileges** is clickable. The effective privileges (the ones against which the server bases its access decisions) are the privileges that are located in the server's memory. Privilege modifications that are made from the **User overview** page are made both in memory and on disk in the mysql database. Modifications made directly to the mysql database do not have immediate effect. The **reload the privileges** operation reads the privileges from the database and makes them effective in memory.

Adding a user

The **Add a new User** link opens a dialog for user account creation. First, we see the panel where we will describe the account itself, as shown in the following screenshot:

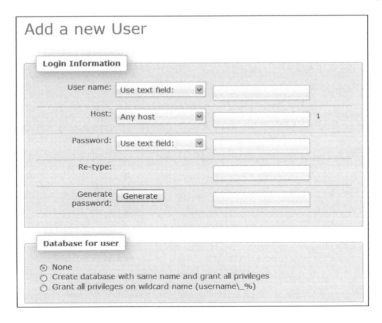

The second part of the **Add a new User** dialog is where we will specify the user's global privileges, which apply to the server as a whole (see the *Assigning global privileges* section of this chapter), as shown in the following screenshot:

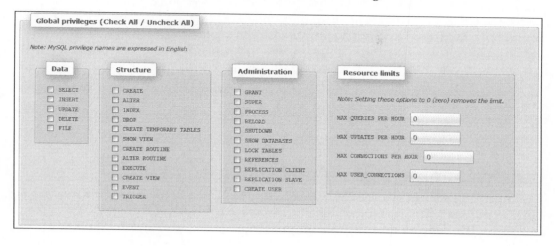

Entering the username

The **User name** menu offers two choices. We can choose **Use text field:** and enter a username in the box, or we can choose **Any user** to create an anonymous user (the blank user). More details about the anonymous user are available at http://dev. mysql.com/doc/refman/5.5/en/connection-access.html. Let us choose **Use text field:** and enter **bill**.

Assigning a host value

By default, this menu is set to **Any host**, with % as the host value. The **Local** choice means localhost. The **Use host table** choice (which creates a blank value in the host field) means to look in the mysql.host table for database-specific privileges. Choosing **Use text field:** allows us to enter the exact host value we want. Let us choose **Local**.

Setting passwords

Even though it's possible to create a user without a password (by selecting the **No password** option), it's best to have a password. We have to enter it twice (as we cannot see what is entered) to confirm the intended password. A secure password should have more than eight characters, and should contain a mixture of uppercase and lowercase characters, digits, and special characters. Therefore, it's recommended to have phpMyAdmin generate a password—this is possible in JavaScript-enabled browsers. In the **Generate password** dialog, clicking on **Generate** button enters a random password (in clear text) on the screen and fills the **Password** and **Re-type** input fields with the generated password. At this point, we should note the password so that we can pass it on to the user.

Understanding rights for database creation

A frequent convention is to assign a user the rights to a database having the same name as this user. To accomplish this, the **Database for user** section offers the **Create database with same name and grant all privileges** radio button. Selecting this checkbox automates the process by creating both the database (if it does not already exist) and assigning the corresponding rights. Please note that, with this method, each user would be limited to one database (user `bill`, database `bill`).

Another possibility is to allow users to create databases that have the same prefix as their usernames. Therefore, the other choice **Grant all privileges on wildcard name (username_%)** performs this function by assigning a wildcard privilege. With this in place, user `bill` could create the databases `bill_test`, `bill_2`, `bill_payroll`, and so on; phpMyAdmin does not pre-create the databases in this case.

Assigning global privileges

Global privileges determine the user's access to all databases. Hence, these are sometimes known as **superuser privileges**. A normal user should not have any of these privileges unless there is a good reason for this. Moreover, should a user account that has global privileges become compromised, the damage could be far greater.

If we are really creating a superuser, we will select every global privilege that he or she needs. These privileges are further divided into **Data**, **Structure**, and **Administration** groups.

In our example, **bill** will not have any global privileges.

Limiting the resources used

We can limit the resources used by this user on this server (for example, the maximum queries per hour). Zero means no limit. We will not impose any resources limits on **bill**.

The following screenshot shows the status of the screen just before hitting **Create user** to create this user's definition (with the remaining fields being set to default):

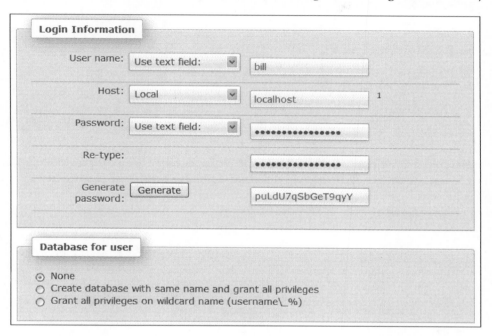

Editing a user profile

The page used to edit a user's profile appears whenever we click on **Edit Privileges** for a user in the **User overview** page. Let us try it for our newly created user **bill**. There are four sections on this page, each with its own **Go** button. Hence, each section is operated independently and has a distinct purpose.

Editing global privileges

The section for editing the user's privileges has the same look as the **Add a new User** dialog, and is used to view and to change global privileges.

Assigning database-specific privileges

In this section, we define the databases to which our user has access, and his or her exact privileges on these databases.

As shown in the previous screenshot, we see **None** because we haven't defined any privileges yet. There are two ways of defining database privileges. First, we can choose one of the existing databases from the drop-down menu as shown in the following screenshot:

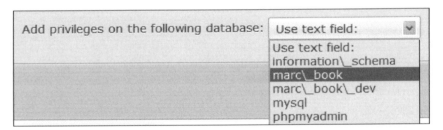

This assigns privileges only for the chosen database. Secondly, we can also choose **Use text field:** and enter a database name. We could enter a non-existent database name, so that the user can create it later (provided we give him/her the CREATE privilege in the next panel). We can also use special characters, such as the underscore and the percent sign, for wildcards.

For example, entering **bill** here would enable him to create a **bill** database, and entering **bill%** would enable him to create a database with any name that starts with **bill**. For our example, we will enter **bill** and click on **Go**.

The next screen is used to set **bill**'s privileges on the **bill** database, and create table-specific privileges.

To learn more about the meaning of a specific privilege, we can hover the mouse over a privilege name (which is always in English), and an explanation about this privilege appears in the current language. We give **SELECT, INSERT, UPDATE, DELETE, CREATE, ALTER, INDEX,** and **DROP** privileges to **bill** on this database. We then click on **Go**.

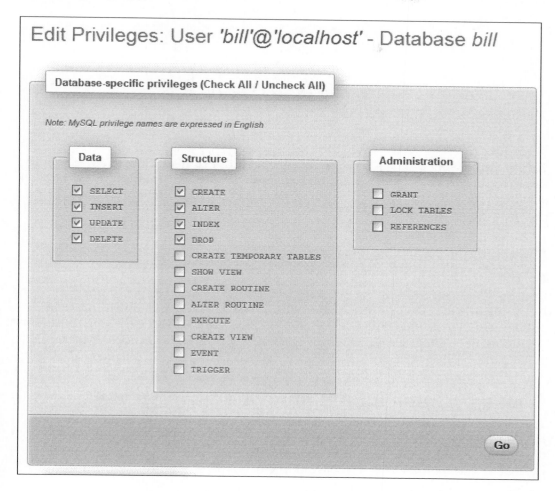

After the privileges have been assigned, the interface stays at the same place, so that we can refine these privileges further. We cannot assign table-specific privileges for the moment, as the database does not yet exist.

To go back to the general privileges page of **bill**, click on the **'bill'@'localhost'** title.

This brings us back to the following, familiar page except for a change in one section:

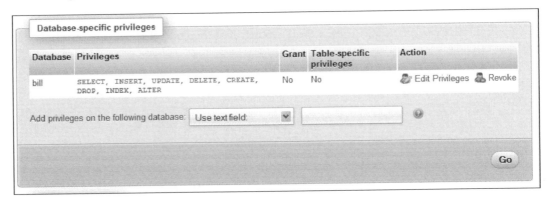

We see the existing privileges (we could click on **Edit Privileges** link to edit or on **Revoke** link to revoke them) on the **bill** database for user **bill**, and we can add privileges for **bill** on another database. We can also see that **bill** has no table-specific privilege on the **bill** database.

Changing the password

The **Change password** dialog is part of the **Edit user** page, and we can use it either to change **bill**'s password or to remove it. Removing the password will enable **bill** to log in without a password. The dialog offers a choice of password hashing options, and it's recommended to keep the default of **MySQL 4.1+** hashing. For more details about hashing, please visit http://dev.mysql.com/doc/refman/5.1/en/ password-hashing.html.

Changing login information or copying a user

This dialog can be used to change the user's login information, or to copy his or her login information to a new user. For example, suppose that Bill calls and tells us that he prefers the login name **billy** instead of **bill**. We just have to add a **y** to the username, and then select **delete the old one from the user tables** radio button, as shown in the following screenshot:

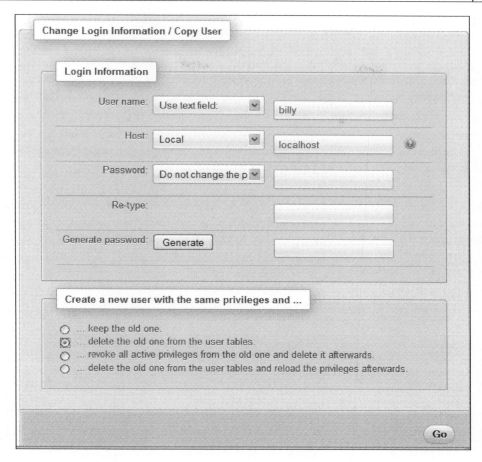

After clicking on **Go, bill** no longer exists in the mysql database. Also, all of his privileges, including the privileges on the **bill** database, will have been transferred to the new user—**billy**. However, the user definition of **bill** will still exist in memory, and hence it's still effective. If we had chosen the **delete the old one from the user tables and reload the privileges afterwards** option instead, the user definition of **bill** would immediately have ceased to be valid.

Alternatively, we could have created another user based on **bill,** by making use of the **keep the old one** choice. We can transfer the password to the new user by choosing **Do not change the password** option, or change it by entering a new password twice. The **revoke all active privileges...** option immediately terminates the effective current privileges for this user, even if he or she is currently logged in.

Removing a user

Removing a user is done from the **User overview** section of the **Privileges** page. We select the user to be removed. Then (in **Remove selected users**) we can select the **Drop the databases that have the same names as the users** option to remove any databases that are named after the users we are deleting. A click on **Go** effectively removes the selected users.

Database information

The **Databases** page is intended to create new databases, and quickly get privileges information for each database. Optionally, it can also be used to obtain global statistics on these databases without having to click on each database in the navigation panel. When we enter the **Databases** page, we see the list of existing databases:

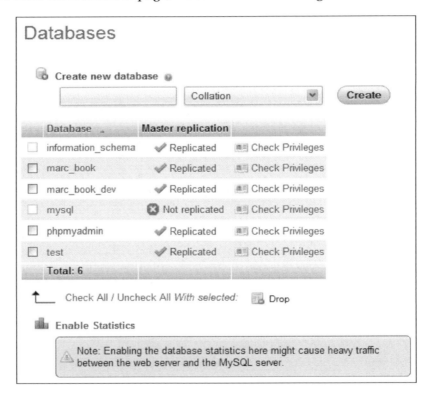

We also see an **Enable Statistics** link. By default, statistics are not enabled because computing the size of data and indexes for all the tables in all the databases may consume valuable MySQL server resources.

Enabling statistics

If we click on the **Enable Statistics** link, a modified page appears. For each database, we get the default collation for tables in this database, along with the number of tables in the database and the total number of rows for all tables. Next, information about the space used by the data portion of the tables is given, followed by the space taken by all indexes, and total space for all tables. Next, the space that could be reclaimed by optimizing some tables in this database is presented under **Overhead** column header. Finally, we can see replication information, followed by **Check Privileges** links:

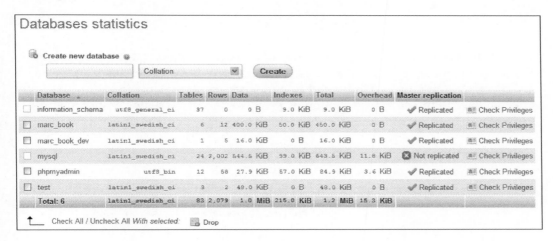

Sorting the statistics

By default, the statistics list is sorted by database name in ascending order. If we need to find the database with the most tables or the database that takes the most space, a simple click on the **Tables** or **Total** column header sorts the list accordingly. A second click reverses the sort order.

Checking the database privileges

Clicking on the **Check Privileges** icon or link displays all of the privileges on a specific database. A user's global privilege might be shown here, as it gives him or her access to this database as well. We can also see the privileges specific to this database. An **Edit Privileges** link takes us to another page, which is used to edit the user's privileges.

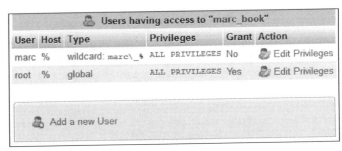

We notice that this panel also contains the **Add a new User** link. Clicking on this link is a convenient way of creating a user that has privileges to the database we are currently examining. Indeed, after entering the user-creation panel from this link, a fourth choice in the database creation or privileges granting dialog is shown and selected by default, as shown in the following screenshot:

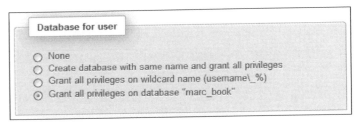

Dropping selected databases

To drop one or more databases, we go to Server view and click on the **Databases** menu tab; put check marks next to the names of the databases to be dropped; and then click on the **Drop** link next to **With selected**. We then get a confirmation screen. Two of the databases (mysql and the virtual information_schema) cannot be selected; the first one to avoid making a big mistake and deleting all of our accounts, and the second one cannot be selected as this is not a real database.

 This is an operation that should not be taken lightly, and it might be prudent to first export the whole database as a backup.

Server information

Both administrators and ordinary users can benefit from monitoring the server and obtaining information about its general configuration and behavior. The **Status**, **Variables**, and **Processes** menu tabs can be used to get information about the MySQL server, or to act upon specific processes.

Verifying server status

The server status statistics reflect the MySQL server's total activity, including (but not limited to) the activity generated by queries sent from phpMyAdmin.

Clicking on the **Status** menu tab produces runtime information about the server. The page has several sections. First, we get information about the elapsed running time and the startup time. Then we get the total and average values, for traffic and connections (where the **ø** indicates average), as shown in the following screenshot:

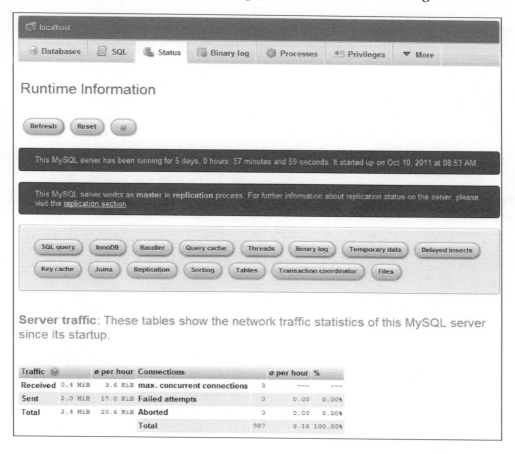

Next, the statistics about the queries are displayed (shown in part in the screenshot). The average number of queries per hour, minute, and second give a good indication of the server load.

The query statistics are followed by statistics about each MySQL statement executed, including:

- The absolute number of times each statement has been executed
- The hourly average of execution
- The percentage of execution for this statement compared to all statements

The presentation order is by descending percentage of utilization; in the following screenshot, we see that the **set option** statement is the one which is most received by this server with **37.40%**:

Query statistics: Since its startup, 6,273 queries have been sent to the server

Total	ø per hour	ø per minute	ø per second
6,273	51.86	0.86	0.01

Query type	ø per hour	%	Query type	ø per hour	%
set option	1,977	16.343 37.40%	insert	40	0.331 0.76%
select	1,525	12.607 28.85%	show create table	26	0.207 0.47%
change db	395	3.265 7.47%	update	24	0.198 0.45%
show variables	187	1.546 3.54%	show keys	20	0.165 0.38%
show table status	181	1.496 3.42%	show grants	16	0.132 0.30%
show tables	167	1.381 3.16%	delete	15	0.124 0.28%
show plugins	121	1.000 2.29%	grant	6	0.050 0.11%
show fields	114	0.942 2.16%	replace	5	0.041 0.09%
show databases	113	0.934 2.14%	drop user	5	0.041 0.09%
show binlogs	99	0.818 1.87%	show create func	4	0.033 0.08%
show master status	63	0.521 1.19%	show create event	4	0.033 0.08%
show slave status	63	0.521 1.19%	show create proc	4	0.033 0.08%
show storage engines	62	0.513 1.17%	show status	3	0.025 0.06%

After **Query statistics**, a **Show query chart** link, when clicked, produces a chart displaying the popular query types on this server, as shown in the following screenshot:

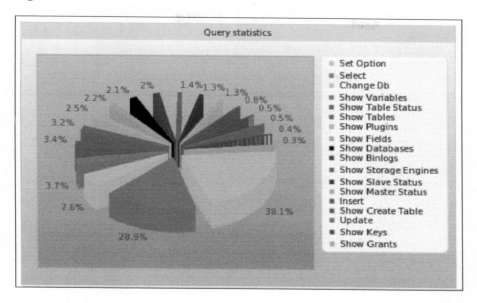

Depending on the MySQL version, many other sections containing server information are also displayed.

Server variables

The **Variables** page displays various settings for the MySQL server, which can be defined in, say, the my.cnf MySQL configuration file. These values can't be changed from within phpMyAdmin.

Server processes

The **Processes** page is available to both superusers and normal users. A normal user would see only the processes belonging to him or her, whereas a superuser sees all of the processes.

This page lists all active processes on the server. There is a **Kill** link that allows us to terminate a specific process, as shown in the following screenshot:

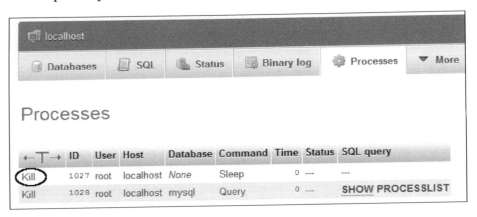

This example has only two running processes, including the one created by the SHOW PROCESSLIST command itself. This process is not killable because it's no longer running when we get to see the page. On a busy server, we would see more processes running.

Storage engines

Information about the various storage engines is available in a two-level format. First, the **Engines** tab displays an overview of the possible engines for the current MySQL version. The names of the engines that are enabled on this server are clickable.

Storage Engines

Storage Engine	Description
InnoDB	Supports transactions, row-level locking, and foreign keys
PERFORMANCE_SCHEMA	Performance Schema
MRG_MYISAM	Collection of identical MyISAM tables
MyISAM	MyISAM storage engine
CSV	CSV storage engine
MEMORY	Hash based, stored in memory, useful for temporary tables

Secondly, a click on one engine name brings up a detailed panel about its settings. Hovering the mouse over the numbers in superscript reveals even more information about a particular setting.

Available character sets and collations

The **Charsets** menu tab on the home page opens the `Server` view for the **Charsets** page, which lists the character sets and collations supported by the MySQL server. The default collation for each character set is shown with a different background color (using the row-marking color defined in `$cfg['BrowseMarkerColor']`).

Examining binary logs

If MySQL's binary logging is active on our server, the menu in the `Server` view changes so that a **Binary log** tab appears. This tab gives access to an interface, through the `SHOW BINLOG EVENTS` command. This command produces the list of SQL statements that have updated data on our servers. This list could be huge, and currently phpMyAdmin does not limit its display with a pagination technique. Hence, we could hit the browser's memory limit, which depends on the particular browser we are using.

In the following screenshot, we choose the binary log that we want to examine (unless the server has only one binary log), and the statements are then displayed:

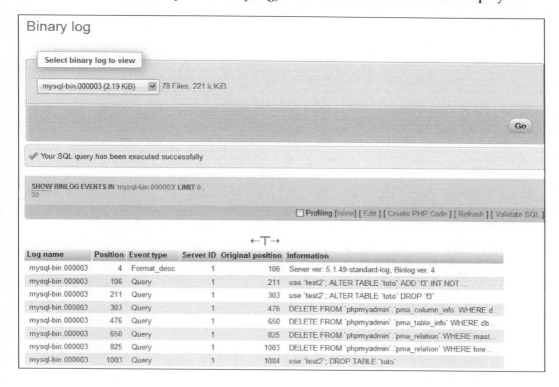

[343]

Summary

This chapter covered various features available to system administrators, such as user-account management, privileges management, database privileges checks, and server status verification. Appropriate knowledge of the MySQL privileges system is crucial in order to maintain a MySQL server adequately, and this chapter proposes exercises centered on the notion of a user and his or her privileges.

Appendix, Troubleshooting and Support, is next, describing where to obtain support in order to make phpMyAdmin run efficiently.

Troubleshooting and Support

This *Appendix* proposes guidelines for solving some common problems, and provides hints on how to avoid them. It also explains how to interact with the development team for support, bug reports, and contributions.

Troubleshooting

Over the years, the development team has received numerous requests for support, and many of them could have been avoided with a few simple verifications.

System requirements

A section at the beginning of the Documentation.html file (which is included with phpMyAdmin's software), discusses system requirements for the particular phpMyAdmin version we are using. It's crucial that these requirements be met, and that the environment be properly configured so that problems are avoided.

Some problems, looking like phpMyAdmin bugs, are in fact caused by the server environment. Sometimes, the web server is not configured to interpret .php files correctly, or the PHP component inside the web server does not run with the mysql or mysqli extensions. MySQL accounts may be badly configured. This can happen on home servers as well as on hosted servers.

When we suspect that something is wrong, we can try a simple PHP script, test. php, which contains the following code block, to check if the PHP component answers correctly:

```php
<?php
echo 'hello';
?>
```

We should see the **hello** message. If this works, we can try another script:

```php
<?php
phpinfo();
?>
```

This script displays information about the PHP component, including the available extensions. We should at least see a section about MySQL (proving that the `mysql` extension is available), which gives information about the MySQL **Client API version**.

We can also try other PHP scripts that make a connection to MySQL, to see if the problem is more general than just phpMyAdmin not working. As a general rule, we should be running the latest stable versions of every component.

Verifying the base configuration

We should always double check the way in which we performed the installation, including correct permissions and ownerships. Typos may occur when modifying `config.inc.php`.

Solving common errors

To help solve a problem, we should first pinpoint the origin of the error message. The following are the various components that can generate an error message:

- MySQL server: These messages are relayed by phpMyAdmin, which displays **MySQL said** followed by the message
- PHP component of the web server: For example, **Parser error**
- Web server: The error can be seen from the browser, or in the web server's log files
- Web browser: For example, JavaScript errors

Seeking support

The starting point for support is the phpMyAdmin official site, `http://phpmyadmin.net`, which has sections on documentation and support. There you will find links to the discussion forums and to various trackers, such as:

- Bug tracker
- Feature requests tracker
- Translations tracker

- Patches tracker
- Support tracker

FAQs

The `Documentation.html` file, which is part of the product, contains a lengthy FAQ section with numbered questions and answers. It is recommended to peruse this FAQ section as the first source for help.

Help forums

The development team recommends that you use the product's forums to search for the problem encountered, and then start a new forum discussion before opening a bug report.

Creating a SourceForge account

Creating a (free) SourceForge user account and using it for posting on forums is highly recommended. This enables better tracking of questions and answers.

Choosing the thread title

It is important to choose the summary title carefully when you start a new forum thread. Titles like "Help me!", "Help a newbie!", "Problem", or "phpMyAdmin error!" are difficult to deal with, as the answers are threaded to these titles and further reference becomes problematic. Better titles that have been used in the help forum include:

- "Import with UploadDir"
- "User can't but root can login"
- "How big can I expect a table to get"
- "Continuous login prompts"
- "Cannot add foreign key"

Reading the answers

As people will read and, almost always answer, your question, giving feedback in the forum about the answers can really help the person who answered, and also help others who have the same problem.

Using the support tracker

The support tracker is another place to ask for support. Also, if we have submitted a bug report, which is in fact a support request, the report will be moved to the support tracker. If you have a SourceForge user account with e-mail forwarding configured in your profile, you will be notified of this tracker change.

Using the bug tracker

In this tracker, we see bugs that have not yet been fixed, along with the bugs that have been fixed for the next version. Bugs fixed for the next version keep a status of "open" to avoid getting duplicate bug reports, but their priority level is lowered.

Environment description

As developers will try to reproduce the problem mentioned, it helps to describe your environment. This description can be short, but should contain the following items:

- phpMyAdmin version (the team, however, expects that it's the current stable version)
- Web server name and version
- PHP version
- MySQL version
- Browser name and version

Usually, it isn't necessary to specify the operating system on which the server or the client is running, unless we notice that the bug pertains to only one OS. For example, FAQ 5.1 describes a problem where the user could not create a table having more than fourteen fields. This happens only under Windows 98.

Bug description

We should give a precise description of what happens (including any error message, the expected results, and the effective results we get). Reports are easily managed if they describe only one problem per bug report (unless the problems are clearly linked).

Sometimes, it might help to attach a short export file to the bug report to help developers reproduce the problem. Screenshots are welcome.

Contributing to the project

Since phpMyAdmin's inception in 1998, hundreds of people have contributed translations, code for new features, suggestions, and bug fixes.

The code base

The development team maintains an evolving code base from which they periodically issue releases. On `http://phpmyadmin.net`, the **Improve** page explains how anyone can contribute, and gives pointers about the project's `git` source code repository. A contribution (translation update, patch, new feature, and so on) will be considered with a higher priority if it refers to the latest code base, and not to an outdated phpMyAdmin version. Another useful page of instructions for using Git, which is used for storing the code base, is located at `http://wiki.phpmyadmin.net/pma/Git`.

Translation updates

Taking a look at the project's current list of 65 languages, you will notice that they are not equally well maintained. Since the project's move to a `gettext`-based localization system, everyone is encouraged to contribute to translations. The project is using a translation server equipped with the `Pootle` software, located at `https://l10n.cihar.com/projects/phpmyadmin`. It's also possible to use this server to translate phpMyAdmin's `Documentation.html`.

Patches

The development team can manage patches more easily if they are submitted in the form of a `git format-patch` against the current code base, with an explanation of the solved problem or the new feature achieved. Major contributors are officially credited in `Documentation.html`.

Index

color-marking rows 89, 90
distinct values, browsing 91
navigation bar 84, 85
query result operations 86
results, sorting 87-89
SQL query links 83, 84
browser's local storage
phpMyAdmin configuration storage,
storing in 68
**browser transformations, MIME type 278,
279**
bug description 348
bug tracker
about 348
environment description 348

C

calendar pop up 116
cell 276
**Change or reconfigure master server link
244**
Change password dialog 334
CHAR
data entry panel tuning 82
character-based columns 179
character set
about 52, 53
selecting, for export file 129
chart
data, displaying as 86
CHECKSUM option 180
Check table operation 176
Choose column to display icon 193
clickable thumbnail (JPEG or PNG) 281, 282
code
executing, with triggers 301, 302
code base 349
CodeGen 141
collation 52, 53
color-marking columns 89, 90
color-marking rows 89, 90
column
adding, to table 107
column attribute, table
editing 108, 109
column-commenting 201, 202

column comments
migrating, automatically 202
column criteria
about 219
exploring 219
column_info function 27
column length
limiting 90
columns
displaying 220
length, limiting 90
selecting, from table 76
sorting 220
Column selector
about 218-220
multiple columns 219, 220
single-column 219, 220
Columns selector 208
comparison results panel 234
complete synchronization
about 235
performing 236
compression 129, 130
conditions
adding, to criteria box 221-223
config
user, authenticating with 32
config.inc.php file
about 12, 13, 38, 270
creating, manually 20
editing, on Windows client 20
false error messages, avoiding on 13
config.sample.inc.php file 13
configuration file
server, defining 38
configuration parameters, phpMyAdmin
about 20
PmaAbsoluteUri 21
server-specific sections 21, 22
**configuration principles, phpMyAdmin
13-15**
configuring
phpMyAdmin 12
Control slave link 244
control user
need for 23, 24
cookie authentication mode 34-36

I

image
  links, adding to 282
Import/Export icon 194
import feature
  about 149, 150
  other limits 151
  time limits 150, 151
  transfer limits 150
Import files menu 150
Import menu 150
in-cell sort 289, 290
index editing 120
indexes
  FULLTEXT indexes 120
  index editing 120
  index problems, detecting 122
  managing 118
  multi-column indexes 120
  optimizing, EXPLAIN used 121, 122
  single-column indexes 118, 119
index management 79
index problem
  detecting 122
information_schema
  using 303, 304
initial QBE page 217
Inline link 84
inline row editing 102
InnoDB
  about 186
  URL 186
Insecure connection message 16
INSERT DELAYED statements 134
INSERT IGNORE statements 134
INSERT statement 213
installing
  phpMyAdmin 9
internal relations
  defining 187, 188
  display column, defining 188, 189
  relation, defining 188
International Electrotechnical Commission (IEC) 64
Internet Protocol (IP) 41

in-transit data
  protecting 43
INT type 78
in use table
  repairing 183
IO Thread Stop only option 244
IP address 288
IP-based access control
  phpMyAdmin, protecting with 41

J

JavaScript client code 8
JavaScript Object Notation. *See* **JSON**
JPEG libraries
  support, asserting 280
JSON 10, 142

K

Kanji support 129
key management. *See* **index management**
keys
  selecting, for tables 79, 80

L

Language selector 50, 51
LaTeX
  about 138
  options 138
Light mode
  about 55
  table name filter 56
  tree display, of database names 56
LIKE criterion 221
LIMIT clause 85
links
  adding, to image 282
LOAD DATA INFILE statement 149, 156
LOAD DATA interface
  using 157, 158
LOAD DATA LOCAL INFILE statement 156
LOCAL CHECK OPTION clause 293
local Linux server
  phpMyAdmin, installing on 11

PHP/MySQL combination 7
PmaAbsoluteUri parameter 21
pmadb 24
pmadb function 27
PMA_langDetails() function 50
PNG libraries
  support, asserting 280
Pretty printing 213, 288
PrimeBase XT. *See* PBXT
printable report
  creating 261
Print button 261
Print view link 261
privileges
  exporting 327
  managing, for users 325
  reloading 328
Privileges page 325
procedures
  about 296
  entering 297
  manipulating 298
  testing 297
Professional Home Page 8
Profiling checkbox 84
profiling queries 92
public bookmarks 253, 254

Q

queries
  editing 211, 212
  executing 225
  profiling 92
  updating 220, 221
Query by example (QBE) feature 217
query generator 217
Query results operations section
  about 86
  data, displaying as chart 86
Query window
  about 46, 70, 71, 209
  appearance 209
  database based SQL history feature 210,
    211
  options 210
  queries, editing 211, 212

session based SQL history feature 210
Query window options 210

R

referential integrity checks 200, 201
relational MySQL 185
relational schemas
  displaying 269-271
  generating 264
relational system 185
relation function 27
relations
  defining 188, 195, 196
  defining, with Designer 192-196
  defining, with relation view 186, 187
relations, defining with Designer
  about 192-196
  display column, defining 197
  foreign key relations, defining 196
  interface, over viewing 193, 194
relation view
  relations, defining with 186, 187
Reload icon 193
remote server
  phpMyAdmin, installing on 11
Rename operation 181
Repair table operation 176
replicated databases 245, 246
replicated tables 246
replication
  configuring 238
  information, obtaining 245
  preparing for 230, 231
  status, gathering 245
replication information
  obtaining 245
Replication menu 238
replication status
  gathering 245
report
  preparing, with data dictionary 264
Reset slave option 244
results
  sorting 87-89
RFC 2616 21
rights, for database creation 330

Thank you for buying
Mastering phpMyAdmin 3.4 for Effective MySQL Management

About Packt Publishing

Packt, pronounced 'packed', published its first book "*Mastering phpMyAdmin for Effective MySQL Management*" in April 2004 and subsequently continued to specialize in publishing highly focused books on specific technologies and solutions.

Our books and publications share the experiences of your fellow IT professionals in adapting and customizing today's systems, applications, and frameworks. Our solution based books give you the knowledge and power to customize the software and technologies you're using to get the job done. Packt books are more specific and less general than the IT books you have seen in the past. Our unique business model allows us to bring you more focused information, giving you more of what you need to know, and less of what you don't.

Packt is a modern, yet unique publishing company, which focuses on producing quality, cutting-edge books for communities of developers, administrators, and newbies alike. For more information, please visit our website: www.packtpub.com.

About Packt Open Source

In 2010, Packt launched two new brands, Packt Open Source and Packt Enterprise, in order to continue its focus on specialization. This book is part of the Packt Open Source brand, home to books published on software built around Open Source licences, and offering information to anybody from advanced developers to budding web designers. The Open Source brand also runs Packt's Open Source Royalty Scheme, by which Packt gives a royalty to each Open Source project about whose software a book is sold.

Writing for Packt

We welcome all inquiries from people who are interested in authoring. Book proposals should be sent to author@packtpub.com. If your book idea is still at an early stage and you would like to discuss it first before writing a formal book proposal, contact us; one of our commissioning editors will get in touch with you.

We're not just looking for published authors; if you have strong technical skills but no writing experience, our experienced editors can help you develop a writing career, or simply get some additional reward for your expertise.

PHP and MongoDB Web Development Beginner's Guide

ISBN: 978-1-84951-362-3   Paperback: 292 pages

Combine the power of PHP and MongoDB to build dynamic web 2.0 applications

1. Learn to build PHP-powered dynamic web applications using MongoDB as the data backend

2. Handle user sessions, store real-time site analytics, build location-aware web apps, and much more, all using MongoDB and PHP

3. Full of step-by-step instructions and practical examples, along with challenges to test and improve your knowledge

PHP Ajax Cookbook

ISBN: 978-1-84951-308-1   Paperback: 340 pages

Over 60 simple but incredibly effective recipes to Ajaxify PHP websites

1. Learn how to develop and deploy iPhone web and native apps

2. Optimize the performance of Ajax applications

3. Build dynamic websites with faster response from the server using the asynchronous call feature of PHP Ajax

4. Using Ajax allows quick and efficient access of data from the server, thus precluding a total web page refresh

Please check **www.PacktPub.com** for information on our titles

Printed in Great Britain
by Amazon.co.uk, Ltd.,
Marston Gate.